PRAIRIE DU CHIEN: FRENCH, BRITISH, AMERICAN

Unabridged, unaltered republication of
the second (1949) edition. Eight pages of
illustrations have been added and a new
cover designed. Published to celebrate
the 300th anniversary of Prairie du Chien.

1985

PRAIRIE DU CHIEN:
French · British · American

By

PETER LAWRENCE SCANLAN, M.D.

1937

Composed, Printed and Bound by
The Collegiate Press
George Banta Publishing Company
Menasha, Wisconsin

Introduction

THE EARLY history of Wisconsin was conditioned by its waterways and particularly by the Fox-Wisconsin waterway forming
the easiest and best known route from the Great Lakes to the
upper Mississippi. Naturally, therefore, settlements grew up at
either end of this great thoroughfare and these were fortified
for protection of the commerce that passed that way. At the eastern
end stood Green Bay, the *La Baye* of the French explorers; at the
western end a large open prairie just above the mouth of the
Wisconsin became a coveted emporium for the fur trade. The
earliest history of Green Bay has been preserved for us by the
Jesuit missionaries, men of education and culture who devoted
their lives to the betterment of savage Indians, at the same time
sending back to France long interesting descriptions of the regions
they saw.

The western settlement, early called Prairie du Chien for an
Indian chief who bore the name of *Chien* or Dog, had no Jesuit
visitors and it is first mentioned in detail in 1766-67 by Jonathan Carver, the earliest English traveler to visit that place. There
is reason to believe, however, that Prairie du Chien had a French
régime of importance and interest. Dr. Scanlan has skillfully re-
constituted this period in the first three chapters of this book,
proving from French documents its first Fort St. Nicolas, and
the constant stream of discoverers and explorers that passed this
site from the time of Jolliet and Marquette (1673) to the cession
nine decades later of the entire region to the British.

Green Bay has had its historians for many years; but a conspicuous lack in the history of Wisconsin has been an authentic
and full history of Prairie du Chien. The groundwork was laid
for such a work by our earlier historians who secured interviews
with pioneer settlers such as Lockwood and Brisbois, and published documents on the forts of the war of 1812 and the first
American posts. Not until Dr. Scanlan undertook the task has
any successful history of Prairie du Chien been put forth. This is
not simply a *local* history of one place in Wisconsin. Because of
its commanding position on the Mississippi at the mouth of the
Wisconsin, Prairie du Chien's history is involved in international

relations. After France's cession of western Louisiana to Spain in 1762 and the revolt of the English colonies that had far echoes in this distant region, Prairie du Chien stood at the meeting place of three great nations, while American, British and Spanish agents vied for the allegiance of the upper Mississippi Indians, and the riches that came from their trade. Although nominally a part of the new republic of the United States after the treaty of 1783, British traders maintained their influence and exclusive trade with the aborigines for thirty years longer and Prairie du Chien became the metropolis of the British fur trade on Spanish and American soil.

After the Louisiana purchase in 1803 Spain's claim to allegiance disappeared, but not until the Americans had fought the second war with Great Britain was this region finally annexed commercially to the United States. After 1816 when Fort Crawford was built by American troops, British traders accepted the inevitable and either withdrew or became naturalized American citizens.

Through all the vicissitudes of this century of struggle the French-Canadian settlers of the Prairie, retired voyageurs for the most part, went their accustomed way. They planted grain, built primitive mills, associated with the Indians, among whom they found their wives and among whom their half-breed children grew up. There were no priests or religious services until 1817, no schools until about the same time; and not until the 1830's did Prairie du Chien begin to be Americanized. The coming of the first American home missionaries and the early American merchants changed the town and adapted it to its new mission as an important center of Wisconsin territorial life.

The competence of Dr. Scanlan for his unique task of portraying this kaleidoscope of change and movement is obvious. He has been a resident of Prairie du Chien for many years; he knows its monuments and remains; he is a friend of the present day French residents and has heard the reminiscences of their ancestors; he is acquainted with the traditions of the place; he has carefully examined the local records in church and court house. When he learned that a history of the place was needed and nowhere written, he prepared himself for his task by searching for records in the collections of the Wisconsin Historical Society at Madison, those of Minnesota at St. Paul, of Missouri at St. Louis, and of Iowa at Des Moines. He also visited the neighboring Mississippi river towns of Galena and Dubuque. He traveled afield as far as Montreal and Quebec for French and British documents and spent months searching the great store of materials at the nation's capital.

Then he set himself to write this book with the aid of his daughter Marian, who is a teacher in a Milwaukee high school. We can unhesitatingly recommend it as authoritative, reliable and thorough. It fills a lacuna in Wisconsin history and it should be in every public library in the state and in every private library that cares for Wisconsiniana.

LOUISE PHELPS KELLOGG

Madison, January, 1937

Foreword

HAD I been a historian instead of merely a lover of history, a better work would have resulted. However, who reads this must be impressed with the multitude of facts assembled in the first sustained account of Prairie du Chien history. Selecting material has been even more difficult than the gathering of material which preceded it. New sources of information have been opened up continuously in the fourteen years during which this book has been in the making. In 1922 when my wife died and I turned to this history as a spare-time hobby, which has changed gradually into an occupation of almost full-time pursuit, I had been actively engaged in the general practice of medicine for thirty-one years. This had meant scant leisure for other interests than my work and my family. Since 1922 more and more of my time has been devoted to historical research. An article on Dr. William Beaumont, published in 1923, was my first writing on Prairie du Chien history.

Tracing to their source legends and facts about people as well as places has necessitated considerable traveling about: many trips to Madison, Wisconsin; several to St. Louis and to St. Paul; one to South Dakota; one along the trail of Nicolet to Montreal, Three Rivers, and Quebec.

An honest effort has been made to sift from the mass of accumulated material those *facts* which have significance and interest. Much has been omitted—some things inadvertently and some things because here and there a "pleasing tradition" has proved to have little or no basis in fact. To keep the truth uppermost has been my aim throughout.

It is a very pleasant obligation to acknowledge, at least in part, the aid of a great number of individuals and organizations and libraries.

To Dr. Louise Phelps Kellogg, Dr. Joseph Schafer, Miss Alice Smith, and others of the Wisconsin Historical Society and its library, are due my first thanks for their continued graciousness in making available to me the resources of the magnificent Historical Library. In St. Louis, Mrs. Nettie Beauregard, Miss Stella M. Drumm, and other staff members of the Jefferson Memorial Li-

brary have been most kind both in personal aid and in correspondence. Miss Grace Nute and her aides in the Minnesota Historical
Library at St. Paul have likewise been helpful on repeated occasions. Rev. Peter Leo Johnson, Professor of Church History, St.
Francis Seminary, St. Francis, Wisconsin; Rev. Raphael N. Hamilton, S.J., Head of the Department of History, Marquette University, Milwaukee, Wisconsin; Rev. M. M. Hoffman, Professor of
History, Columbia College, Dubuque, Iowa; and Rev. Lawrence
Kenney, S.J., formerly of St. Louis University have permitted me
to consult manuscripts and books in the libraries of the seminary
and the universities and have been of frequent aid in correspondence.

I wish also to make acknowledgment to two distinguished
Canadian gentlemen who have been of material aid. Through the
generosity of M. Pierre Georges-Roy of Quebec, I am in possession of the four volumes of the *Rapport de l'archiviste de la province de Quebec* upon which I have drawn so extensively. Mr. Lawrence J. Burpee, Secretary of the International Joint Commission,
Ottawa, secured for me valuable biographical information from the
London files of the Hudson's Bay Company.

Our late Senator, Honorable John J. Blaine of Boscobel, and
our Congressman, Honorable Gardner R. Withrow, made possible the innumerable courtesies shown me in the three months
which I spent in Washington, D.C. in 1933. From official records
in the offices of the Adjutant General, the Quartermaster General, Inspector General, Judge Advocate General, and the Interior
Department, I obtained invaluable information, especially for the
chapters on Military Affairs and Civilian Affairs. Many officers
and clerks in these government offices assisted in giving me access
to these records, and I wish to express my appreciation. The Library of Congress, too, proved a rich source of scattered information.

Official records at the Land Office of the State of Wisconsin;
at the county offices of Crawford, Grant, Chippewa, and Eau Claire
counties, Wisconsin; of Jo Daviess County, Illinois; of Clayton and
Dubuque counties, Iowa; and unpublished church records at Prairie
du Chien and elsewhere have been studied carefully in an effort to
reconstruct family histories and establish points of dispute between
fact and legend. This would have been an extremely difficult task
without the cooperation of those in charge of such records. Many

persons in Prairie du Chien and elsewhere have loaned precious books, manuscripts, maps, and pictures. It is not possible to name them all, but I am deeply grateful to all who have aided in any way.

For a critical reading of this manuscript, I express my gratitude to Dr. Joseph Schafer, Rev. Peter Leo Johnson, and Dr. Louise Phelps Kellogg. To have an introduction by Dr. Kellogg, whose research and writing in Wisconsin history are so widely and so favorably known, is a privilege indeed, and to her I am truly grateful.

And, above all, I thank my daughter Marian whose help and sympathy have made possible the publication of this volume. To her I dedicate this book.

P. L. SCANLAN

Table of Contents

PRAIRIE DU CHIEN: FRENCH, BRITISH, AMERICAN
Corrections and Additions
1949

p. 53, footnote. Paul Cardinal, born in 1775. In 1818 the government refused his claim to 800 arpens of land at Charette, Missouri. (American State Papers, III, 324) May 31, 1819, Paul Cardinal, then of St. Charles, deeded to the Hempsteads his share of the property of Jean Marie Cardinal at St. Louis. (St. Charles Records. Jefferson Memorial Library, St. Louis.)

p. 54 should read visits to Prairie du Chien, also Mississippi in footnote should be inserted.

p. 56 Paul Cardinal received his share of his father's estate at St. Louis. He held land at St. Charles, Mo. and was an American soldier at the battle of "Sink Hole" May 24, 1815.

p. 57 Julien Cardinal is not buried at Eastman. It was a Potawatoine probably half-breed named Cardinal.

p. 61 line 10. "Prairie du Chien" not "Prairie les Chiens". ("Dog Plain", so designated as the property of an Indian chief whose name was literally translated by the French to "Dog".)

p. 65 line 7. "We" is a typographical error. It should be "he".

p. 67 Linctot died about 1783. He was made Major in Indian affairs by Governor of Virginia in 1779.

p. 71 line 20. Further research has proved that this body was that of Augustine Ange.

page 71 line 35. Pierre Antaya (Peltier) was alive in 1820.

p. 72 line 17. "Prairie du Chien" not "Prairie Les Chiens".

p. 74 line 2. The Mackinac merchants at Kaskaskia about 1780 to 1785 were spoken of as the Mackinac Company, however, the real Mackinac Company was not organized until 1806. Apply this correction also to the interpretation of line 29.

p. 76 line 35. The trader, Augustine Dubec was not the father of Julian Dubuque.

p. 77 line 29. Henry Monroe Fisher came to Prairie du Chien in 1792 as a clerk for Andrew Todd. Fisher became an independent trader in 1794.

p. 77 line 37. Speaking of Archibald Campbell and his son John here is an error. They are one and the same man and his proper name was Archibald. He was the Indian Agent at Prairie du Chien from December 1807 to August 1808. He had two sons, John and ———— by a white wife, and three sons, Duncan, Colin, and Scott by a Sioux woman. There were two half-breed daughters, Margaret and Nancy. Margaret was Hercules L. Dousman's Indian wife and the mother of George and Emma Douisman (Mrs. Charles Barrette). Nancy married Bourke and lived on the Red River of the North in Canada. Archibald's son, John, married Margaret, the half-breed daughter of Joseph Ainsse (Heins). She is the woman listed as a widow with seven children in the 1836 census of Crawford County. She was frozen to death near Winona in 1838. Their son, John married a half-breed Winnebago, Sophia, daughter of Joshua Palen, an Indian trader who died of Cholera at Keokuk in 1833. There is a street named after him in that city.

In Prairie du Chien there is a coulee named after Campbell.

p. 78 line 4. Fisher lived on Main Village lot 8, and Dickson lived on lot 12.

p. 83 Campbell.

There was no Hudson's Bay Co. at Prairie du Chien.

p. 85   line 34. This repeats the error of Archibald and John Campbell being father and son. See correction for page 77, line 37.

p. 86   line 13. Again note that Pierre Antaya was still alive in 1820.

p. 87 George Aird died in 1805. (Old Cathedral Records, St. Louis, show that he was buried April 1, 1805.) The statement about him —line 5— cannot be true.

p. 90   line 6. Governor Howard's statement is incorrect. The Hudson's Bay Company never had a post at Prairie du Chien.

p. 109   line 31. Jacques Vieau came to Milwaukee in 1795.

p. 109 Aiken not Aikens.

p. 123 Redford Crawford was buried at St. Louis June 11, 1811. (Old Cathedral Records).

p. 124 Captain Morgan left Fort Crawford October 1816, and Colonel Talbot Chambers came April 22, 1817.

p. 125 Rolette was court-martialed by the British first in 1813 and also January 5, 1815 at Prairie du Chien, but acquitted both times. Rolette was banished by Americans because he was a foreigner.

p. 126   line 27 Colonel Chambers' initials were not C. A. His name was Talbot Chambers and he was at St. Louis at that time. Maybe that is why Hayne got the wrong initials.

p. 127   line 9. Long measured only the south side of the fort which was ten feet longer than the other sides. Its correct measure was 110 yards square.

p. 127   line 31. Muhlenberg took three outside rooms off the barracks for a hospital. (Mr. Cooper's location of the hospital was wrong.) There the experiments on Alexis St. Martin's stomach took place.

p. 137. 'Sentry post" is a misnomer. These were rock posts to support the porch floors of the hospital.

p. 139   line 16. It was Lt. J. A. Davis not Jeff Davis who drove horses to the pinery on the ice.

p. 139   line 32. The officers barracks were not 46x30 as stated. I believe they were 40x40. There was six feet between buildings.

p. 139 Jefferson Davis was at Fort Winnebago in February, 1830. (Adjutant General's Office) Major Garland's order of February 14, 1830, must have been intended for Brevet Second Lieutenant J. A. Davis, also of the First Infantry, who was stationed at Fort Crawford at that time.

p. 144   line 35. It is definite that the rock work on the barracks was all done in October, 1833.

p. 150   line 26. Re-emphasizing that Jeff Davis did not participate in the Black Hawk War. Also that Dr. Beaumont never saw cholera in Prairie du Chien.

p. 167. Wisconsin became part of Michigan 1818.

p. 169 Should be 1818 not 1805. Under Illinois from 1809 to 1818.

p. 170   line 30 ff. The John Campbell mentioned here is Archibald. Correction for page 77 clears up this confusion in regard to the Campbells. John Johnson was his second in the duel.

p. 171   line —— Prairie du Chien. (Boilvin, 1811).

p. 177   line 23. Boilvin did not take his family in July 1814. The family was left at Prairie du Chien.

p. 179. Note on Rolette. Rolette was arbitrarily banished for the winter by the Commanding officer, outside of what was later called the burrough of Prairie du Chien. Rolette secured a permit from the Sec. of War to return to his family and business.

Michael Brisbois was treated as a traitor, because he had been appointed a Lieut. of Prairie du Chien militia by Gov. Ninian Edwards of Illinois, in 1809. But in war of 1812, he was accused of siding with the British and because of that, he was arrested for treason, but was never tried. A Senator from Missouri was his attorney and sent him home. M. Brisbois had no choice, for Prairie was under the British. Besides his bills to the Indians would not have been paid by the British.

p. 180. Among the Lisa "Papers" (Jefferson Memorial Library, St. Louis) is a statement, credited to the Trappists, that Reverend Rogation Olivier resided at Prairie du Chien in 1810. I have found no verification of this, however.

p. 182 line 30.   Major Stephen Long's statements as to the origin of the name, Prairie du Chien, are incorrect. There were no "dog Indians".

p. 183 line 33. The early deeds at Prairie du Chien were recorded by the Clerk of Probate Court.

p. 184 line 10. In addition to Lockwood's narrative, there is also a Michigan Territory record of the first Crawford County officers.

p. 184. The Mann Hotel was the place of the first meeting of Crawford County in 1819. Perhaps Doty held court in it in 1823.

p. 184 On November 1 0, 1819 there was filed at Detroit a list of the civil and military officers of Crawford County. They were appointed on May 10, 1819 by the Governor of Michigan Territory. List of officers of county court:

Chief Justice, John W. Johnson

Associate Justice, Nicholas Bolvin and Francis Bouthillier

Judge of Probate and Justice of the Peace, Wilford Owens

Commissioners of County, James McFarlane, Pierre LaRiviere and Louis LaBlanc, also known as Provincale

Justice of the Peace, John W. Johnson, Denis Courtois and Nicholas Boilvin

Sheriff, Thomas McNair

Coroner, John B. Faribault

Register in Probate, John P. Gates

Clerk of County Court, John L. Findley

Supervisors of Roads and Bridges, Hyacinth St. Cyr and Oliver Cherrier

Constables, John L. Findley and Peter Barrette

The military officers were:

Captain, Thomas McNair

Lieutenant Charles La Pointe, Ensign Scott Campbell

Michael Brisbois was later made County Treasurer

p. 185. The first coroner was Jean B. Faribault.

p. 185. Barnard, not Bernard.

Boilvin died at St. Louis May 18, 1827, and was buried the following day. (Old Cathedral Records).

p. 188 Lyons survey showed the east boundary of the Old Frenchtown Cemetery to be the road. It was 8 arpens (1540 feet) and ran back to the Marais de St. Friole. Now about 120 feet square is fenced

p. 189 line 23. The first term of Doty's court at Prairie du Chien began October 17, 1823.

p. 191 line 14. In Thomas G. Anderson's description of Prairie du

Chien he speaks of "framed" log houses. In 1800 some of the log houses were made by putting up four grooved corner posts and then fitting the horizontal logs into these grooves. There were also log houses made by vertical logs sunk in the ground, in addition to the common log house. In 1853 an Octagon house was built. Posts were put on the corners and mortar and rock filled in between.

p. 195   line 24.   The title of the picture   referred to   should read "Prairie du Chien in 1829" Rolette's house.

p. 196   line 30.   Refers to page 188 line 10.

p. 196.   Brigadier General J. M. Street moved into a house built for him by John Dowling in June 1832. It later became Rialto Hotel. It was here where Judge Mills stopped on his arrival in 1834. James Humprey about 1870 opened a soap factory in the building. There is a residence now on the site. Street planned to sell it to the government. He was the only Indian Agent who lived in it.

p. 200   The Julian LaRiviere home was logs and these later were covered with siding and enlarged. His father Pierre lived there, so did his son Sam. It may have been built as early as 1802.

p. 201.   Father Francis Vincent Badin records of St. Gabriel's church were found by Twaites and he had a photostatic copy made. Marian Scanlan made an English translation. She and her father went to Montreal to see these records. They were kept by the French Jesuits at St. Joseph College. They failed to see them. Some years later Mr. Bernard Kennedy saw them, but they would not give them up, although he had a request from St. Gabriel's to get them.

p. 202   line 29.   Reverend Alfred Brunson, superintendent of the Methodist Episcopal Mission, was not the first Protestant minister to make his home in Prairie du Chien and work among the civilians. In 1818 a Reverend Mann of the Reformed Church lived on Main Village lot 19, and he preached in the log school house several Sundays in succession. Also, one of Street's sons, a Presbyterian, preached at Cassville, and probably at Prairie du Chien.

p. 203.   The Episcopal organization took place at the hospital of Fort Crawford November 20, 1837. Reverend Cadle came to Prairie du Chien November 8, 1837. He was made chaplain at Fort Crawford June 10, 1838 and resigned effective July 1, 1841. In the late summer of that year he was in the eastern part of the state. (Howard Greene, Richard Fish Cadle, privately printed by David Greene Corporation, Waukesha, 1936. pp. 105, 120.)

p. 203.   Keyes, in his 'Journal," 1818 (Manuscript Department, Wisconsin Historical Library) says that   Reverend (Benjamin)   Munn (Mun, Mann) preached in the new school house Sundays from September 6 to November 16. The only available reference to this man is in The History of Pike County, Missouri, published in 1883. (Jefferson Memorial Library). Here he is noted as a Reformed preacher.

p. 204   line 6.   The first contract for the school building to be built specified a building 20x24 feet. However, the building that was actually built measured 20x30 feet. This school house was located on the golf course just west of the new dining hall at Campion and diagonally across from Lawler Hall at the corner of Minnesota St. and E. Campion Blvd.   The school was built in 1846?

p. 209   line 29.   The statement that the Diamond Jo Steamship Line built a large warehouse on the island is in error. The warehouse was built in 1857 by the Mississippi and Milwaukee Railroad.

PART I

Before 1800

CHAPTER ONE

Backgrounds

IN A NARRATION concerning the lands and people who have claimed possession of this city of Prairie du Chien, it is not amiss to go back to early visitations of North America by Europeans, particularly such visitations as affected control of the Mississippi and St. Lawrence rivers and their tributaries.

Columbus on his fourth voyage to the New World, skirted the Central American coast from Nicaragua to Panama. By whom the Gulf of Mexico was first visited is not known, but Pineda sailed along the Texas coast in 1517, and it is likely he was the first white man to visit and ascend the Mississippi River. Garay's map, printed in 1523, traces very distinctly the delta of the Mississippi —the Rio del Espiritu Santo (River of the Holy Ghost). In 1528 De Narvaez set out from San Domingo to explore the lands west of Florida. Cabesa De Vaca, one of the survivors of this expedition, who with three of his men escaped Indian slavery after four years, was the first white man to traverse the United States from sea to sea, for on his journey to Mexico City, which he reached in 1536, he had wandered as far west as Lower California.

In 1539 Friar Mark started eastward from California to explore the country of fabulous wealth of which De Vaca told. Hernando De Soto in the same year set out from the Atlantic coast of Florida, fought his way through the hostile Indian country, reached the Mississippi about 1541, crossed it, explored the Arkansas and much of the country north (nearly as far as the Missouri River) and returned to die and be buried in 1542 in the Mississippi at the mouth of the Arkansas. Moscoso became the leader of the De Soto survivors. Turning westward, he hoped to reach California. On his journey he met an Indian woman who told of Friar Mark's men with whom she had come and from whom she had escaped a few days earlier. Moscoso and Friar Mark missed each other because the former had no faith in the Indian woman's story. Moscoso returned to the Mississippi, built boats, and descended the river to its mouth. He began this trip July 2, 1543. The Indians killed many of his men. The survivors reached Tampico after sailing down the Mississippi River "a thousand miles" and coasting along the shores of the Gulf of Mexico. Tristan in 1559 under the guidance of De Luna reached the Mississippi again. After much trouble his men returned to Mexico whereupon the Spanish seem to have lost all interest in further exploration of the Great River. It is said that a Portuguese navigator sailed up the river in 1630, but the proof is not conclusive.

By reason of her discovery of the mouth of the Mississippi Spain in accordance with the custom of nations claimed all the lands drained by the Great River and its tributaries. Until 1634 when Jean Nicolet entered the territory of the present state of Wisconsin, no white man or nation contested the Spanish claims. The claim to the lower river was not challenged openly until the French approached the upper waters of the Mississippi and traced the river to its mouth. Then La Salle by his *proces verbal* April 9, 1682, formally claimed for the French king all these lands drained by the Mississippi and its tributaries.

By 1700 the French controlled the mouth of the Mississippi. The line between the Spanish and French was never definitely fixed. Neither one sought lands primarily for settlement, but for exploitation of furs and minerals. Their traders intermarried with the Indians. They were less offensive to the natives than the aggressive Englishmen or Americans who came later to dispossess the Indian of his hunting grounds.

While the Spanish access to the river was from the south, the French approached from the waterways of the north and east. On this passageway from the St. Lawrence to the Gulf of Mexico, Prairie du Chien—located at the junction of the Mississippi and Wisconsin Rivers—was destined to be an important point.

The Spanish flag might have waved over this peaceful village had it not been for the defense of the Sioux chief, Wabasha, who turned back an armed vessel sent out by Spain to prevent British and American trade incursions which were made upon the Spanish territory across the Mississippi, with Prairie du Chien as a base. The flags of France, England, and the United States have successively shown the possession of these three nations.

Upon the discovery of America a new interest was aroused in sciences, arts, religion, and in political alignments. The great commercial nations were the first to see, reach out, and take advantage of the era the new world had opened up. While commerce and gain were very active motives in the strife for possession on the new continent, there were other motives, of which religion was the most potent. France was only semi-commercial during this period of discovery. Her people were religious, filled with great zeal to spread the doctrine of Christ, and the savage red men furnished a fertile field for their endeavor.

In 1535 Jacques Cartier sailed up the St. Lawrence River and took possession of the abutting lands in the name of France. The desultory visits of the French until the great soldier of fortune Samuel de Champlain became interested in the exploration of the great basin of the St. Lawrence, were feeble and unavailing in result. Champlain, however, was personally active in exploration. He made the voyage up the St. Lawrence river in 1603 and upon his third visit in 1608 established Quebec. Two years later he explored and named Lake Champlain. In 1629 he was taken prisoner by the English who captured Quebec, but following the restoration of Quebec to France in 1633 he was made lieutenant governor under viceroy Condé. In the meantime the "Company of the Hundred Associates" had been formed for the purpose of trade and exploitation and incidentally the exploration of the new country. Champlain at the head of this organization in Canada, is to be credited with selecting a group of fearless and capable interpreters and explorers to carry on the work.

Jean Nicolet was sent by Champlain when quite a young man to live with the Indians and learn their language that he might become an interpreter for the Canadian government. Born in France, Nicolet came to Canada in 1618 and almost at once was sent to Allumette Island in the Ottawa River to learn the Algonquin tongue. The years from 1623 to 1631 he spent with the Nipissing, living with them as a member of the tribe. In 1627 he was made an official interpreter for the Company of the Hundred Associates. Other young men were going through the same course to learn the Indian language and habits. Among these may be mentioned Marsolet, Brulé, and Le Tardif, the latter a partner and brother-in-law of Jean Nicolet.

The attention of the traveler today is called to many points of interest along the course taken by Nicolet to Wisconsin in 1634. At Sault Ste. Marie a monument marks the place near the Canadian locks where Brulé and his companion reached the outlet of Lake Superior about 1622. Also there is a marker in the Canadian city of Sault Ste. Marie, telling of Nicolet's reaching there in 1634.

Even today, traveling by automobile, one is wearied by the length and difficulties of the journey from Green Bay to Three Rivers; what must have been the hardship of the voyage of Nicolet who traveled three hundred years ago by water and portaged the numerous rapids of the rivers? He had no guides and anywhere along his course he might expect to encounter savage enemies. To the west of Lake Huron lay unknown land. With seven Huron Indians he set out on this long journey by canoe to visit the "Men of the Sea" (Winnebago) to make a trade treaty with them. In his mind was the prevailing dream of the time—that perhaps these Men of the Sea were Orientals; perhaps he was to find the means of access to the Pacific Ocean.

July 4, 1634 Nicolet was at Three Rivers and saw the first pickets for a fort put up. He left Allumette Island in September, and there is nothing to show that he was accompanied by any white man after he left the Ottawa River. From the Ottawa by a short river, the Mattawa, and a difficult portage of four miles to the River de Vase (Muddy River), he reached Lake Nipissing and went down its outlet, what is now French River, to Georgian Bay and then into Lake Huron. He kept along the north shores, entered St. Mary's River, and thus came to Sault Ste. Marie. Returning to Mackinac strait, he entered Lake Michigan, keeping along its northwest shore into Green Bay where he landed presumably at Red Banks, nine miles northeast of the present city of Green Bay.

His bright Mandarin robe, embroidered richly with designs of birds and flowers, and the pistols he bore in each hand and discharged, impressed the Winnebago. They came to meet him, called him Manitou, and carried him and his load to their village. Willingly they entered council during which four thousand warriors feasted him on six score beavers. Whether he went up as far as the Wisconsin River or even sailed on it is not known, but it is more than likely that he learned from the Indians of the Great River. He spent the winter with the Hurons and was back at Three Rivers in July, 1635.

The governor who succeeded Champlain did not encourage discoverers, so Nicolet settled down at Three Rivers as clerk and interpreter for the remainder of his life. On account of the death of Champlain and the fierce wars made upon the French by the

Iroquois it was years before the government put forth any further effort to explore Wisconsin.

However, a group of fugitive Huron Indians came down the Wisconsin and up the Mississippi about 1656 and established themselves in northwestern Wisconsin before 1660.

In the meantime a few venturers, emissaries of the fur trade of New France, traversed Lake Superior and entered Wisconsin at other points. Of all these, the most adventurous were Radisson and Grosseilliers who made their first visit to the West in 1654. Later they penetrated into the wilds along Lake Superior and are credited with having spent a winter in northern Wisconsin, enduring hunger and cold with a band of Indians. Radisson learned of the Great River. Because his Journal says: "By the persuasion of some of them we went into ye great river that divides itself in 2," some historians have claimed that Radisson saw the Mississippi at its junction with the Wisconsin, but recent research disproves this claim.*

When Radisson and Grosseilliers returned from the Upper Country to Montreal in 1660, it took a fleet of Indians to bring their furs. Since these men had ventured without government permission, their pelts were seized and they realized only a small amount on them. Because of resentment over this, Radisson deserted the French and went to Hudson Bay where his action resulted in the chartering of the Hudson's Bay Company, thereafter a powerful factor in the growing fur trade of North America. The estimated $200,000 worth of furs which Radisson and Grosseilliers brought had come from territory never before seen by white men. Since these men were the earliest traders in Wisconsin the fur trade in the northwest may be said to begin with them.

In 1660 Reverend Menard came west along the southern shores of Lake Superior and finally sought his former Huron converts who were located on the headwaters of the Black River. He perished in the woods near the Indian village, his companion having reached it safely. Thus the first Jesuit priest on Wisconsin

---

* Miss Grace Lee Nute, of the Minnesota Historical Society, whose recent study of the Radisson manuscripts in England is to appear soon in published form, says definitely that Radisson did not visit this place. Even assuming truth for the Radisson Journal, it served New France no purpose, as it was not published for a long time after the exploration period and was not published in the United States until 1885.

soil became the first martyr, the first white man to die in this state. By 1665, the Jesuits had a mission at La Pointe.

In 1667 or close to that year Nicolas Perrot, a young, venturous trader, came to Green Bay. He was apparently one of eight Frenchmen who met Reverend Allouez there when he came in 1669 to establish at present-day De Pere the mission of St. Francis Xavier. In 1670 Perrot left Green Bay with a fleet of nine hundred Indians carrying furs to Montreal. The next year Perrot was busy assembling the Indians to meet at Sault Ste. Marie where St. Lusson enacted the *proces verbal* June 14, 1671, in the presence of the Jesuits and Perrot, and in the presence of fourteen different tribes there represented. St. Lusson took over all the country in the name of the French king.

The first reliable historical record of white men at the junction of the Wisconsin and Mississippi Rivers was made by Jolliet and Marquette June 17, 1673. There is no question about these men and the date that they were here; in 1674 the facts were made known to the Governor General of Canada who had sent them on this voyage of discovery. That certainly entitles them to the credit and honor of authenticated discovery of the Mississippi River at this point, and for that reason local Prairie du Chien history rightly begins with them.

CHAPTER TWO

The Early French at the Mouth of the Wisconsin

JOLLIET and Marquette were the first of a long line of French who came to the site of Prairie du Chien. Some of these men were explorers; some, missionaries; some, traders; and some few, travelers. We owe to Frontenac, aggressive Governor General of Canada, the selection of Louis Jolliet as the person to extend the dominion of France to the western lakes and rivers.

Jolliet was Canadian born and twenty-four years old, son of a blacksmith, who had begun his education in a Jesuit college but left it for the love of adventure and the lure of trade and riches. He had made many excursions and had been on Lake Superior.

On his great voyage of discovery he was accompanied by Reverend Jacques Marquette, S.J., who was at that time stationed at the mission of St. Ignace and who had been stationed at La Pointe. Here he had talked to Illinois Indians who on their visits to Chequamegon Bay told of their knowledge of the Great River. Jolliet arrived at St. Ignace December 8, 1672, with Frontenac's orders to discover the Great River; he and Marquette spent the winter together and laid their plans.

May 17, 1673 Jolliet with two Frenchmen and Marquette with three set out in two birchbark canoes.* The way to Green Bay was a known route even at that time, and they arrived at the mission of St. Francis Xavier where they were welcomed by the Jesuits. They proceeded up the Fox River until they reached the Mascouten, a tribe who had been instructed by the Jesuits the preceding year. Here they secured two Indian guides who accompanied them to the portage of the Wisconsin River upon which they entered their canoes alone and finally, June 17, 1673, entered the waters of the Mississippi "with a joy that I can not express," Marquette wrote.

The *Relation* of Marquette does not make it clear as to the hour of the day or whether they landed or whether they turned their

* Because Marquette was not supposed to row and Jolliet was, there were three men with Marquette and only two with Jolliet. Names of three of these men are known.

boats up or down the stream, but it does describe the Mississippi River at Prairie du Chien, as they viewed it from the bluffs or actually went over it, because the *Relation* assures us there were no Indian footprints found. The latitude was taken which while not exact, was at least such that there could be no future danger of mistaking the location. The bald hills, the level plains, the embosomed islands, the double channel of the river, could not have escaped Marquette, and if he made his calculation of the latitude from the stars he must have landed to do so. Did he encamp on the plain that served as a landing for Carver in 1766 or did he prefer the Iowa side where Pond encamped a hundred years later?

It is hardly thinkable that these explorers were not curious to know whence the Great River came and what was its source. It seems plausible that they landed on the present site of Prairie du Chien. Some days after they left the confluence of the Wisconsin and Mississippi, Marquette wrote of the mosquitoes; so there were probably none here when they stopped. These men would not be very far from their canoes in case they landed. When they left their men later to go to the Indian village, they gave strict orders about staying by the canoes. There were many suitable places along the river bank to land and encamp. There were no trees to hide the vision, and so it is not unlikely that Prairie du Chien was Marquette's and Jolliet's first stopping-place on the Mississippi. Evidently there was no Indian village here at that time, or mention of it would have been made. The passing of these Frenchmen marks the first historical event of which we have any written record. The Indian mounds that were found here were not noted by him, as they have been by more recent observers.

We may, in fact, must, conjecture that following the lead of Jolliet and Marquette many adventurous men went over the same route, but no trace of them was left; no record of their travel remains. The man to whom all official honor is due is Jolliet who represented the government and was in full command; however, Marquette, who was twelve years older, better educated, and represented the church, was much respected and his advice and counsel no doubt ruled all their movements. The maps and journals of Marquette were preserved to hand down to students of history the record of the journey; while the bold and fearless Jolliet lost everything at La Chine Rapids, just as he was in sight of Montreal. When his boat overturned, Jolliet's maps, his memoranda, and all were lost, even the little Indian slave boy given him by the Illinois chief to take to the Governor of Canada.[1]

During the winter of 1678-9 Rene-Robert Cavelier de La Salle had sent a Recollect priest, Reverend Louis Hennepin, and Henri de Tonty to build a ship to sail the Great Lakes in order to facilitate La Salle's trade. Tonty, of Italian birth but an adopted son of France, was much feared by the Indians, partly because they knew him respectfully as "the man with the iron hand." La Salle himself was a man of unbounded ambition, intolerant, and over-bearing to his subordinates. These qualities were the very ones that ruined his adventures and later cost him his life.

The *Griffon,* the ship La Salle ordered, was the first ever built on the Great Lakes. It was built and launched near Niagara Falls, a sailing vessel of sixty tons burden. The *Griffon* set out on its first and only voyage August 7, 1679. It sailed successfully on Lakes Erie, Huron, and Michigan, and reached Green Bay. Here it anchored to take on furs to be transported to La Salle's trading-place, established at Mackinac on this voyage. Joutel, La Salle's trader at Green Bay, had gathered from the surrounding country pelts which were loaded on the *Griffon.* The boat set sail on its return voyage but never reached Mackinac and was never heard of again.

La Salle himself, with Tonty and Hennepin, proceeded from Green Bay to Peoria Lake, where January 4, 1680 he started to build Fort Crevecoeur. One historian thinks that La Salle sent Hennepin at this time to build a fort at the mouth of the Wisconsin River; at any rate, in 1682 La Salle wrote a letter, objecting to Duluth's going into the Sioux country by way of the mouth of the Wisconsin because Duluth would kill buffalo on which La Salle claimed a monopoly and more particularly because La Salle had an establishment at that time on the Mississippi at the mouth of the Wisconsin.[2]

It was from Fort Crevecoeur that Hennepin, with two of La Salle's traders, set out February 29, 1680 down the Illinois and up the Mississippi, perhaps expecting to find La Salle's traders at the mouth of the Wisconsin River. They were captured at noon April 12 near the mouth of the Wisconsin by the Sioux, who compelled them to go to the principal Sioux village at Mille Lacs, above the falls on the Mississippi to which Hennepin gave the name St. Anthony's. Here they were held as prisoners for a time and then brought down the Mississippi with a band of Sioux. They were rescued by Duluth who took them before the Sioux chief with whom he had smoked the calumet the year before. Hennepin's narrative of his experiences in New France is not considered trustworthy. In his later years he tried to take the honor of discovery of the Mississippi away from Jolliet and Marquette in favor of La Salle and assume a great deal of credit for discoveries himself, even pretending that during the time he was among the Sioux he was not a prisoner.[8]

Daniel Greysolon Duluth (Du Lhut) had gone with a small group of men by way of Superior into the Sioux country in 1678 without the permission of the government of Canada and had concluded a trade treaty with the Sioux at Mille Lacs. When he was on his way down the Mississippi July 25, 1680, he heard that white men were prisoners of the Sioux and made an effort to find them. Hennepin and his men were released through his influence, after being taken by Duluth to Mille Lacs. Thereupon Duluth with his four men (Lamatrie, Bellegarde, Masson, and Pepin) and Hennepin with his two (Michel Accault and Antoine DuGay Auguel *dit* Picard) went down the Mississippi and at the mouth of the Wisconsin stopped to dry meat for their journey up the Wisconsin, across the portage, and down the Fox to Green Bay, stopping to rest at the mission of St. Francis Xavier at De Pere. They spent the winter at Green Bay or at St. Ignace and in the spring went to Quebec where Duluth was held prisoner until 1681 when *coureurs de bois* were granted an amnesty and Duluth came again into the favor of the government.

The next recorded presence of white men at the mouth of the Wisconsin was in the summer of 1683. Duluth with thirty men came to Green Bay with goods for the Indian trade, bringing Reverend Philippe Pierson, S.J., as chaplain, according to the custom of the time, to restrain the vicious whites and to influence the Indians who had learned to respect the "blackrobe" as a manitou, whether good or evil, who must not be injured by them. They stored their goods at the Jesuit mission and went forth to meet the Fox Indians, who were unfriendly and did not want them to proceed to the Sioux country. However, finding Duluth heavily armed and with a considerable force of white men, the Foxes agreed to let them pass unmolested.

Duluth's party went up the Fox and down the Wisconsin, thence up the Mississippi to the Sioux country where reputedly they built a fort, probably at the headwaters of the St. Croix. All returned the same way they came.

It is not clear that Duluth himself went to the Sioux country that fall because he left Mackinac August 26 and was at Sault Ste. Marie in October, trying three Indians for the murder of two French traders near Keweenaw Bay. With a group of twelve of his own men and about eighteen other French who came to his assistance from Keweenaw Bay he cowed a large concourse of Indians who were assembled, and tried and executed two of the murderers in the presence of all the assembled tribes. This bold move was made to protect his traders in the Indian country. By what authority he tried these Indians is uncertain.

In 1685 Duluth made a second trip to the Sioux country by way of Green Bay and Prairie du Chien, but whether he returned by this route or by Lake Superior is not known. In a ten-year period Duluth had accumulated enough to retire to Montreal, where he spent the rest of his life in luxury. Just prior to his retirement from trade, he was at Prairie du Chien on his last trip to the Northwest.[3] That year, 1688, three prominent men—Duluth, Perrot, and La Hontan—came down the Wisconsin River to its mouth.

Nicolas Perrot had been well known at Green Bay before the Jesuit mission was established. Some say he was there for the first time as early as 1665. Be that as it may, he surely was there in 1667 and was well known by the Indians. He wrote much; he was a man of intelligence, an active trader, a fearless officer, and a power in handling the Indians who loved and feared him.

In 1683 he was accompanied by Monsieur de la Durantaye to Green Bay where they arrived soon after Duluth. Pursuing his purpose of making friends with the Sioux, he followed the Fox and Wisconsin waterway to the mouth of the Wisconsin where he may have established Fort St. Nicolas (designated by Prairie du Chien people as the old French fort in "Lowertown") that year. Within this enclosure Boisguillot, a French Canadian officer, exercised his military authority as late as 1689 while driving a successful trade with the Indians. Boisguillot, a brother-in-law of the elder Langlade, was then in partnership with Perrot.

Perrot was made governor of all the Northwest in 1685 and proceeded to Green Bay, thence to the mouth of the Wisconsin. Any delay at Prairie du Chien might account for his not being able to reach his destination on the upper Mississippi and being obliged to spend the winter at Trempealeau where he erected a winter fort. Reverend Jean Joseph Marest, S.J., was his chaplain. The next spring, 1686, he moved to Lake Pepin where he built Fort St. Antoine. On both of these expeditions Perrot was accompanied by soldiers who passed by the present site of Prairie du Chien on their way to the Sioux country.

In the summer of 1686 Perrot returned to Green Bay where he received orders to evacuate his fort in the Sioux country and proceed to the war against the Iroquois. He said he could not get boats to remove the goods from his fort, and there is nothing to show that he did. While at Green Bay he gave a silver monstrance to the church there, upon which his name was inscribed. It was said that it was given to the Jesuits to keep their good will, and perhaps the governor of Canada had bought it in France. Perrot had furs stored with the Jesuits at the mission and when he went to Montreal to help fight the Iroquois, the pagan Indians burned the Jesuits' storehouse, causing a loss of over forty thousand livres to Perrot, making him a poor man.

With de la Durantaye, he spent the winter of 1687-8 in Lower Canada; Perrot returned to the Sioux country in 1688 and traded that year and the following year. May 8, 1689 in the presence of Reverend Marest, Le Sueur, and Boisguillot who was commanding officer at the mouth of the Wisconsin, by *proces verbal* he took over the entire country in the name of the French king. It does not appear that Perrot was an officer in the French army, but he was a government interpreter for many years, and at this time, authority having been delegated to him, he had a right to command, not as a trader, but as a government officer in charge.

About 1690 a Miami brought Perrot samples of lead, which he pretended he did not care for; however, he promised he would establish a fort within twenty days near their village in the neigh-borhood of the lead mines.* The last act of Perrot in Wisconsin was taking some Indian chiefs to Montreal in 1695.[4]

Baron La Hontan came to Canada with the French marines in order to assist the French against the Iroquois in 1684; at the close of the campaign in 1687 he was made commanding officer of Duluth's fort near Detroit, now the site of Fort Gratiot. This fort he abandoned and burned August 27, 1688. He then went

---

* Supposedly located within the present limits of East Dubuque, Illinois.

to Mackinac where he stayed until September 24, when he left for the Mississippi country. Journeying by way of Green Bay, the Fox and Wisconsin rivers, with a detachment of soldiers, five good huntsmen of the Ottawa, and ten Fox Indian guides, he reached the mouth of the Wisconsin October 23, 1688. He said he landed on an island of the Mississippi and the day after crossed to the other side of the river. November 2 he came to the mouth of the "Longue" River, which, his map shows, empties into the Mississippi a short distance above the mouth of the Wisconsin, from the west. He made some observations in his book, but the "Rive Longue" he described does not answer to the description of any known river, and many feel that he may not have been very far away from Prairie du Chien on the Mississippi. Apparently he reached the mouth of the "Longue" River in one day's travel. He went down the Mississippi and wrote of having sailed on the Missouri and returned on the Illinois, stopping at Tonty's fort where he said he found twenty illegal traders; by way of the Chicago portage and Lake Michigan, he returned to Mackinac, arriving there some time before September 28, 1689, the date of writing this account.

His manuscript, like Hennepin's, is not reliable, but it is possible that it was never intended to be the truth but a burlesque on other travelers' reports. Many of his comments are of interest. He wrote of Green Bay as a place of great trade for skins and Indian corn which the savages sold to the *coureurs de bois* who came and went by the nearest route to the Mississippi. He spoke enthusiastically of the maple sugar which the Indians made and expressed himself as better pleased with the company of the wild Indians than the whites.[5]

Pierre Charles Le Sueur is the next leader whose activities on the Mississippi River affected the history of Prairie du Chien. Le Sueur was born in Artois, France, in 1657 and came to Canada as a young man. Although he was sent to the Jesuit mission at Sault Ste. Marie as a *donné*, the lure of the fur trade was so great that he left the Jesuits to become a trader. Le Sueur said that he came down the Wisconsin for the first time in 1683, and he was a witness at the time of Perrot's *proces verbal* at Fort St. Antoine. From 1683 he was in active trade with the Sioux, and from the time of Duluth's withdrawal from the trade, he was really Duluth's successor in the Lake Superior country.

In 1693 Le Sueur established a fort on Lake Superior and another either at the same time or two years later just above Lake Pepin near the mouth of the St. Croix on an island in the Mississippi, thus keeping the route from the Sioux country to Lake Superior open. His furs were sent to market this way. By 1693 a very large amount of furs went to Montreal from the western country. Boisguillot was affiliated with Le Sueur in the trade in 1695. That year Le Sueur took to Montreal a Sioux chief who died there and so Le Sueur did not feel obligated to return to the Indian country, from which the Canadian government had just recalled all traders.

There was no possibility of securing a new trader's license in 1698, since the fur trade was entirely prohibited on account of the superabundance of furs on the French market; so Le Sueur tried to get permission to go into the Sioux country to explore and to work some mines which he had discovered on the Chippewa River. The Canadian authorities refused him permission because they believed that he would trade in furs, especially as he asked for fifty men to discover lead and copper mines when only six men and one canoe were needed to discover mines.

In 1698 Le Sueur went to France where, by some arrangement, he secured from the French king what had been denied him by the Canadian government—the right to work mines. With two boats, the *Renommée* and the *Gironde* and thirty men, he entered the mouth of the Mississippi at Biloxi, December 7, 1699. The Canadian officers were still opposed to his going into the Sioux country to search for mines, as they were sure he would enter the fur trade and sell guns to the Sioux, thereby causing trouble among the Indian tribes. However, the French officers on the lower Mississippi were willing to overlook the wishes of the government, since they would profit from his illicit trade.

With a Spanish felucca, unlike any boat ever seen on the upper Mississippi, he started up the river, making his first stop at the Illinois settlement where he acquired two men and received a letter from Reverend Gabriel Marest, S.J., telling him to beware, as the Indians were on the warpath. The Sioux had threatened to punish the Illinois for the death of three Sioux who had been killed by the Tamarois, one of the Illinois tribes. The Illinois chief asked Le Sueur to appease the Sioux if he should meet them, and this he did.

An idea of the amount of travel and traffic on the Mississippi at this time may be gleaned from Le Sueur's account of the parties he met. Thirty-one leagues above the mouth of the Illinois he met four Canadians going down to the Illinois country; seventeen leagues farther up he met seventy Sioux in seven canoes going down the river to avenge themselves on the Tamarois. These Indians Le Sueur induced to return.

He took lead out of a place which we believe from the description must have been Snake Hollow, now Potosi, Wisconsin. About at the mouth of the Wisconsin (eleven leagues above the mouth of Grant River) he met five Canadians who had been robbed and one of whom was dangerously wounded in the head. They had one wretched gun and five or six charges of powder and ball. Their story was that while they were descending from the Sioux to the Tamarois, forty leagues above, they had met nine canoes with ninety Indians who had plundered and cruelly beaten them. This was a party of Foxes, Sauk, Potawatomi, and Winnebago who were going to make war on the Sioux.

Le Sueur passed the mouth of the Wisconsin September 1. Just below La Crosse he discovered some canoes of Indians that the Canadians recognized as the ones who had robbed them. Le Sueur arranged to defend himself, but the Indians pretended to be friendly and said the Sioux had taken all they had. He gave them powder; this was done, he said, to provide safety for a missionary who was to go into the Sioux country, probably Reverend Gabriel Marest.

Le Sueur's record speaks of a lead mine three leagues up the Chippewa River and of a copper mine higher up. He speaks also of a cave on the Mississippi near the St. Croix, dangerous to enter because of rattle snakes. Just below the mouth of the St. Croix, he met a group of forty-seven Indians of several different nations dwelling east of the Mississippi River. They brought a Frenchman, Denis, who told Le Sueur that they had accidentally killed La Place, a deserter from the Canadian army.

Just below St. Anthony's Falls Le Sueur left the Mississippi and went up what is now the Minnesota, then called St. Peter's, some say in honor of Le Sueur himself, whose first name was Pierre (Peter). Later, he left the St. Peter's River and went up what is now known as the Blue Earth to a point where he expected to work the mines of blue and green clay. As he landed, he met nine Sioux who told him that he was on the lands of the Iowa and Oto.

October 3, 1700, he received several Sioux in his fort, called Fort L'Huillier in honor of his benefactor. The last day of September when he started building his fort, one half of his men went hunting, killing four hundred buffaloes. While the fort was being built, seven traders from Canada who had been plundered and stripped naked by the Sioux came to the place. Le Sueur had known one of them in Canada and he furnished them with clothes. They stayed all winter with Le Sueur. The Sioux who had robbed them came to the fort to trade and made some amends. They brought for trade four hundred beaver robes—each robe made of nine skins sewed together. Le Sueur bought these and many others.

At the beginning of May, 1701, Le Sueur launched on the water his shallop loaded with the green earth taken from the mines and with pelts from his trading. He had about three canoe-loads of furs. Before he started, he held a council between three Sioux chiefs, who were brothers, and Monsieur d'Eraque, a Canadian gentleman, at which council it was agreed that the Sioux would maintain peace with d'Eraque who was left in command of the fort and twelve Frenchmen. Le Sueur made the Sioux presents and then departed.

On leaving, he promised to send a canoe loaded with ammunition from the Illinois. When he arrived at the Illinois settlement, he did send three men with a canoe laden with powder and lead to the value of two thousand livres; but nearly opposite to Perrot's mine the canoe split in two and all was lost. The three men in charge proceeded down to the fort of St. Denis, a short distance above the present site of New Orleans. Bienville and St. Denis immediately sent a canoe with ammunition and food with orders to hasten it to Fort L'Huillier to replace the one lost. In the meantime Le Sueur unloaded his furs and went down in his shallop to Biloxi where d'Iberville was getting two ships unloaded. In the spring of 1702 when d'Iberville sent a transport to St. Denis at his fort on the lower Mississippi, he found there d'Eraque and the Frenchmen from Fort L'Huillier. After the Fox Indians killed two Frenchmen working in the woods near the fort, the rest of the party cached the goods and came down the Mississippi, abandoning the fort. There is nothing of further interest to us concerning Le Sueur.[6]

Other events were pending in the French possessions in America, while these numerous bold and wilful violators of the law were roaming the wilds of the upper Mississippi. Disunion arose between Louisiana and Canada—as to disputed boundaries, policies governing the treatment of Indian tribes, and rules of trade. New France had forbidden the beaver trade in her territory and called in all of the commanding officers, many of whom either worked at or profited from the illegitimate trade.

D'Iberville came to Louisiana in 1699 to colonize it and to exclude the Spanish and English from the Mississippi. It is said that soon after his arrival, d'Iberville and his brother Bienville, who was acting as commanding officer, met a British vessel at the mouth of the Mississippi on its way up the river. By subterfuge Bienville induced them to return to the Gulf of Mexico, telling them they were not on the Mississippi River at all. This would indicate a timely arrival of the French to head off the British, for a while at least. D'Iberville and Bienville, while hostile to British and Spanish discoverers and traders, permitted and assisted Le Sueur and other French to violate the Canadian trade laws.

We have seen that Le Sueur was allowed to go up the Mississippi with thirty men to work mines. The three canoeloads of furs that he acquired in the Sioux country, the richest robes ever received, were accepted at Bienville's fort. Other *coureurs de bois* who were forbidden to trade for beaver likewise acquired large quantities of furs and found ready sale for them in Louisiana. Thus, while the governor of Canada was trying to restrain illegal trading, the governor of Louisiana was receiving goods and thereby demoralizing the trade. At one time when traders were ordered to Montreal, instead of following instructions, one hundred *coureurs de bois* went down the Mississippi to the Louisiana territory, secured ammunition, and reaped large financial rewards. The recall of the commanding officers and missionaries removed all restraint from those who sought this rapid road to wealth. The governor of Canada on different occasions asked that *coureurs de bois* be given reprieve on condition that they would return to the colony. Some did; others ignored the opportunity and followed in their natural course of illegal trade, going either to the French on the lower Mississippi or to the British on the Ohio.

Because of the difficulty of preventing illegal traders like Le Sueur from plying their trade in the upper country, it was proposed in 1700 by a new Canadian trading company which had displaced the Hundred Associates that a series of trading forts be established for the purpose of preventing *coureurs de bois* from going to the English and also for the purpose of stopping English traders from entering the Northwest country.

The Sioux beaver trade was best because of the great number of valuable animals in their country; also, as the whites advanced from the east, the fur-bearing animals were no longer to be found in the original hunting-grounds. Better methods of trapping and killing, an increase in the number of traders and in the intensity with which they sought out people who had furs to sell had marked effects. Explorers had to go farther to seek new territory to ply the trade,—the more territory, the more aggrandizement for the mother country.

Possession was nine points of the law, and different European nations plunged forward and found men filled with love of adventure and greed for gain who stopped at no consideration in extending the territory of their mother countries. The French resented particularly the inroads of the British. In the absence of the commanding officer at Mackinac in 1685 some English traders went to Mackinac and after a large trade returned in safety to Albany.

Three forts were projected—at the mouth of the Wisconsin River, near Detroit (this to replace the former stronghold at Mackinac), and at the mouth of the Ohio. The first of these evidently was not erected. A fort was established near Detroit in 1701. This was to be the gateway of all Canadian trade between Montreal and the Northwest. It was especially intended to prevent the recurrence of English intrusion. However, the greed of the commanding officer at Detroit, Cadillac, led to much dissatisfaction, and in 1713 the fort at Mackinac was reestablished and was ever afterwards the main entrepot to the Northwest. The establishment of a fort at the mouth of the Ohio had long been a cherished wish of Canada and Louisiana, but it was not until 1702 that the actual establishment took place. Charles Juchereau Sieur de St. Denis, a resident of Lower Canada, was the man chosen for the undertaking. A fort was built at the mouth of the Ohio on the site of the present city of Cairo, Illinois, but St. Denis himself lived only two years after its erection, and upon his death it was abandoned.[7]

This St. Denis was a brother of Louis Juchereau *dit* St. Denis, an officer under Bienville in Louisiana. The brothers had worked

at Levis with Bissot (father of the founder of Vincennes, Indiana),
who among his many activities owned and operated a tannery which
proved to be his most profitable investment.

In the spring of 1702 Charles St. Denis set out from Detroit
with Reverend Jean Mermet as chaplain, for Mackinac. There he
established a tannery and then proceeded to Green Bay and down
the Wisconsin and Mississippi until he reached the mouth of the
Ohio.[8] It is easy to believe that he bought buffalo skins on the way,
as he passed through country where there were plenty of buffalo.
At the portage of the Wisconsin the Winnebago would not let him
pass until he gave them a canoe load of goods valued at $5,000.
These Indians had been exacting tribute of the traders for some
time, and it was dangerous to go that way to the Mississippi.[9] Although St. Denis left Mackinac with eight canoes manned by four
men each, he reached his destination somewhat crippled in necessi-
ties because of his heavy loss. After the fort was built, his men
were all taken sick with fevers and in two years St. Denis and nearly
all of his men died. Reverend Mermet left the deserted fort and
went to the Illinois settlement.

St. Denis had hired Kickapoo Indians to bring buffalo skins to
his tannery, and much leather was allowed to rot on the ground
when the fort was abandoned in 1704. Had St. Denis located with
his tannery at Prairie du Chien, where he would have found it
healthy, it might have meant much to him and to Prairie du Chien.

Many adventurers lost their lives in the upper country. Often-
times a French name along the routes of travel marks the tragedy
of some *voyageur*, as a man's name was frequently given to the
place where he lost his life. This was a French custom followed by
the Canadians.

In 1700 the Governor of Canada sent Captain Alphonse de
Tonti to Mackinac to cause the Frenchmen who remained there to
come down to the colony. He brought back only twenty; the others,
eighty-four in number, for the most part proceeded to the Mississippi where thirty of them with ten canoes loaded with beaver sold
to d'Iberville. Later, after his departure, ten more canoes reached
his establishment on the Mississippi. It is no wonder Le Sueur met
so many French on his trip up the river in 1700. The king advised
that these men be allowed to settle in Louisiana and many of them
did. At this time it was planned to move the settlement from
Mackinac to Detroit. However, Reverend Jean Joseph Marest was

retained at Mackinac as a missionary, from 1700 until the reestablishment of the fort there in 1713.

Much detailed information concerning individuals in trade is gleaned from a study of the licenses granted traders. France and later England believed it necessary to keep a record of those men who went into the Indian country themselves or who engaged boatmen to go for them. Contracts for these engagements included the names of the contracting persons, a statement of the length of the engagement, and the party's destination. They were signed, witnessed, and recorded at the city of departure—most often Montreal.[10]

April 23, 1704, Raymond Jean *dit* Godon was engaged by Francois Marie Bouat, a prominent merchant and outfitter and Canadian officer, to go to the Mississippi River. His name does not appear later in the records, although the year before he had engaged with the Company of the Colony to go to Lake Erie. We have no further record in this case.

Le Sueur's wife (Marguerite Messier) also engaged a man in April of this year to make the journey to the mouth of the Mississippi. This same year Bouat sent to the Mississippi Charles Dasny, but no future engagement appears; however, he may have remained in the western country. At that time too often the goods of the outfitter were carried to the Illinois country and the men did not make any returns; furthermore, Bouat had many boats consigned to Detroit, some of which were sent to the Illinois country, from which the illegal traders had an outlet either at the mouth of the Mississippi or with English traders on the Ohio River.[11]

From 1700 to 1708 very few canoes came down from the upper country, but in 1708 there were sixty. It was advised that a fort be placed at Mackinac and a limited number of licenses granted in order to increase French trade and prevent Indians from going to the English Hudson's Bay Company. It was seen that few Indians came to Montreal during those years, and the *coureurs de bois* feared the loss of their goods and possible imprisonment if they returned to the colony.

From 1700 until about 1740 the governor of New France was either not able or not willing to pay much attention to the Northwest. Queen Anne's War (1701-13) was a disturbing element in the colonies, as the rival nations incited the Indians to war on the whites. So far as Wisconsin was concerned, the Fox Indians resisted white civilization the longest and were the most troublesome, the most warlike, and the least understood. The Fox wars were long and bloody and costly to the traders. These Indians were jealous of the traders' selling guns to the Sioux who were their bitter enemies and were a menace to the smaller Indian tribes because of their number. The exacting of tribute from all who attempted to go by the Green Bay and Wisconsin route to the Mississippi practically prevented any traffic over that route.

In spite of the difficulties, many French lived with the Indians. Famous interpreters like Maurice Menard and Jean Baptiste Reaumé were well versed in the language of Foxes and Sioux by 1715. The Jesuits, too, maintained their mission at De Pere until its abandonment in 1728, but fewer missionaries were sent into these distant parts of the Northwest.

Efforts were made in 1712, 1716, 1726, and 1728 to pacify or quell the Foxes, but they were so treacherous and fierce that it became the policy of the Canadian government to wage a war of extermination against them.

The French hoped that after Lignery's negotiations at Green Bay in 1726 there would be a lasting peace. The cheerful version of affairs sent by Duplessis, commanding officer at Green Bay, in 1727 was misleading in the extreme.

The First Sioux Trading Company was formed in Montreal June 6, 1727, to carry out a plan, cherished since 1723, of building an establishment in the Sioux country. The danger of passing through the territory of the Foxes had delayed the accomplishment of this purpose. The establishment was to be "useful for discovery of the western sea" as well as advantageous to all the settlements on the Mississippi. Furthermore, the conversion of the Sioux was the great motive of the two Jesuit priests who accompanied the expedition.

The contract between the government and the company was comprehensive. Excerpts are of interest. "They shall not be permitted to trade on the Ouisconsin nor on the portage by which they must pass to reach the Sioux. . . . Should they be stopped on the way in the country of the Renards, or beyond, or should they when they reach the Sioux country, be compelled by superior force to return this year, they shall be permitted to trade their goods wherever they think proper. . . . They further undertake to purchase three or four extra canoes when they reach Michilimakinak in order the more easily to traverse the River of the Renards, and that of Ouisconsing and to carry in such canoes 600 pounds weight for the missionaries . . ." It was signed by Beauharnois, Longueuil, La Corne, d'Aigremont, Saint George Dupré, Youville, Pierre Daillay [Dumay], Marin,* Etienne Petit, Garrau [Garreau], Francois Campeau, Francois de May, Pierre Richard, Jean Baptiste Boucher de Montbrun, Francois Boucher de Montbrun, and Jean Garrau.[12]

The expedition left Montreal June 16, 1727, and in five weeks reached Mackinac. It included, besides the signers of the contract, the boatmen and soldiers, together with René Boucher de la Perrière, commanding officer; Pierre Boucher of Boucherville, his nephew, who was second in command; la Jemeraye; Maurice Menard, interpreter; and Reverends Guignas and Gonner, S.J. Descendants of many of this group of men live or have lived in Prairie du Chien.

They left Green Bay August 15 and arrived at Lake Pepin September 17. Two miles from the present railroad station of Frontenac, Minnesota, on the west side of Lake Pepin they chose their site and built Fort Beauharnois, so named in honor of the Governor General. After the winter was past, de la Perrière and Reverend Nicolas Gonner started back, leaving Pierre Boucher, nephew of de la Perrière, in command.

Lignery's report to the Canadian government dated at Green Bay August 30, 1728, said that he had arrived at Mackinac August 4 and with about 1200 men including 400 whites and Indians of many tribes proceeded against the Foxes. Liberal promises of trade were made to those who would accompany Lignery on this expedition. He surrendered four old men who were captured to the savages to be tortured and burned the Fox villages which had been deserted by the Indians, who had fled upon warning of the approach of the army. Because of the failure of the commanding officer in Illinois to head them off at the mouth of the Wisconsin, the Foxes were not pursued on their retreat into Iowa.[13]

Lignery, aware of his failure, burned the fort at Green Bay and retired, with the missionaries, to Mackinac, leaving Damours, sieur de Clignancourt, a trader, alone during the winter of 1728-9. Before leaving Green Bay, Lignery, who realized that his expedi-

* Claude Marin, because he is the one who had a license to the Sioux country that year.

tion had served only to exasperate the Foxes and that the Sioux Company men were in grave danger, sent five French with two Menominee through the woods, across Wisconsin from Green Bay to Fort Beauharnois to notify the French there to look out for the Foxes and to warn them to return by way of La Pointe and Lake Superior.

After hearing from the runners from Green Bay, Boucher held a council at Fort Beauharnois September 18, 1728, to decide what to do. October 3 twelve of the number—among them Reverend Guignas and the Montbrun brothers—started down the Mississippi in three canoes, hoping to reach the Illinois country. Because the rivers were low at this time, traces of a party of Foxes were found at the mouth of the Wisconsin. October 16 the French were captured by Kickapoo between Rock River and the Des Moines and held captives at their main village nearby. The Kickapoo said that they had learned from six Frenchmen and two Menominee that Lignery had driven the Foxes from their country. Boucher made presents to the young men in an effort to win their favor. By some means the Montbrun brothers and another man escaped, to the Illinois country. Their escape influenced the Kickapoo not to harm the others. They protected them from the Foxes and in the spring all were allowed to go to the Illinois. All had suffered greatly, and Reverend Guignas especially arrived in great distress. From the Illinois, they were sent home.

The French who spent the winter at Fort Beauharnois were not molested by the Sioux. The Winnebago and Foxes came and camped near the fort and induced la Jemeraye, an ensign, a nephew of de la Perrière, to bring some Fox chiefs to St. Joseph's. They detained him twenty-one days, after which fourteen of them went with him in safety to St. Joseph's, but the chiefs would not go farther. Those who remained at the fort during the winter returned home by way of Lake Superior.

Peace being restored with the Foxes, Beauharnois again entered into a contract with another group of merchants to exploit the Sioux country. The contract was signed at Montreal June 6, 1731. René Godefroy de Linctot was made commanding officer with Pierre, son of Rene Robineau, Sieur de Portneuf, second in command, Reverend Guignas, missionary, and about twenty traders.[*14]

* The traders were the Sieurs Mouet, one of whom was Augustin, Sieur de Langlade; Linctot the younger (Hubert); Coulonge; Giguières; Toussaint; Sieur

This Second Sioux Company was a larger and better equipped organization than the one sent out in 1727. There were licenses granted to several for the Sioux post in 1731. Charles Langlade's father and uncle were members of this company and continued in the trade many years, apparently as small and independent traders. Linctot wrote from the Sioux country that these men were not able to get to Fort Beauharnois on time but were compelled to winter (1731-2) at Trempealeau where, on account of scarcity of food, some men went to neighboring villages to live with the Indians. (Antoine) Dorval, a member of the Second Sioux Company, was sent to winter with the Fox Indians at the mouth of the Wisconsin.

While Dorval was in this region, a Fox village about twelve miles east of the site of Prairie du Chien was destroyed by Iroquois and Hurons. The official report of this attack mentioned the existence of two settlements "a village of forty-five cabins near Ouisconsin [on the Grand Gris] in which were ninety men, besides nine other cabins at a distance from the former." From this report and from Dorval's account we are sure of the existence of an Indian village of "nine cabins" at Prairie du Chien as early as 1732.[15]

In the summer of 1732 a large number of canoes went to the Sioux post. The next year a group of Illinois of the village of Le Rocher sent thirty of their young men against the Sioux. Near the Wisconsin they fell on Chippewa, Menominee, Sauk, and Nipissing, killing three men, three women, and a baby, and capturing two little girls whom the chief of Illinois promised to bring to Mackinac to be returned by the commanding officer to the Chippewa.

In 1735 Louis Nolan took a score or more of *engagées* to the post of the Sioux. This seems to be the largest trading fleet ever sent into the upper country by an individual trader. This year, in the face of Indian troubles, the receipt from beaver skins was considerable. Between the posts of the west of Lake Superior and

---

de Portneuf; (Pierre) Richard; Du Bau (Dubeau); Pierre and Charles Le Duc; Francois Guyon (*dit*) Desprez; St. Michel *dit* Charles du Chesne; Antoine Lanouette; Joseph Joliette; (Francois) Campeau, blacksmith; name of interpreter not shown. All signed except Giguières, Toussaint, Pierre and Charles Du Chesne, and Du Bau who could not write.

the post of the Sioux, nearly 100,000 good skins were received, valued at 178,000 livres.[16]

St. Pierre, who succeeded Linctot as commanding officer among the Sioux, said that the Indians seemed to be well-intentioned and some planned to go down to Montreal in 1736. Trading continued until 1737, all of the canoes traveling over the Wisconsin-Fox route to Green Bay and Mackinac.

An earlier census of Indians of the Mississippi River and Northwest listed for Green Bay one hundred fifty Sauk warriors, one hundred Foxes, eighty Kickapoo, sixty Mascouten, one hundred Potawatomi, and ten Miami. This indicated a small Indian population in comparison with what Nicolet had found. The report on the Sioux to be compiled by Linctot was not received. The Sioux visited the French fort many times during the winter of 1736-7.

After St. Pierre started to build another fort farther up the Mississippi, he learned that the Sioux had changed their feeling toward the French; perhaps their massacre of Verendrye's son and Reverend Aulneau and the convoy that was taking men to the forts of the western sea had excited in them a lust for blood. At last the Sioux attacked the Chippewa near the fort, and after a consultation with Linctot the younger, second in command, and Reverend Guignas May 30, 1737, the French abandoned and burned Fort Beauharnois. Then the Chippewa-Sioux war made it unsafe on the upper Mississippi. However, thirty *coureurs de bois* insisted on going into the Indian country in spite of danger and in violation of the laws.[17]

Tradition has it that some of these men returning from Fort Beauharnois in 1737 established themselves at the mouth of the Wisconsin and formed the nucleus of the future Prairie du Chien. Lockwood, an early American settler, said that "about 1737 the French established a trading post here and built a stockade around their buildings to protect them from the Indians."

Of all the travelers familiar with the confluence of the Mississippi and Wisconsin, Perrot alone is known with certainty to have established a storage fort at this point. There is a legend, however, that there was a fort at Prairie du Chien in 1755, built by one of the Marins. The Marins will be discussed in the following chapter. In a resolution in Congress on land claims in 1817, the citizens of Prairie du Chien asked that claims be extended as far east as the

Kickapoo River, using as leverage for the claims the former existence of Marin's fort.

Certainly this place was an important entrepot for the Sioux
and other upper Mississippi trade, and for almost thirty years after
1727 no name was more important in trade here than the name
Marin.

CHAPTER THREE

The Marins

WHETHER or not the Marins had a fort at Prairie du Chien, all of them knew the location well. There has been much confusion as to the identity of the three Marins—Pierre Paul, Joseph, and Claude—and it is with the idea of clearing this confusion as also of showing the extensive travel and varied government service of many French of the period that the biographies of the Marins are given in as great detail as the records show. These biographies will tend to prove that, despite the persistence of a legend to the contrary, none of the Marins built a fort here, particularly in 1755.[1]

The Marins were well-connected and were untiring servants of the French government, save as the interests of the fur trade caused them to conceal their activities from a too solicitous home colony. Pierre Paul Marin was the father of Joseph Marin and the older brother of Claude. All three were traders and soldiers of importance.[2]

Paul Marin's wife, Josette, daughter of Joseph Guyon, was a cousin of Therese Guyon (St. Germain), a daughter of Denis Guyon, who married the commanding officer at Detroit, La Mothe Cadillac. Jean Guyon Dubuisson, commanding officer at Green Bay from 1729 to 1732 was perhaps an uncle to Paul Marin's wife. Claude Marin's wife was a daughter of De Villiers, commanding officer at Green Bay, and widow of Francois le Febre Duplessis, both of whom lost their lives at the hands of the Sauk Indians in 1733. In 1737 she married Claude Marin, Sieur de la Perrière, and after his death, in 1758 she married Damours, Sieur Clignancourt, the lone trader who remained at the deserted fort at Green Bay in 1728. She spent the greater part of her life in Lower Canada, in all probability.

Pierre Paul Marin was perhaps the most striking, as he was the most illusive, character who came to Wisconsin to trade. He was born at Montreal March 19, 1692, and married Josette Guyon Dupres in 1718. Most of the early part of his life seems to be hidden in obscurity. However, because of his connection with Bouat, it is likely he traded out from Detroit prior to 1718. Marin was sent to Chequamegon Bay as an ensign with St. Pierre in 1722 and continued in trade at that point until he was appointed in command of a convoy for the traders of the Lake Superior region in 1726. The next fourteen years he spent in private trade and in the service of the government.[3]

The first recorded notice of Paul Marin, Sieur la Malgue, as a trader, is a written contract between him and Montigny and Bouat dated 1719 when he was spoken of as an ensign in Illinois.[4] He was engaged in the western trade in 1727-8 and then in 1729 was at Green Bay. This year he got licenses for two canoes to Green Bay and he and nine men arrived in the late summer and rebuilt a palisaded fort upon the site of the Menominee Indian fort. That was the year that the Fox Indians had been attacked by a group of other tribes on the Wisconsin when they were returning from a buffalo hunt.

Beauharnois reported an attack, which may be this one or a similar one about the same time, in which it was said that one hundred Foxes were slain, thirty warriors and the rest, women and children. This perhaps was the cause of the Foxes' attacking the Winnebago, who sought the aid of the Menominee and Marin. Marin left four of his men at the fort and took five white men and thirty or forty Menominee warriors with him to go to the assistance of the Winnebago. After several days the Foxes withdrew from their attack. He induced the Menominee and Winnebago not to pursue them, lest they be defeated. Marin returned to Mackinac, where Dubuisson, commanding officer, with four hundred men, was ready to set out against the Foxes. Marin returned to Green Bay with him, and it seems reasonable that the severe defeat of the Foxes, instead of being administered by Marin and nine men, was more likely to have been caused by Marin reinforced with Dubuisson's troops.[5]

If Dubuisson had been ordered to go to Le Rocher in Illinois to assist the other commanding officers, he did not go, for he was at Montreal before news of defeat of the Foxes reached there. Neither Dubuisson nor Marin is reported as having been there, although the two left Mackinac together in 1730. Dubuisson was censured for his expedition against the Foxes because it was carried out without orders from the higher authorities. It may have been to protect Dubuisson that Marin took upon himself the responsibility for the overwhelming defeat of the Foxes at Butte des Morts in 1730.

Paul Marin was trading at Mackinac in 1732 and at Nipigon on Lake Superior the next two or three years. In November, 1738, he was given orders to proceed to the Sauk village on the Mississippi at the mouth of Rock River to make headquarters.* In the winter and spring of 1739 Marin was seriously sick. In 1740 he was commanding officer at Green Bay and continued in this position until 1743.

June 20, 1740 there was a council held by Beauharnois at Montreal at which the Menominee objected to the Chippewa going through their country to war on the Sioux. Marin, who had plenty of difficulties with the Indians during this period, had brought Foxes, Sauk, Winnebago, Ottawa, and Menominee chiefs to Montreal, arriving June 16. This year the Sioux did not come. They were afraid of the Ottawa because they had killed a man and his wife of that nation in the spring at the portage of the Wisconsin.

At the mouth of the Wisconsin, Marin had a talk with the Sioux January 18, 1741, and ransomed a Chippewa woman who was a prisoner among them. The Sioux claimed she was held as hostage because of Chippewa attacks. Their chiefs were willing to go down to Montreal to see the Governor-General if some one would go with them, but Marin could not go because he was too badly needed to keep order. Just at this time Sieur L'Ecuyer arrived from La Pointe with news that the Chippewa had attacked and killed a large number of Sioux. Marin wrote that with the aid of Sieur L'Ecuyer he did his best to stop the Chippewa and Sioux from warring on each other.

The Indians had moved westward and south because of difficulties with the French at Green Bay, but Marin wrote June 13, 1741, that the Winnebago had already returned and the others would return if the French sent no traders to Chicago.

August 6, 1741, Marin wrote that all was quiet at Green Bay and he was going to Mackinac to try to prevent the Ottawa and Chippewa from going by way of Green Bay against the Sioux. That year eight cabins of Mascouten wished to settle among the Miami because they feared the Foxes and Sioux on the Wisconsin River. A party of Sioux and Foxes went against an Illinois tribe to surprise them, but the Sauk had warned them to be on their guard.

* About this time, by a Sauk woman, Marin became the father of a daughter who was later the mother of Keokuk's wife.

Marin took a number of chiefs to Montreal in 1741 for another council. The English were secretly sending agents to various Indian tribes to induce them to desert the French and trade with the English. Among these agents were Foxes who had sent war parties against the Illinois. Beauharnois at his house held a secret council to consider the matter of warring on the Fox tribe.* They were secure in their position, however, and difficult to deal with because, in case they desired to retreat, the Iroquois had secretly agreed to harbor them, and the Sioux of the Prairie were equally willing to afford them asylum in case of need.

During Marin's absence—perhaps in Montreal—fifty Illinois (Pimetous) went against the Foxes at the mouth of the Wisconsin and killed four women and wounded one man. Thereupon the Sauk went in great number and surrounded the Illinois as they returned down the Mississippi in canoes. The Sauk killed nine and took five prisoners. When the Illinois were recognized, the Sauk regretted their act. It was believed that this encounter might lead to a war between the two nations.

The summer of 1742 Marin was at the council with Beauharnois at Montreal.† He appeared to be chief representative of the Sioux at this time. Joachim Sacquespee Sieur Gonincourt, one of Marin's traders and an ensign, was left in charge of Green Bay in his absence. Sacquespee was sent with a chief's son to settle an affair in which the Menominee had killed two Foxes. It is not clear where this village was to which they were sent. Marin wrote from the Portage of the Great Calumet (on the Ottawa River) that the Chippewa and Ottawa had killed a Sioux and a Fox and he would have difficulty in settling the affair. However, August 29 Sieur de Sacquespee wrote from Green Bay that all was quiet there, and on his return trip Marin wrote from Mackinac September 8, 1742, that he arrived there September 3.

During his command, very few licenses were given for the post. Paul Marin and his brother Claude had many licenses to Mackinac

* Present: Baron de Longueuil, Messrs. De la Chassaigne, La Corne, de Lig-nery, La Noue, and Duplessis-fabert.
† Present: Sauk, Foxes, Menominee, Chippewa, and Sioux and Winnebago of two villages—one near Green Bay and one on Rock River. Speaking to the Menominee, Beauharnois said: "I give the principal chiefs and the distinguished women presents." This indicates that the Indian women were not always left at home when there was tribal business on hand. Glory-of-the-Morning was no doubt at this council.

during this time and later. Whether Claude traded in Wisconsin or whether any other traders, either legal or *coureurs de bois,* traversed the territory over which Paul Marin had a monopoly does not appear. However, Jean Garreau St. Onge* was in Mackinac in 1739, and often traders did not return the same year they went into the upper country. Probably he and others pushed trade wherever they could.

In 1742 Marin requested leave of absence so he could go back to France the next year. In recommending the leave, Beauharnois said that Marin had been continuously on detached duty among the savages except for a leave of absence granted in 1736. He said that Marin had enemies due to envy and jealousy "as happens in this country. On my arrival in 1726 he was recommended as a good man who had been among the savages all his life. He always commanded respect at a post."[6]

Following 1742 there is an interim of about seven years during which Marin was active elsewhere than in Wisconsin. To be commanding officer of a western post was understood to mean an opportunity for personal aggrandizement. So long as a semblance of order and a degree of friendliness of the Indians for the French were maintained, other activities of the commanding officers were practically unrestricted. The Governor General of Canada was not above accepting his share in illicit trade. Paul Marin made huge profit from his office, but he was fortunate in the periods when he held command. As a soldier, he was usually recalled from the West when there were grave Indian troubles and at such times the profit from trade was lessened by the difficulty of transporting goods past the country of hostile tribes.

In 1743 the policy of the Canadian government was changed. Trading rights for Green Bay and its dependencies were sold for

* Not one of the older Garreaus. He was an active trader in the Northwest for many years. He had a license for La Baye in May, 1743. Twice he appeared in a partnership. In 1744 he appeared again as a licensed trader. He had been one of the traders of the First Sioux Company and knew about the Indians and the good furs of the upper Mississippi. Whether he made his headquarters at Green Bay or went into the Sioux section or perhaps lived at the neutral ground at the mouth of the Wisconsin he no doubt obtained the furs from the upper Mississippi.

Among the men who held licenses early from the British are several men of this name. Jean Baptiste St. Onge for Detroit in 1769; Charles St. Onge for Lake Superior in 1770; boatmen: Francois St. Ange, 1775; Francois St. Onge in 1769; Jean Bapt. St. Onge, 1769; Jean St. Onge, 1770, and a St. Ange, 1772. Perhaps these are all the same family. Also, we know Jean Garreau as St. Onge, and there was an Etienne Auge at Green Bay.

8100 livres to Joseph de Fleury Sieur de la Gorgendiere* who transferred his rights to Louis Dailleboust, Sieur de Coulonge, and other traders. This sale took place at the Chateau St. Louis, Quebec, March 26, 1743. Under the new arrangement† Marin was recalled and the commanding officer, Lusignan, became a figurehead. He found the traders more difficult to handle than the Indians and complained of them as independent and insubordinate. The Foxes and Sauk were at this time assembled near Green Bay except for ten cabins at Chicago and two at Milwaukee.

With no garrison, Lusignan was unable to arrest illegal traders, and the "farmers" of the post entered into contract with eight or ten *coureurs de bois* who came the first of May to purchase six thousand livres' worth of beaver skins for which they were to be supplied with goods. Lusignan's wrath was aroused particularly by Sieur Auger,‡ one of the worst traders, whose return to Montreal was threatened.[7]

King George's War disturbed trade with England in 1744. Goods were scarce and only a few canoes went into the upper country.§ The Shawnee, now French in sympathy, had captured eight English traders, and it was expected that the British Indians would soon treat the French in the same manner. Paul Marin, who was likely in France in 1743, the following year found work in eastern Canada, where he was selected to lead an expedition of western Indians and Canadians against Acadia. He was to have the help of the Acadians and local Indians so that when he appeared around the Basin of Minas in June, 1745, practically all of the Acadians declared for the French. He was welcomed and supplied plentifully with provisions and stores for which he paid partly in money and partly in notes. He was summoned to go with his western Indians to the relief of Louisburg in Acadia, but he arrived after Louisburg had surrendered. Then he was assigned to the north coast of New England where he was so dreaded because of his cruelty and his great influence upon the Indians that the British put a price upon his head.[8]

* In 1702 Gorgendiere had married Claire, daughter of Louis Jolliet.

† Paul Marin's last license for Green Bay was granted in August, 1742. Joseph Marin had a license to Green Bay July 25, 1742.

‡ Francois Ange (Anger, Auger) representing himself and company hired (among others) for Green Bay Joseph Papineau *dit* Montigny. Etienne Anger was killed later at Green Bay by a Menominee.

§ One Louis Delerigé, sieur Delaplante engaged men that year, for the Upper Country (especially the North) and for Mackinac.

The end of the war was in prospect in 1747 when Vercheres was appointed new commandant at Green Bay and new farmers* contracted with Montreal merchants "to exploit the post of La Baye des Puans" (Green Bay) under certain conditions. The farmers were to have "Exclusive Trade with the Savages and the French settled throughout the whole Extent of the said post, to Wit: with the Puants, folles avoines, Renards, Sakis, and Scioux, Being careful to treat the latter with circumspection And to attract them as much as possible." They were not to trade below the Rock River. Licenses and names of *engagées* were to be registered. Not more than four pots of brandy for each *engagée* were to be carried. However, each year thirty or forty casks of sixteen pots each might be conveyed for consumption of the post. The commanding officer was expressly forbidden to carry on trade but was bound to protect the new farmers and drive out or arrest all who encroached on their rights. In return for fuel and lodging provided by the farmers, the commanding officer was to turn over to them all presents received from the Indians. The contract was to run three years from 1747 and the consideration was to be "5000 livres each October in wartime" if they were able to get their trade through; if the trade ran below normal, they were to pay 3000 livres; if the war should end and goods become abundant, they were to pay 6000 livres.[9]

One hundred ninety-two Indians, eighty of them from Green Bay, were brought to Montreal from Mackinac by La Corne, Commanding Officer. His perils deterred the farmers somewhat. Some of the men who held licenses refused to make the journey. Seven licenses were given gratis to induce the traders to carry on the trade, as it was essential to the Indians. Only nine canoes went up to Mackinac September 22, 1746. The merchants in Montreal were willing to permit postponement of departure of their canoes. None expected to get away until they received favorable news, for the Chippewa, Ottawa, and Hurons were in a warlike mood against the French because of English influences among them. The Mohawks, too, were greatly feared. Goods had to be convoyed and often it took a hundred men to secure safety.

Vercheres was convoyed from Montreal to Mackinac and arrived there October 3, 1747. It was optional whether he should go or send St. Pierre to Green Bay to see if the Indians were friendly.

* Lemoine (Moniere) and L'Echelle, merchants—Louis Damours, Sieur Clignancourt, Jean Garreau St. Onge, Etienne Ange, Paul Leduc.

Evidently he went himself. Six canoes went to Green Bay that month, but of all the canoes that had gone into the upper country only thirty-three at that time had returned to Mackinac, these convoyed by Duplessis.

Not more than 100,000 to 120,000 beaver skins were received by the Company of the Indies who had sent four hundred and fifty pieces of scarlet cloth to be divided among the *voyageurs*. The *coureurs de bois* were reported as worse that year than ever before, and it was suggested that they be sent in punishment into slavery in San Domingo.

Very few licenses appear for Green Bay during 1747 and 1748 because goods were high-priced and hard to get and furs were low-priced. However, in 1748 each of those men who were to farm Green Bay in 1747 had a permit to trade, taken out in the individual's name instead of as a company, the company apparently being broken up. The commanding officer at Mackinac said he could get only two traders to go to Green Bay—Garreau and Clignancourt. These men paid him one thousand livres each for their trading privileges. The ending of the war (1748) left the Indians in a more peaceful mood. There was no outbreak at Green Bay and tribes along the borders were again becoming friendly. St. Pierre, in command at Mackinac, was able to apprehend the Indians who had killed the French the year before and they were brought to Montreal from Green Bay. Vercheres had some trouble with the Indians at this time, part of it supposedly caused by the traders. Paul Marin was charged with being an inciting cause, but there is no assurance of this. He did hold a license for the Sioux issued November 27, 1749, and the following year returned to the West as commanding officer at Green Bay.

The new governor-general of Canada, the Marquis de La Jonquière, was an able naval officer but unscrupulous and grasping. He began his administration in 1749 and picked Paul Marin for the western post because he was an ardent trader as well as a fearless leader. Apparently neither one paid any attention to the restrictions put upon trade, as he and Marin and Bigot farmed Green Bay during Marin's appointment. The Illinois had been induced by envoys of the Miami, who were in part gone over to the English, to trade and the Indians at Detroit and Mackinac were being tampered with until the French were not safe. Goods into the upper country had to have convoys, and it was decided to enlarge the garrison of the forts. Indian tribes were again at war with each other and all was confusion in 1750 when Marin arrived and soon brought peace.[10]

When the Sioux requested that Marin build a fort in their country, the government thought it wise for him to do so because in addition to the rich trade, the friendliness of the Sioux was necessary to western exploration. That year Marin had a large fleet of boats with licenses for Mackinac, Green Bay, and the Sioux.[11] This was the most formidable trading outfit ever sent up to the western country, and no wonder, for he had a private understanding with La Jonquière to exploit Green Bay and dependencies, especially the Sioux.

Leaving Sieur Villebon, second in command, at Green Bay, Marin went into the Sioux country where he established a fort on the west side of Lake Pepin and proceeded to pacify the Sioux preparatory to making explorations.[12] He made peace between the Sioux and the Christinaux who had been warring many years, and he returned a son of a Christinau chief who had been kept among the Sioux.

Marin and La Jonquière and Bigot in partnership held the monopoly of Green Bay and its dependencies and made an annual profit in the years 1749-50-51 of 156,000 livres, a sum of money which in our day would amount to about $500,000.[13]

Bougainville, making a report on the conditions during the early part of the French and Indian War (1757), said that it was a custom of traders to get a license for a few canoes and not report the full number that they took into the Indian country. This is exemplified in the Marin trading because the reports said he had eight or nine canoes while the licenses show that there were about one hundred eighty canoes sent up, sixty each year for these three years.

The new governor had given Marin eight or nine canoes of goods to distribute as presents to the Indians. The boats sent to Mackinac may have been for Marin's son Joseph who was commanding officer at Chequamegon at this time and who no doubt was to share in profits of exploitation of the Sioux. Paul Marin made no explorations beyond his Sioux fort in 1751 but promised to exert himself to reach the headwaters of the Mississippi with the idea that beyond the watershed a river flowing into the Pacific Ocean might be found. It is likely that he exerted himself more in

the fur trade than in any idea of discovery. Probably his son made
what discoveries and explorations were made on the Missouri. Paul
Marin was to go to Montreal in 1751 but he was detained at Green
Bay to keep the Indians quieted. While the nations about Green
Bay were much disturbed, yet the *voyageurs* carried on a good trade
at that place.

War parties of Wisconsin Indians were being formed in 1751
to attack the Missouri. Marin did not prevent—or perhaps try to
prevent—the expedition of northern Indians against an Illinois
tribe in 1752. This was the largest group of warriors ever to
assemble at Prairie du Chien: Sioux, Foxes, Sauk, Menominee, and
Winnebago. One hundred eighty canoes of nine warriors each
gathered on the Wisconsin, descended the Mississippi to the Mitchigami village near Cahokia. They fell upon these Illinois and anni-
hilated the whole tribe June 6. The French who might have
defended the Mitchigami were at Fort Chartres observing the
religious festival of Corpus Christi. The act was in retribution for
some Sioux who had been killed some time before. A statement of
the Governor would indicate that he was in sympathy with the
avengers and felt the Illinois deserved punishment for attempting
to desert the French cause earlier.[14]

After the death of La Jonquière, his successor Duquesne selected
Paul Marin to build a series of forts between Lake Erie and Pitts-
burgh. Marin was sixty years old at this time and yet he willingly
responded to the orders and left the western country never to
return. In spite of scurvy among his Indians as a result of poor
food, he continued his assigned work—the building of Fort Le
Boeuf in Pennsylvania—until his death there October 29, 1753.
He had been a captain of infantry and at his death was "com-
mander-in-chief of the army of the Beautiful River." He did not
live to receive the Cross of St. Louis, an honor which had been
refused him earlier, but which Duquesne secured for him.

Joseph Marin* was recalled from Chequamegon to succeed his
father as commanding officer at Green Bay and the Sioux fort in
1752. Beauharnois recommended him as a strong and vigorous man
of great promise; "he has the support of all the best people and
deserves the favor of the king."[15] In his early youth, although

---

* He was a sponsor at Mackinac July 31, 1750, July 18, 1753, and August
15, 1754. Also he was a witness to the marriage contract of Charles Langlade at
Mackinac August 11, 1754.

sickly, he accompanied a detachment sent to Illinois in the Indian wars. Perhaps his father insisted, in spite of the protests of other officers, upon the efficacy of the Marin name as a fighting power. He had a license to Green Bay in 1742 and again in 1744. In 1749 he was sent to La Pointe to make peace in the Chequamegon region between different tribes and between the French and Indians and to open up trade, which he claimed to have done in two years' time. He was called to perform services at Quebec in 1751 and then the following year sent to relieve his father on the upper Mississippi. Of his activities in 1752 he himself wrote: "I had an order . . . to make discoveries among the nations, who were as yet unknown. This I did during two years, covering on foot more than two thousand leagues sometimes in snow, sometimes amid ice, running a thousand dangers among barbarous nations and wearied by fatigues of every sort. I conquered, in these two years, more than twenty nations, that I made submissive to France, and these have since waged war for us. I had peace made between the Renards, Sakis, Puans, Sioux of the Lakes, Sioux of the Prairies, and Folles Avoines and the Illinois. This peace was of the greatest consequence, for if these nations had not been reconciled, the French of the colony established at the Cahau [Cahokia] at the forts of Chartres and the Cas [Kaskaskia] would have been obliged to abandon their settlements."[16]

As it was, the French at Cahokia were saved from the slaughter meted out to the Mitchigami only by the fact that they were at Fort Chartres on the day chosen by the northern Indians for the massacre. Joseph Marin, like his father, omits reference to this massacre.

Rigaud, a brother of the governor of Canada, was first given the farming of Green Bay in 1753 for three years and then repeatedly until England took over Canada.* He was never at any time actually at Green Bay, his interests being handled by Marin and later commandants. His reappointment was urged by his relative for two contradictory reasons: if the war continued he could only exploit the post at a loss; he was in financial straits because of his own

* At the time the British took over Canada, Rigaud and his wife were said to have been granted landed interest in La Baye by his brother. This claim, made by an ingenious Englishman who maintained he had bought La Baye from the Rigaud family, was disallowed. Rigaud had no interest at Green Bay except a trader's interest and he farmed it to get every penny that could be extracted in peltry and also in favors, as will be seen later.

extravagance as an old Canadian officer, the illness of his wife in France, the increase in the price of goods and decrease in the price of furs, and the loss of 30,000 livres of furs burned at the post of Green Bay.[17]

While few licenses appear in his name during his office at Green Bay, Marin* was in partnership with Rigaud, who had control of trade and needed no license. The trade was not so profitable for Joseph as it had been for his father; still, he and Rigaud made 312,000 livres in three years. Whatever may be said of the peculations of the Marins, they were no greater than the exploitation commonly practised by others in high places, and one thing which is conspicuous throughout their lives in the wilderness is their intense loyalty and patriotism toward France.

Joseph Marin was ordered to Lower Canada in 1754 to help in war. This was the year that Washington precipitated war by firing on a detachment of French who had been sent out from Fort Duquesne to scout. Jumonville, the leader, with eight men, was killed by the first volley, and that same year the De Villiers brothers caused Washington to surrender at Fort Necessity after both sides had sustained many casualties.† The cause of these clashes was the conflict between French and English as to control of the Ohio River and its tributaries. The land was claimed by France because discovered by La Salle and thereafter continuously occupied by French forts; on the other hand, the English were inciting the Indians to claim ownership and to permit them to enter into trade in this valley.

The next year Joseph Marin was sent back to the West to quiet the Indians and keep them friendly to the French. How well he performed his mission can be read in the numbers of Redmen of every nation of the West who came down to Montreal to help the French against the English. The turbulent Sioux, the untamed Fox, the Winnebago, the Menominee (always friends of the French), Ottawa, Iowa, Kickapoo, Mascouten, Huron, Chippewa—all sent warriors as soon as actual war was announced. All western forts were ordered abandoned in 1756 as the French needed every man. The Sioux fort was abandoned, but a commanding officer and a few soldiers were left at Green Bay. It is worthy of note that all

* He had two licenses in April, 1755.
† It was the father of these two De Villiers men who was killed at Green Bay in 1733. Of his eight sons, seven were killed fighting for the French cause.

of the western Indians were a unit for the French when the war began. This was due in no small measure to the Marins.

1755 is the year the Marin fort at Prairie du Chien was supposed to have been established, but it is extremely unlikely that Joseph Marin, obeying orders to evacuate his Lake Pepin fort, would establish a new fort at a time when the interests of France demanded men in Lower Canada and the Ohio valley. On his return to the East he captured a group of British traders on Lake Erie. He was a captain and participated actively in the war, entering the campaigns of 1757 and 1759. He was captured at the surrender of Quebec, after which time there is no record. Probably he was sent as a prisoner to France. The Cross of St. Louis, coveted by his father, was bestowed also upon him.

The son had even greater influence than his father with the Indians. There probably was no greater appreciation of his services shown than when at Montreal in the pardoning of two Iowa who had murdered two Frenchmen and been brought to Montreal by the Iowa themselves to be executed, Marin and St. Luc were selected to carry out the ceremonies of pardoning (June 23, 1757). At that time there were present at Montreal eighteen hundred Indians ready to go against the English.[18]

It is likely when the Canadian records are searched more carefully and available for study by competent men, the dark spots in the Marin family will be removed and much of the fiction that legend has handed down of this elusive period of Wisconsin history will be made clear; not until then can we visualize the ability, foresight, and aggressive activity of the Marin family. They never forsook their country; when Paul Marin was called to the mission of building a line of French defenses to the Ohio at an age when men are not called to war, he cheerfully left a profitable business and did not use his age as an excuse but died in service to his country. His son was of the same timbre and went to Lower Canada to do the bidding of the Governor in defense of the only country he knew, New France: a country that gave him birth was to him worth fighting for.

Of the third Marin there is little to write. Claude Marin was ten years younger than his brother Paul. Appearing first in 1727 as a trader of the First Sioux Company,* he appeared on the records

* Credit transaction; 1727: 1872 livres from Charles Nolan for the post of the Sioux.

as holding many licenses in the succeeding years, some to Mackinac and some to St. Joseph's, where he was commanding officer in 1747. He was in partnership with Dequindre and apparently stayed in the upper country, for on one or two occasions his wife sent up canoes and goods in her name. Licenses issued to Mackinac were frequently for goods intended for more distant points in the upper country. His place in Wisconsin trade is obscure, even the time of his death uncertain, although probably he died in 1754. The last license in his name appears in 1752, and his widow remarried in 1758.

In the last years of the Marins in Wisconsin, other men were coming into prominence here through their military and trading activity. Charles de Langlade, son of one of the French traders of the Second Sioux Company, was one of these. He had checked English trade efforts on the Ohio and struck terror to the hearts of the Miami in 1752. This tribe had renounced their French allegiance and gone over to the British. With two hundred forty men—Indians and French—Langlade captured their fort at Picka-willany, killed their chief, and took eight English traders and a large bounty. Much like children, the Indians were apt to fear the victorious and unite with the successful. Like the younger Marin, Langlade was an active leader of Wisconsin Indians in the French and Indian war, his part in the defeat of Braddock a matter of proud record.[19]

Rigaud's aides for the Green Bay trade changed, but for the remainder of the French period his abuses continued to be the scandal of the trade, despite repeated efforts to clean up the offenders. When the privilege of farming was less profitable, other systems of graft came into vogue. One was to get few licenses and send out many canoes; another was to get certificates of expenses allowed by the government. This last was easy money, but with the end of the war the trade at Green Bay was demoralized by a sudden influx of aggressive English traders.

Couterot, who came in 1756, was the last commanding officer at Green Bay under the French. In 1757 Rigaud's farming contract was with Jacques Giasson* and Ignace Hubert,† prominent

---

* There is not much known of J. Giasson; traces of his trading at Prairie du Chien are found. He married Angelique Hubert in 1745 and died in 1762. He spent some time at Mackinac, and in 1758 brought a sick soldier from the West who died and was buried at Mackinac October, 1758. Charles Giasson, a trader

merchants of Montreal. Before the end of this three-year agreement all the territory was in the hands of the British, and Rigaud's grant had passed out of his hands forever.

A change of policy by the French Canadian government in treatment of the Indians was proposed in 1755. Instead of trying to keep them at peace with each other, they were to be allowed to carry on intertribal wars so that they would thus wear each other down, and the French would not be involved. It was even suggested to foment trouble among them in order to keep them engaged. However, the king of France did not approve such a policy but insisted it was better that the French play the part of protectors and peace-makers among them. It was no longer the policy to gather them in settlements around the French posts but to leave them where they naturally established themselves, even allowing them to roam so long as they did not introduce strangers among them.

In his office as Governor General of Canada, Duquesne issued a new ordinance on the fur trade in the upper posts May 29, 1755. He said he did this because many *voyageurs* multiplied the number of their canoes and carried brandy in excess of the quantity allowed. He required traders to report to the commanding officer of the post for which their licenses were made out and required the commandant to be responsible for any abuse, either the practice of immorality with savage women or the practice of going to places where they had no license. Confiscated goods were not to be burned but used as presents for the Indians.

A résumé of affairs of the trading posts was made in 1757 by the new Governor General.[20] Some of his suggestions are interesting. He thought each officer should have a parcel of land ninety arpents in depth by a league in front* and his soldiers be made to cultivate it and to build small houses for themselves. When a soldier married, he should be given a cow and a sheep and a pair of oxen as well as a plow and other necessary implements for work, and cooking utensils. The oxen should be only loaned to him and

---

in Wisconsin later, who was Clerk of Probate Court of Crawford County in 1829, may have been of the same family.

† Ignace G. Hubert *dit* La Croix married Angelique Porlier in 1746 and while we do not find his name, Dominic, Joseph, Paul and Pierre held English licenses in Western trade after 1769 and these might have been his sons.

* An arpent is 192.6 ft.; a league is about 3 miles.

when he raised others, be returned to the government. To save time and expense of transportation he suggested larger boats to sail the lakes, boats which would need fewer men. These could go as far as Green Bay. A bark canoe carried about four thousand pounds and seldom lasted more than a year. At this time eighty bark canoes went up to Mackinac each year with six or seven hundred men. This he considered wasteful of manpower, for these men could be used to augment the number of laborers in Lower Canada. Five or six men could go on the lakes in a 40-ton bark. This would materially lessen the cost of goods in the upper country.

He reported of Green Bay that it was an established post, farmed for 9000 francs. All expense to the king had been suppressed: there were neither presents nor certificates nor interpreters' wages; all the cost was at the expense of the lessee, Rigaud. The commandant, Hubert Couterot, was interested in the lease and ran it for his own profit and that of his associates. This post included also the Sioux. The largest number and the best quality of furs came to Green Bay from the Sioux country by way of Prairie du Chien. The savages who came there to trade were the Folles Avoines (Menominee), Sakis (Sauk), Outegami or Renards (Foxes), Puants (Winnebago), Mascouten, Kickapoo, Sioux des Prairies, Sioux des Lacs. From this post, one of the best in the upper country, there came in an ordinary year five hundred to six hundred packages of furs.

As one of the men interested in the monopoly of trade, the commanding officer at Green Bay likely visited Prairie du Chien to watch his own interests in trading seasons or at times of transportation of goods and furs. It is not certain whether any soldiers were on the Mississippi River at this time. It is difficult to visualize the large number of men who, with the Indians, spring and fall held those fairs at Prairie du Chien of which a later writer speaks.

In 1758 the Menominee at Green Bay killed eleven French and pillaged the storehouse, the commandant afraid or unable to prevent them. This tribe sent seven prisoners to Montreal to atone for the murders; three were shot and the other four sent to the war. The Governor General remarked with justice: "This submission of an independent nation more than five hundred leagues distant, does great honor to the French name."[21] This year the firm of Giasson and Company were to take over the merchandise according to inventory with a ten per cent profit that was held by the outfitter for Green Bay, Monsieur St. Ange.*

The next year the reports from the upper country showed the Indians more firmly attached to the French, the savages showing great affection for them. This year Langlade came down to Montreal with one thousand Indians. Six or seven hundred Indians came from Detroit under Linctot and as many more from the Illinois on the Mississippi River. La Verendrye was bringing Christinaux and Sioux from Winnipeg and the Dakotas.

The farmers of the posts were not only exploiting the fur trade but were imposing on the government as well. Rigaud had produced at Green Bay between $500,000 and $600,000 in our money at a cost to him of not more than 30,000 livres. Couterot, his nephew, was just as devoid of honesty as his uncle.

The Intendant protested an expense account of 500,000 livres in certificates of Rigaud which his brother Vaudreuil had signed. Couterot produced letters of Rigaud authorizing him to make a great quantity of certificates. The Intendant's wrath found expression thus: "Never have theft and license gone so far."²² He wished to give only 40,000 livres to satisfy the demand, but finally 200,000 livres was paid on this imaginary debt.

On the surrender of Quebec the Indians and French fell back to Montreal and September 3, 1760 Langlade received orders to return to Mackinac. A few days later, before reaching Mackinac, he received word of the surrender of Montreal and the upper forts. He was told that he would pass two companies of English deserters† on his way, and he was commanded to keep the Indians at peace with them and give them provisions. Langlade took over the fort at Mackinac and remained there a year from the time of its evacuation in the fall of 1760 to the actual British occupation September 28, 1761. A month later (October 12, 1761) the British took Green Bay where Lieutenant Gorrell said the fort was quite rotten, the stockade ready to fall, houses without cover, firewood far off at best and not accessible at all when the river closed.

In October, 1760 Beaujeu, Captain of Canada, evacuated the post at Mackinac with four officers, two cadets, forty-eight soldiers,

---

* Invoice as shown by outfitters Messieurs Toussaint & Hery.

† These were chiefly from the Royal American Regiment, recruited by foreigners in the United States, largely Germans from Pennsylvania, New York, and Maryland.

and seventy-eight militia and retired to the Illinois country by way of Green Bay. At Green Bay he was joined by Couterot with his force who went with him down the Fox and Wisconsin, reaching Rock River where the ice stopped them and they were compelled to winter with Sauk and Foxes at the village where Black Hawk was born seven years later.

In their misfortune and retreat the French who had more than once resolved to destroy the Foxes were befriended by them and taken in as brothers; yet the French gave them much goods while staying there, as was the custom then—and always—that when you do a favor, a larger one is expected in return.

The retreating Beaujeu entered the Mississippi River at the mouth of the Wisconsin in the fall of 1760, bringing to a close after more than a hundred years the domination of France at Prairie du Chien. No doubt many of the English deserters who were trekking into the Northwest reached Prairie du Chien before or soon after the last of the French and began trade at once among the savages, having French *coureurs de bois* to help, caring little who governed if they might enrich themselves before law and order were established in the Indian country. Early missionaries had controlled the Indians until French officers were sent to posts, but now there was no semblance of order except the will of the trader when he was strong enough to exert it. It was nearly fifty years later that any civil authority was established at Prairie du Chien.

CHAPTER FOUR

The Cardinals

LIKE OTHER French-Canadian families of the period, the Cardinals were of numerous branches, but all apparently from the same stem. Christian names were identical in various branches; even in one family there might be two or more members bearing the same Christian name. This makes for confusion in research. The Abbé Tanguay has elaborately outlined the descent of the family from its earliest appearance in Canada up to 1800, as revealed through the scattered parish records of New France—Quebec, Montreal, La Prairie, St. Constant, St. Philippe, Prairie du Rocher, Detroit, Ste. Genevieve. But even he was not able to show the gene-alogy of certain of the Cardinals. The parish records of the cathedral of St. Louis, Missouri, and of St. Gabriel's church, Prairie du Chien, Wisconsin, afford subsequent but incomplete information.

A further source of valuable data on the family is the civil records given in the Report of the Archivist of the Province of Quebec and only recently published. These voluminous French records show the parties to trade contracts—traders, *bourgeois,* and *voyageurs*—and the destination and licensing of all canoes out-fitted for licit Indian trade between the years of 1670 and 1778. They show credit transactions and often indicate the relationship of persons to each other. Where women were parties to trade, the married and maiden names are usually given, and when as widows they carried on the trade of their husbands this also is shown in the records.

During the period of English control, licenses were issued first by the commanding officer at any of the British forts and later—up to 1791—by the central authorities at Montreal. A partial list of these also is available for research in the United States.[1]

Two great difficulties in tracing the genealogy of the family arise from the fact that some individuals severed their connection with the Catholic church, whose records were the chief source of accurate vital statistics at the time, and from the fact that some families had no male children and the names of the female members were lost through marriage.

The Cardinal family history is here traced in detail for two reasons: it is representative of the complexity of the French-Canadian genealogies; furthermore, Cardinal is the name of the first permanent white settler at Prairie du Chien.

As early as the first French record of trade, there were Cardinals engaged in voyages to the "Upper Country." This term included all the reaches of land and water, known and unknown, extending west and north from the headwaters of the St. Lawrence, as opposed to the "Lower Country," which included the Canadian territory below the Great Lakes to the mouth of the St. Lawrence. Beyond Mackinac there were no well-established posts and the destination was necessarily vague.

Jacques Cardinal was probably among the first group of men to come down the Wisconsin River after its discovery. We know that, with Jean Lefevre and Jean Dupuy, he held the third recorded license to go—in 1683—to the "Ottawa." Duluth's licenses also were for the Ottawa, and we know that he went down the Wisconsin River in that same year. In 1688 Simon Cardinal and his brothers Jean and Gabriel were *engagées* with Boisguillot to the "Ottawa," and we know that Boisguillot was trading this year at the site of Prairie du Chien with Nicolas Perrot who also held a license to the "Ottawa." In 1689 one of the Cardinals went to Fort St. Louis in Illinois. Le Sueur, who had forts at Chequamegon Bay and at the mouth of the St. Croix river, engaged Gabriel Cardinal for the Upper Country in 1692 and again in 1695. Charles Juchereau St. Denis was accompanied to the Mississippi River in 1702 by Pierre Cardinal.

All four of these Cardinals were sons of Simon-Jean (I), one of the original ancestors.

The Company of the Colony sent Jacques (II), son of Simon (I), and his son Jacques (III) to Detroit as original settlers under the régime of La Mothe Cadillac. Jacques was the first Cardinal and was the one referred to as Sieur Cardinal. This family settled in the Illinois country. Marie Cardinal, widow of Jacques Hubert Lacroix* and daughter of Jacques Cardinal (II) got credits in 1730 for eight thousand two hundred five livres to be expended in trade in the Upper Country. A little later Pierre Cardinal appears in the records as a settler of Detroit.

The family of Pierre Cardinal (II), son of Simon (I), were of Detroit. One son, Daniel, went to Mackinac as a boatman in 1717

* She married Lacroix in 1707 and married Jean Baptiste Menard in 1731.

and again in 1729; another, Francois-Marie, went to Detroit in 1724 and to the Miami two years later. Francois was a famous *voyageur* who went into the Indian country many years. He may have made the trip with the First Sioux Company in 1727. He worked for both Claude and Joseph Marin and for Rigaud. Marie-Francoise, who was a daughter of this Pierre (II) married Pierre Hubert Lacroix in 1721 and Poncelot Batillo de Clermont in 1750. Simon, probably her brother, went into the Upper Country with de Villiers and Marin Urtebise.

Jean Baptiste Cardinal, son of Pierre (III) and grandson of another Pierre Cardinal, (II)—son of Pierre (I), was arranging for credit to make a voyage to the Upper Country in 1727, and in 1728 he had a boat to Green Bay. Three years later he was an independent trader, as is revealed by a credit transaction which shows he owed Pierre Couraud de la Coste 542 livres and seven sols to be paid upon return from journey to the Upper Country. In 1733 this Jean Baptiste Cardinal (IV) made a voyage to Green Bay for the Company of Francois Lefevre, commanding officer.

His son, Jean Baptiste (V), had the most spectacular career of any of the Cardinals.[2] This was partly because the period and place of his activity coincided with the time and place of Indian and British coalition to drive out the Americans and, without official sanction, also the Spanish. Traders plied their occupation with hazard. All French settlers were assumed to be British subjects and therefore to owe allegiance to the British cause in the Revolution.

Jean Baptiste Cardinal lived at the village of St. Philippe where he married Angelique Dupuis. With his wife, he was living in the American Bottoms near Piasa (Alton, Illinois) when he and Charles Gratiot* entered into partnership to send a boat of provisions and ammunition to Prairie du Chien in 1780 under a Spanish license. They borrowed money enough from Charles Sanguinet, a wealthy trader at St. Louis, to bear the expenses necessary for the trip. Jean Baptiste Cardinal was placed in command with five men to take the boat up the river. At the mouth of Turkey River they were captured by the Indians and British and brought to Prairie du Chien as prisoners where their provisions and ammunition were

* Gratiot was a resident of Montreal who came to Prairie du Chien in 1777 as an agent of John and William Kay, settled at Kaskaskia in 1778, and moved to St. Louis in 1780. (See Billon—*Annals of St. Louis*.)

used by the Indians who had made a rendezvous at Prairie du Chien for the attack on St. Louis.[3] Thus unwittingly they helped their enemies. Jean Baptiste Cardinal was put in irons and sent to Mackinac with his five men, and the boat was also sent there and used for the purpose of transferring the fort on the south side of Mackinac to Mackinac Island in 1780. Cardinal was not humble enough to Sinclair, commanding officer at Mackinac, and the irate Irishman sent him to Montreal in chains with some other prisoners while his boatmen escaped from Mackinac and got back to St. Louis the same year. Three of them sued Gratiot for their wages and the case was tried by three judges—Cerré, Caheil, and Linctot—who decided against the men.

After Jean Baptiste Cardinal was in prison in Montreal for a considerable time, he was paroled to his merchant friends on promise that he would not leave the city of Montreal, and the next year (1781) General Haldimand wrote to the commanding officer at Mackinac to know what the charges were against Cardinal. The answer was conspiracy and treason to the British government. He was then thrown into jail again and so far as we know kept there until the end of the Revolutionary War. The next we know about him, he was trading on the Mississippi on the site of the present city of Alton. He probably lived until about 1796, when we find his heirs claiming his property.

During his absence it is not certain that his family had any word from him, but because of fear of the Indians they moved to Cahokia. Gratiot never lost faith in Cardinal during all the anxious waiting of his family for news. He said Cardinal would not desert his family or his Spanish government and while the time of his return seems not to be recorded, yet he surely was back in 1783. Thus the fifth Jean Baptiste Cardinal in line from the time the French began to go into the Indian country returned to civilization and a home and family awaiting him to settle down. The ease, comfort, and culture of the white man appealed to him at last.

Still another Jean Baptiste Cardinal was resident at Prairie du Chien. There was a Jean Baptiste born at Ste. Genevieve, Missouri, in 1757, son of a Francois-Amable Cardinal, whom Tanguay is unable to connect with any of the other families. However, there are indications that this Jean Baptiste of Prairie du Chien may have been the son of Jean Marie Cardinal, the first white settler here. At any rate, Jean Baptiste Cardinal lived at the north end

of the prairie on a lot in the immediate locality of the first permanent settlement. In 1820, at the time of the examination of the
land claims, his wife, Marie Souligny, also known as Marie Lavigne
and Dame Cola, testified that he had occupied farm lot number
three in the Fisher or Mill Coulee as early as 1788.[4] This couple
owned land and must have lived at St. Louis, because there is in
St. Louis a joint will in which each left to the one who survived all
the property because they had no children.*

Before considering the principal Cardinal, Jean Marie, we must
speak of one more man of the name. During the Revolutionary War
Francois Cardinal was a trader at Mackinac. In 1780 he was one
of a company of small traders who asked protection of the commanding officer because they feared the Americans might capture
them. In 1786-7 when Joseph Ainsse was sent by the merchants
of Montreal to Prairie du Chien and the Upper Mississippi with
presents for the Indians, among other traders that he encountered
at Prairie du Chien was Francois Cardinal. On the 11th of May,
1787 he bought "from M. Cardinal two hundred fifty-six pounds
grease."[5] When Ainsse was court-martialed and charged with using
the goods intended for Indian presents for his own purposes,
Francois Cardinal was a witness. There is no further trace of this
man at Prairie du Chien. His home was probably at Montreal. He
may have been closely related to Jean Marie Cardinal.

For the story of Jean Marie Cardinal we must return to 1754,
a time when, as we have seen, peace and harmony prevailed at the
mouth of the Wisconsin River, since all the western Indians were
then friendly toward the French.

* Why was this woman known by four different names? This may be the
answer: her maiden name was Lavigne and she married successively Souligny,
Cola, and Cardinal. Another possible answer is that Cola and Cardinal are names
for the same person. Still another is that Cola is derived not through the Cola
connected with the Cardinals but through a member of the St. Jean family who
were known as Colas in Prairie du Chien.

Farm Lot Number 15 at Prairie du Chien had been owned formerly by Marie
Souligny who had built a house on it as early as twenty-one years before 1820.
There had been a house on it for four or five years before that, and the land was
cultivated. Upper Village Lot Number 2 formerly belonged to lands claimed by
Marie Lavigne. Testimony on Farm Lot Number 30 showed that Michel Brisbois
bought this at auction in 1797 when it was sold as property of Francis Lavigne,
who was perhaps the father of Marie. Rolette made an agreement with Marie
Souligny after the death of her husband, Cardinal, in 1823 whereby she should
transfer her property to him on condition that he would support her for the
remainder of her life. She died in 1824. This woman was spoken of at her death
as Dame Cola.

In approaching the subject of where the earliest white settlement at Prairie du Chien was located and the time and manner of the coming of Jean Marie Cardinal, Senior, I do not always have recorded deeds or written history to vouch for what probably happened.*

From what we know of him as recorded facts from reliable records, we feel reasonably sure of our surmise that he was the first white settler, that he came in 1754 or earlier, and that he located in the Mill Coulee near a large spring one mile above the present "river road" approach to the coulee.

The only narrative of the coming of the Cardinals to Prairie du Chien is contained in the reminiscences of B. W. Brisbois, son of an early settler. The legend in its entirety is quoted: "At an early period Jean Marie Cardinal, with his wife, and a Mandan Indian slave, named Nicholas Colas, arrived, and settled about a mile and a half above the present court-house, at what is known as the Middle Village. Cardinal had ascended the Mississippi as far as the Cannon River, just above where Red Wing now stands; but preferring the Prairie du Chien locality to any point he had visited, he returned and made a permanent settlement there. Mrs. Cardinal used to relate, that when they first arrived, the buffalo were so numerous as sometimes to impede the progress of the three adventurers in their frail bark vessel, and that they had to wait for the vast horde to cross the river before their canoe could pass in safety. It was, too, a time of an unusual flood in the Upper Mississippi: the waters were so high that they came up from the mouth of the Wisconsin, in their bark, next to the bluffs, where the ground was some feet lower than the rest of the plain; and she declared that she had seen no such great flood since that one at the time of her arrival. She died in 1827, and her age was computed at about one hundred and thirty years. Mr. Brisbois, however says she did not appear to be so old."[6]

The picturesque Mrs. Cardinal, taking to herself, at the age of 120 years, a third husband, has appealed to the interest and imagination of subsequent writers. Unfortunately, the records controvert Brisbois's statement of her age beyond any shadow of doubt.

In 1781 some reputable knowledge of the name of the first settler and members of his family would be expected. And it was

* I believe that he was a son of Pierre Cardinal (II), son of Pierre (I). If so, his father was head of the Montreal family and he was likely born there.

in that year that B. W. Brisbois's father first came to Prairie du Chien. How is it possible to determine with assurance the exact year of the Cardinals' coming if the legend is inaccurate in this particular? There is no hesitancy in Mr. Brisbois's statement that the settler's family comprised Jean Marie Cardinal,* his wife and Nicolas Cola, an Indian slave. Had there been children, this would certainly have been noted. The date of birth of Jean Marie Cardinal's oldest child so far as we have records to show, is 1755. Eight children of the couple were baptized at the same time in 1776 at St. Louis. It was the common practice of the French who were in the Indian country to take their children with them to a priest to have the children baptized and their own marriage legalized at the same time. This record included a statement that ". . . and . . . his wife acknowledge as their legitimate children Genevieve, Ursule (Charlotte), Marguerite, Susanna and Catherine (twins), Felicite, and Jean Marie, Junior."† The youngest child of this marriage was born in 1775. The place of birth is not given, for any of the children, but it is certain that the family lived in Prairie du Chien at least part of the time and it is reasonable to suppose all of this time and to suppose that the family were brought before the priest when they returned to St. Louis from the Upper Mississippi where there had been no chance to receive the rites of the church. If Cardinal had been living anywhere in the Illinois country from the time Father Gibault went down in 1768, the ceremonies could have been performed by him or one of his as-

* Another Jean Marie Cardinal not to be confused with this one was at Detroit in 1749 and at that time had a child born of an Indian woman baptized there. He came to Detroit as a *voyageur*, but there is only one voyage listed.

† The complete church records at St. Louis show:

1. Genevieve born 1755; married 1) J. B. Vifarenne June 6, 1777 m. 2) Jacques Marechal June 30, 1784. (The baptismal records do not give date of birth but give age; e.g., Genevieve was recorded as being twenty-one years old in 1776.)

2. Ursule (Charlotte) b. 1758; m. 1) Joseph Desnoyer November 25, 1779 m. 2) Joseph LaMarche April 2, 1795.

3. Marguerite b. 1766 m. Charles Valle February 25, 1783. (In *WHC* Vol. XIX p. 92 appears the baptism of Pierre about three years old son of Chas. Vale and a savage mother. Is this one of her children?)

4. Susanna, 1768, twin mate of Catherine, died December 7, 1782.

5. Catherine, 1768, twin, married Nicholas Fail February 28, 1791.

6. Felicite, 1771, twin mate of Jean Marie m. Anton Girardeau February 28, 1792.

7. Jean Marie, Jr., 1771, twin, m. Elizabeth (Isabel) Antaya.

8. Paul—born in 1775.

sistants. In 1754 Cardinal was probably twenty-five years old and his wife about eighteen.*

There is no official record of flood years on the Upper Mississippi as early as this. However, even within the memory of living men it has been possible to reach the bluffs by canoe here in time of high water and the Cardinals came in a year of "high water." Reason for considering 1754 a likely year for settlement was that peace prevailed among the Indian tribes on the Upper Mississippi. A Frenchman was safe anywhere along the river and especially was this true if he had an Indian wife. That Mrs. Cardinal was an Indian, a Panis Maha, is attested in her marriage record.† There can be no doubt that some of Cardinal's ancestors had familiar knowledge of the locality of Prairie du Chien and it is reasonable to believe that Jean Marie Cardinal, coming down the river from Lake Pepin, would go to the bluffs by the nearest and most navigable stream. Cardinal may not have wished to live too close to the Foxes who occupied the lower part of the Prairie at the time. While they were at the moment leagued with the French, they were the most treacherous and fickle of all the tribes. Neither did Cardinal wish to be in the path of the Sioux, who made use of the Sioux coulee (five or six miles to the north of the Cardinal location) to prepare themselves with paint and feathers for their visits to the neutral grounds on the prairie.

Cardinal was a hunter, trapper, and small trader. He would seek a location which in addition to supplying wood and water and tillable soil for his home would provide good opportunity for fishing and hunting. The bluff-tops were bald, but on the slopes there was heavy timber to shelter game and fur-bearing animals and, in the coulees, meadow and swampland and streams to harbor fish and beaver and musk-rat.

There is no other place than the Mill (or Fisher) coulee where a canoe could ascend the stream so far. The first land entry for a farm lot in this coulee was made by one Jean Baptiste Cardinal, maybe a son of Jean Marie.[7] At about a mile and a third from the mouth of the coulee is still to be seen the spring from which it may

---

* Jean Marie Cardinal at his death in 1780 was estimated as being fifty years of age. In 1776 at the time of the marriage ceremony the age of Mrs. Marie Cardinal was estimated at forty years.

† The Panis-Mahas were captured and sold to the French as slaves more than any other nation. In early days they dwelt on the west bank of the river and also very early maps show a trail from the mouth of the Wisconsin westward to the Missouri river where the permanent settlement of the tribe was later.

be surmised that Jean Marie Cardinal and his family drew water. It is located on the north side of the coulee at the foot of a bluff later prospected for a gold mine.

An early Missouri historian spoke of "Cardinal's fountain" as being located in a field he was opening up at the time of his death on White Ox Prairie in what is now the city of St. Louis. Thirty years before this, Cardinal may well have called the spring in Mill Coulee Cardinal's Fountain because it must have seemed to him a necessary and most welcome addition to his home.

In a clash between French and English traders on the Wisconsin River at English Prairie (now Muscoda, Wisconsin) in the winter of 1762-3 one Cardinal and one Tebeau were said to have killed Lansing and his son, British traders from Albany.[8] Perhaps to escape the consequences of this encounter the two crossed the Mississippi River into Spanish territory. We know that Jean Marie Cardinal had a mining lease along the west side of the Mississippi near the "Tuque" River in 1769.* Reverend Samuel Mazzuchelli in his memoirs said that one Cardinal and his partner antedated Julien Dubuque at Dubuque's mines.[9] Dubuque came there in 1788. If Cardinal was dealing in lead or furs he would naturally use St. Louis as a market for trade. To have acquired such extensive holdings so early, he must have found his trade extremely profitable. Another reason for believing that Cardinal was well-to-do is that his half-breed daughters married into good families among the French of St. Louis.

The first record of his presence in St. Louis, outside of the statement that he came to St. Louis from St. Philippe in 1765, is the record of his visit with his entire family in May, 1776. It was on this occasion that there occurred his marriage and the baptism of his children by Reverend Bernard de Limpach, a Capuchin priest then stationed at St. Louis. At the time of his death he owned a house in St. Louis at the corner of Christy and Main Streets, and he was opening up a farm on the prairie.†

Cardinal was killed in the British expedition from Prairie du Chien against St. Louis May 26, 1780. His married daughter, Genevieve, living with him in the *caveau* escaped, but Cardinal himself,

* Some historians have located Tuque River, not on the Mississippi, but on the north side of the Missouri River, higher up than St. Charles, near the village of Chorette where a Paul Cardinal did live in 1804.

† The Cardinal estate was settled in 1799 and division made of the property held in common with his partner, one William Lemme. The St. Louis real estate was sold to a Dr. Watkins.

either taken wholly by surprise or unwilling to recognize the danger, remained outside the fort enclosure and met his death in his own field. Six other men on the outskirts of the city met the same fate in this attack. All the cattle in the path of the British were slaughtered, but the attack failed as a military move for reasons which we shall see later.[10] Cardinal was buried on the very spot where he was killed. This place was apparently not far from the avenue in St. Louis which bears his name. This short avenue probably lies wholly within the land which he held. Forest Park is in the locality of his land.

The family remained in St. Louis. Susanna died in 1782. All the other daughters married, the youngest in 1792. Some of them married twice. In 1784 Mrs. Cardinal went to the authorities of St. Louis and said that she was a widow with seven children and that she was without means and asked that her deceased husband's personal property be sold to afford her means of support. It was so ordered. This personal property comprised the following appraised at 1600 livres total: personal effects, 510 livres; a pair of oxen, 500 livres; a cow, 200 livres; a horse, 150 livres; a mare and colt, 300 livres.* [11]

Of Paul we do not have information. Jean Marie, Junior, and his mother returned to Prairie du Chien where Mrs. Cardinal lived until her death in 1827. She was then about ninety-one years of age—certainly not one hundred thirty! Why did Mrs. Cardinal return to Prairie du Chien? Why does the she-wolf return to the den where her young brood first nestled up to her? This woman had the instinct of her race and came back to the old home where civilization had not yet driven out the Indian. Although Jean Marie, Junior, was not twenty years old at the time, she took him with her as a helper. However, it was not long before she married Nicolas Cola, the Indian slave who came with them on their first arrival and after his death she married Jo Crelie who, tradition tells, regretted his marriage to her.†

The early settlers at Prairie du Chien seemed to think that there were Cardinals here when they came in 1781. There may have

* There is a marriage record for a Marie Cardinal, widow of Jean Marie Cardinal, to Franchere Urbain in 1783. This is evidently not the Marie Cardinal of whom we have spoken, or she would not have been allowed to establish her claim as a widow of Cardinal in 1784.

† Testimony on land claims shows that Jean Marie, Junior, was occupying Farm Lot Number Six in 1790, and in 1791 he owned Farm Lot Number One, which he sold in 1817 to Stephen Hempstead. This deed was signed by Jean

been some of other branches of the family but neither Jean Marie, Senior, nor his son could have been here at that time.

Of Jean Marie, Junior, we are more certain than of his father. His baptism in St. Louis shows that he was a half-breed Panis. He was a strong supporter of the United States government during the War of 1812. He no doubt did not forget or forgive the killing of his father by the British and not only he but other French coming from the Illinois country were American sympathizers. In 1816 he was working for Johnson, United States factor, doing some mason work—underpinning a building. In 1820 he made a claim for Upper Village Lot Number Eight which is nearly on a line with the north line of the present incorporation of Prairie du Chien, but this claim was not confirmed.

There is no record of a marriage, so far as we can find out but the baptisms of his children in Prairie du Chien show them all to be the children of Jean Marie Cardinal and his wife Elizabeth (Isabel) Antaya (Peltier).* Jean Marie probably died in 1823. His name appeared on a petition as late as 1821. In 1824, however, his widow married J. B. Ouillemette (Wemette, also known as Albert). That Mrs. Ouillemette died before 1829 is evidenced by the fact that upon Ouillemette's death in 1829 his only heir was a son by a prior marriage. Pierre Cardinal was a voter in Prairie du Chien in 1832 and in 1840 was sponsor for a baptism. The youngest and last of the family, Julien, died a bachelor between 1890 and 1895 and was buried from St. Wenceslaus' church at Eastman, Wisconsin. His grave, although unmarked, is said by those who dug it to be located at the northwest corner of the Catholic cemetery there.

With the death of Julien, the name Cardinal drops out of Prairie du Chien tradition and records after slightly more than two hundred years.

Marie Cardinal but marked by his wife Isabel (Elizabeth). However, concerning Farm Lot Number Eleven, Denis Courtois and Michel Brisbois said that Jean Marie Cardinal claimed the land in 1794 and made no use of it for several years except to cut hay off it. The said Cardinal died and Nicolas Cola came into possession by marrying the widow. Afterwards it was sold at auction to Joseph Rolette. This testimony is at variance with the facts we have presented, but on these land claims indirect testimony is not always trustworthy.

* Children baptized in 1817 were Eustache, born in 1808; Helie b. in 1810; Pierre b. 1812; Paul (?). Julien, b. 1821 was baptized in 1827. Between Paul and Julien there were probably at least two daughters—perhaps more. Marie Cardinal married Joseph Boothe about 1840 and another Cardinal girl married at St. Paul.

CHAPTER FIVE

The British Period (1763-1780)

THE CARDINALS were illegally in the Indian country and at the sufferance of the Indians; but they were not the only ones. As shown earlier, whites were certainly staying with a village of Foxes at the mouth of the Wisconsin River in 1732. We have reason to believe that stragglers from the Second Sioux Company made the site of Prairie du Chien their headquarters after the evacuation of Fort Beauharnois in 1737.

According to his own testimony in 1781, Joseph Baptiste Parrant had trading headquarters on the Mississippi twenty miles below Prairie du Chien and had been trading at Prairie du Chien from 1759. He held a Spanish license. If he got his supplies at St. Louis after the Spanish occupation, he must have had some special arrangement with the Spanish government, as Laclede had been granted a monopoly of the Spanish trade from 1762. Parrant was arrested by the British at Prairie du Chien in 1780 as a man who had never had a license for trade. At the time of his arrest, his mother was living in Detroit and he seemed to have some business connections with Mackinac, for he was paroled to Etienne Campion, then journeying to that place. Parrant was only one of several political prisoners, some of whom were unaware of regulations which they were charged with violating. There was much illegal trading throughout the period.[1]

English commanding officers at all posts issued some licenses for the Indian trade before 1769, but the older traders seem to have taken out Montreal licenses as usual up to 1778 when the last one was granted from Montreal. This multiplicity of licensing officials may have created some confusion. Many men went into the trade without any permits at all, willing to risk either British or Spanish arrest.

After the final encounter of the French and Indian War, a British detachment under Captain Belfour came to assume British possession of Wisconsin, arriving at Green Bay October 12, 1761. Two days later, according to the official report of Lt. James Gorrell, the captain departed and Gorrell was left at the fort with one sergeant, one corporal, and fifteen privates. The Indians were away hunting so the garrison spent the winter repairing the old French fort and building houses. Gorrell held his first council with the Menominee and three Winnebago chiefs May 23, 1762. He had a French interpreter, and there were also in Green Bay British traders, two of whom—McKay of Albany and Goddard of Montreal—accompanied the soldiers. Where McKay traded this winter is not told, but Lottridge and Goddard traded near Green Bay. Goddard promised to send his trader in the spring to Milwaukee to bring goods to the Indians.[2]

On hearing of the approach of the military in the fall, several French traders with permits from British commanding officers and goods from English merchants had gone down the Wisconsin to the Sioux lands where they tried to incite the Indians against the British. These traders probably never returned to the British but established themselves on the Mississippi. Some may have remained at or near Prairie du Chien.

Because Lt. Gorrell was suspicious of Gautier, his interpreter, Moran gave him an English interpreter. Pierre Leduc (Souligny), —who was Langlade's brother-in-law,—Jourdain, and other inhabitants of Green Bay seemed to be stirring up the Indians against the British. Even Langlade, Senior, was suspected. On the Wisconsin St. Pierre,* Lariviere, and Fantaisie did all they could to discredit to the Indians the tales of other traders. One Le Vorn came from Illinois to prevent the Foxes, Sauk and Winnebago from going to Montreal for their goods. He induced Indians to go to Illinois where he and other Frenchmen would bring them supplies. This promise stopped the Indians from bringing their peltry to the English.[3]

During the winter of 1762-63 the French and English traders clashed on the Wisconsin River† at a place known as English Prairie, now Muscoda. Here two British traders, Lansing and his

* St. Pierre, probably half-breed son of commanding officer of Mackinac, was the one who was supposed to have stolen goods from English traders in 1763 and hidden them where they had hidden Ezekial Solomon from the Indians during the capture of Mackinac—in Amable Lariviere's storehouse.

† The French known to have been on the Wisconsin on this "voyage" were Jourdain and J. Bte. Lebeau (relatives, who lived at Green Bay), Martoc, Lariviere (Amable, no doubt), St. Pierre, Maurice La Fantaisie, and Antoine La Fortune, later a resident of Prairie du Chien, as shown by the fact that he had a son born in January, 1765, above the mouth of the Wisconsin on the Mississippi. Because Marchesseau sponsored this child at Mackinac, it would appear that La Fortune might have been working for Marchesseau.

son, were killed. The following spring Lansing's partner was told by the French and Indians that the murderers were two Frenchmen, servants of Lansing—Tebo and Cardinal—who had made their escape to Illinois after the murder.[4] Apparently there was no Cardinal in the Upper Country this winter except Jean Marie who was living at Prairie du Chien.

Because the Indians had captured Mackinac, the British garrison left Green Bay June 21, 1763 with the English traders and friendly Menominee, Sac, Winnebago, and Fox Indians in order to assist the former commanding officer of Mackinac who was in the forest at the mercy of the Ottawa. Of the traders, Bruce, Fisher, and Roseboom returned to Green Bay in July with the Indians with whom they had come to Mackinac while the Ottawa accompanied the English soldiers to Montreal. During the traders' absence the French had stolen the goods left at Green Bay and either sold them or given them away to the Indians.

Immediately after the Pontiac war ended in 1764, the government discouraged traders from going to Green Bay and its dependencies and so there were no French licenses issued at Montreal in 1764, and no British licenses in 1765; but in 1765 one French license was given Sieur Pierre Cardinal who sent Charles Chevalier to Green Bay. In 1768 Richard Livingstone had a French license for Green Bay. In the meantime there can be no doubt but the French and Spanish had sent traders to Prairie du Chien during these years. When the English got a treaty with western Indians to which Pontiac finally consented, British traders rushed into the territory newly conquered.

In 1766 this place was visited by Jonathan Carver, a native of New England and a former soldier who came to Mackinac where he had some connection with the commanding officer Rogers who supplied him with goods for the Indian trade on the Upper Mississippi. Carver's only permission to be on the river must have come from Rogers. Carver insisted that he was a "traveler," but this seems to have been a screen to cover his connection with trade and intrigue. It appears that Rogers planned to establish a government independent of England either at Mackinac or Prairie du Chien. To this end he was in communication with Hopkins and Tute at Prairie du Chien, where Tute was wielding a large influence over the trade, giving the Indians French gorgets as presents to secure their friendship and discouraging the Indians from trading with anyone else. It was their purpose to gather a force of French and Indians to capture the British fort at Mackinac at an opportune moment. Ainsse, interpreter at Mackinac, testified that Rogers tried to bribe him to escort him to the Mississippi.[5]

This was the unsettled condition of affairs at Prairie du Chien when Carver arrived in October. His writings gave an accurate description of the route he took and of the people he met here and elsewhere on the river. He mentioned the three hundred huts which comprised the "large town" for the first time historically designated as "Prairie Les Chiens" (Dog Plains). "He saw there many horses of good size and shape. This town was the great mart where the adjacent tribes, and even those who inhabited the remote branches of the Mississippi, annually assembled, about the latter end of May, bringing with them their furs and peltries, to dispose of to the traders; and it was determined by a general council of the chiefs whether it would best conduce to their interests to dispose of the products of the chase at this place, or to transport them to Mackinaw on the one hand, or Louisiana on the other."[6]

This last is significant as showing the sources of trade and also indicating an open competing market at that time. Laclede's Spanish monopoly reached as high as Prairie du Chien as early as 1766 and by 1773 this company had a large trade in provisions: ham, sugar, rum, and ammunition.

Not finding goods awaiting him at St. Anthony's Falls, Carver returned to Prairie du Chien in the spring. Here he was no more successful but remained in the Northwest until 1768. He told very little of what he did, but as his friend Rogers was by this time a political prisoner, he might have served himself best by silence on what was going on about him.

Another visitor of note was Reverend Pierre Gibault, first resident secular priest of Illinois, who journeyed to Kaskaskia with his mother and sister in the summer of 1768. He traveled in the company of traders and under protection of the British government who issued him a license to come as a priest to the Illinois, provided that "he behaveth as becometh."[7] Later, when his influence was widely exerted in the American cause, his bishop issued an interdict because he had taken an oath of allegiance to England when his license was issued. The influence of Father Gibault affected, among others, those Prairie du Chien settlers who came from the Illinois country.

The French who came from Canada had not used large amounts of liquor in the trade. The British estimated the amount sent before the end of the French period as one hundred and eight barrels annually. Just how large these "barrels" were is uncertain, but perhaps not our present standard. From the time the British began to issue licenses, an unrestricted supply of liquor went with each canoe. The British liquor policy was a source of trade advantage throughout the history of the fur trade and led to illicit American liquor traffic which grew to such proportions that in 1832, in spite of government prohibition, the American Fur Company sent over nine thousand gallons from Mackinac into the Northwest.

From 1769 to 1773 a number of significant names appeared in the trade records. Jean Marie Ducharme had a license to Green Bay in 1769 (and perhaps before). One of his boatmen was Francis Lavigne, whose name has already been mentioned as a landowner at Prairie du Chien. Augustin Rocque came as a trader to Green Bay the same year, and he had with him a Lavigne, a Laviolette, a Lemire, a Gilbert—all names familiar to the student of Prairie du Chien history. Another trader, Henry Jeannot Bourgignon, was variously known in Prairie du Chien records as Bourk, Bourgues, La Chapelle, and Perillard. A Pierre Antaya came this year as a boatman to Mackinac and Green Bay. Since his name appeared as *voyageur* to Mackinac as early as 1753, he was probably the father of the Pierre Antaya* who was one of the earliest settlers at Prairie du Chien. Zacarie Urtebise (1769), a descendant of Marin Urtebise (a famous trader on the lower Mississippi) was at Green Bay this year, having among his men Jacques Mayrand. Pierre Urtebise (1772), a cousin of Zacarie, was a trader and finally a resident of Prairie du Chien, although both made their homes at St. Joseph for many years.

In 1770 because of restlessness and fear of an Indian uprising no licenses were issued for Green Bay, but the traders who had been trading there took out permits which read "Mackinac" but which may easily have been used for Green Bay and perhaps the Sioux country. In 1772 Sieur Coste who had a license to Green Bay had with him one J. B. Trottier Desruisseau Belcour. Laurent

* This Pierre Antaya came into the Upper Country with Marchesseau in 1763 and was an independent trader at Mackinac and Prairie du Chien with one Hamelin as partner.

Ducharme whom the British considered "esteemed above all the other French" in 1762 again had canoes to Milwaukee this year and came again to Green Bay, unless perhaps he had remained during all this time. Mathieu Damours, Sieur Clignancourt, sent a canoe to the Iowa tribe on the Mississippi River, this year and Joseph Howard provided goods for the trade on the Des Moines River, neither of these paying any attention to their encroachment on Spanish territory. Other men licensed for Green Bay in 1772 were Nicolas Marchesseau and Alexis Sejourne *dit* Sans Chagrin, Paul LaCroix (son of Francoise Cardinal), James and John Mc-Gill, Hypolite and Barthelmy Janis.

In 1773 Jean Marie Ducharme had a license to Green Bay, but we find him trading on the Missouri River, where he was arrested by the Spanish and imprisoned at St. Louis because they would not recognize his British license.

Peter Pond and his partner came to Mackinac this year as traders and Pond proceeded to Green Bay and Prairie du Chien and up the Mississippi to St. Peter's River, having nine clerks who located on rivers tributary to the Mississippi above Prairie du Chien. In his quaint, confident style, using bad grammar, Pond tells much about this trip which was so successful that on his return to Mackinac the next year he secured another consignment of goods for his return to Prairie du Chien. He says that when he and another trader and their men encamped, they set their hooks, and caught large catfishes, one of which weighed one hundred and four pounds. Next morning they crossed over to the other side and about three miles above came to the "Planes of the Dogs (Prairie du Chien) the grate plase of rondavues for the traders and Indans Before thay Disparse for thare Wintering Grounds." He stayed ten days, leaving in October to go to St. Peter's River. He said that they had plenty to eat on the way up the Mississippi: fat geese, ducks, bears' meat, flour, tea, coffee, sugar, butter, spirits, and wine. The wild crab apples had been touched by the frost and were good to eat. In his own words we will let him tell about Prairie du Chien at that time:

"I . . . Desended the River to the Mouth which Emteys into the Masseippey and Cros that River and Incampt. . . . Next Morning we Recrost ye River which was about a Mile Brod and Mounted about three Miles til we Come to the Planes of the Dogs. . . . Hear we Meat a Larg Number of french and Indans Makeing out thare arrangements for the InSewing winter and sending of thare cannoes to Differant Parts—Like wise Giveing Creadets to the Indans who were all to Rondoveuse thare in Spring.". . .

"To be Intelagabel [intelligible] I Go back to the Planes of the Dogs . . . this Plane is a Very Handsum one Which is on the East Side of the River on the Pint of Land Betwene the Mouth of Wisconstan whare it Emties in to the Masseppey & the Last River. The Plane is Verey Smooth hear. All the traders that Youseis [uses] that Part of the Countrey & all the Indans of Several tribes Meat fall & Spring whare the Grateist Games are Plaid Both By french & Indans. The french Practis Billiards—ye latter Ball. Hear the Botes from New Orleans Cum. Thay are navagated By thirty Six men who row as maney oarse. Thay Bring in a Boate Sixtey Hogseats of Wine on one . . . Besides Ham, Chese & c—all to trad with the french & Indans. Thay Cum up the River Eight Hundred Leages. These Amusements Last three or four weakes in the Spring of the Year.

". . . Drifted Down with the Currant till we Came to the Plane whare we Saw a Large Colection from Eavery Part of the Misseppey who had arived Before us. . . . Even from Orleans Eight Hundred Leages Belowe us. The Indans Camp Exeaded a Mile & a half in Length. Hear was Sport of All Sorts. We went to Collecting furs and Skins. . . . By the Different tribes with Sucksess. The french ware Veray Numeres. Thare was Not Les than One Hundred and thirty Canoes which Came from Mackenaw Caring from Sixtey to Eightey Hundred wate Apease all Made of Birch Bark and white Seder for the Ribs. Those Boates from Orleans & Ilenoa and other Part ware Numeres. But the natives I have no true Idea of thair Numbers. The Number of Packs of Peltrey of Differant Sorts was Cald fifteen Hundred of a Hundred wt Each which went to Mackana."[8]

Pond concludes by saying he had the larger share of peltry, going to Mackinac. While at Mackinac news of Indian troubles caused the commanding officer to call the traders together to have them bring peace belts into sections into which they were going. It fell to Pond to bring the beaded belts, which were symbolic of peace, and to make the speech for the Sioux. This he did successfully, and thus ensured a profitable trade among them. He spent only two seasons on the Mississippi; in 1775 he was beyond Lake Superior where he and others formed the Northwest Fur Company in 1778. The profits of this organization enabled him to withdraw early and go back to his old home in Connecticut to retire in 1787.[9]

Organization to secure greater profit and protection from numerous independent traders who were operating to reduce profits was a tendency to which Pond was receptive. One would hardly think Pond would need greater profit, for he did so well his first year that we was able to pay off his partner and pay cash for nearly all his outfit for the second year; after fifteen years he was able to retire with a competence. Neither would one expect him to need protection, for he had been a soldier in the Revolution and in his few years in trade was credited with killing three opposing traders, in duels or otherwise. He said that he came down to Montreal expecting to be tried but was told Montreal had no jurisdiction. The trader's word in the western country was law. It was a case of the survival of the strong.

Pond overshadowed all others in trade in 1773-74 and left a full account which has been useful in understanding Prairie du Chien history. The trade to Illinois and New Orleans must have been extremely profitable, as rum cost less to make where cane was a main product and Illinois had plenty of grain and livestock by this time.

In 1775 the last license granted by Montreal to the Mississippi River was given to Charles Patterson, William Kay, and John Kay—for Green Bay. Whatever goods came from Canada after that carried a British license granted under direction of the General of Canada, first Murray and later Guy Carleton until licenses were abolished by them in 1791.

The reason Pond did not return to Prairie du Chien no doubt was the capture of Montreal by the American troops in 1775. He was more interested in making money than in soldiering; although as a young man he had considerable experience fighting for England, he was unwilling now to become involved in Indian troubles between French and British which were being incited by the Spanish even as far north and east as Prairie du Chien and Green Bay and Milwaukee.

The war was early called to the attention of the western posts and the British felt it necessary that traders be sent among the Indians both to make presents and to trade. During the earlier years of the Revolution, the British licenses were granted for Green Bay. Also, the British continued their policy of arresting traders who had no licenses. Some time during 1777 Thomas Bentley, who had lived in Philadelphia but who had married a French-Canadian and was then living at Kaskaskia, brought goods to Mackinac; but he was suspected of being American in sympathy and was arrested and held as a political prisoner for almost two years until he escaped.* His goods were in the name of another man who brought them back by way of Green Bay.

July 4, 1776, the very day Congress passed the Declaration of Independence, Charles Langlade received orders from De Peyster, British commandant at Mackinac, to take the French-Canadian Indians of many nations gathered there to help General Carleton at Montreal and annoy any Americans they might meet on the way. Langlade probably met Carleton at Isle aux Noix but returned to Mackinac in the fall.[10]

The next spring Langlade was commissioned to secure Indian auxiliaries. In April he began and by June 4, 1777, was at Mackinac with sixty Indians with whom he set out the next day for Canada, some of his Menominee deserting on the way. Louis Chevalier came with Potawatomi from St. Joseph and Charles Gautier came still later with Sauk and Foxes from Prairie du Chien. These were sent after Langlade and reached Quebec July 14. They were then sent to join Burgoyne at Lake Champlain, but the Indians were not pleased with the British general and left within a month. Gautier was at Mackinac in October; perhaps Langlade was, also. Their Indian auxiliaries had gone from the Mississippi to Quebec and Lake Champlain and returned home that summer. Thus far the Indians had been of no service to the British except insofar as they were kept friendly. They never proved amenable to the military discipline of the whites.

May 10, 1778 De Peyster issued orders to all traders to embark one or two savages each and bring them to Mackinac where, he said, Langlade would furnish provisions. Gautier had spent the winter of 1777-78 at and near Prairie du Chien visiting western tribes, persuading them to join the British. June 2, 1778 he arrived at Green Bay with two hundred and ten recruits and four days later he and Langlade started for Mackinac. They left there for Montreal late in June, but whether they joined the Mohawks in raids or stayed in Canada is uncertain. The Menominee were back

---

* A Joseph Howard had goods stored at Mackinac but he was under arrest accused of helping Bentley to escape and also of violating his license.

at Mackinac in August. Old King, their principal chief, always felt proud of a certificate of chiefship he received at Montreal August 17, 1778 from General Haldimand, Carleton's successor.[11]

Langlade was under orders from the commanding officer at Mackinac (October 26, 1778) to go to Grand River and St. Joseph to arouse Indians to the aid of Colonel Hamilton, then planning an expedition against Illinois in which Gautier, Louis Chevalier, and Ainsse were to help. In case their services should not be needed, Langlade was to go to Green Bay and Gautier to the Mississippi to keep the Indians well disposed. July 1, 1779 Langlade got orders to "raise" Indians along the western shores of Lake Michigan, including Milwaukee, and join Lt. Bennett who was sent from St. Joseph against Peoria. Having suffered a defeat on their way at the hands of the Americans under Linctot who had a large force of Indians, they returned to St. Joseph. De Peyster's successor at Mackinac was not enthusiastic about the services of Langlade and Gautier. The latter was displaced by Joseph Ainsse and Langlade's claims were unheeded as is apparent from the fact that Mrs. Langlade, in Montreal, appealed directly to General Haldimand for six months' back pay due her husband in order that she might go to him.[12]

Godefroy sieur de Linctot Laine (Benclo), who defeated the Langlade-Gautier expedition, had only recently joined the Americans. His allegiance was valuable because of the prominence of his father as commanding officer of the Second Sioux Company and because of his own familiar knowledge of the Indian country. With his younger brother Hubert he had been employed in and near Prairie du Chien with Patterson and Kay, and his brother remained with them and loyal to the British until his death in 1778. The elder brother was given a major's commission by General George Rogers Clark and also appointed Indian agent on the Mississippi as far north as Prairie du Chien. However, the British had a price on his head and Linctot never dared come to Prairie du Chien again during the war.[13]

There was considerable trade activity in 1779 despite the war. Some of the traders of this period claimed Prairie du Chien as their residence, among them Jean Marie Ducharme and two Gravelles. Also, Pierre Antaya, Augustin Ange, and Basil Giard were living here. During this year two agreements were made among traders at Mackinac to establish general stores there.[14] These men were trying to protect themselves against losses they might sustain in the war going on and they claimed the protection of the commanding officer against actual losses and as a means of recovery of losses from the government if the enemy destroyed or confiscated their outfits. The volume of traffic is indicated by a statement of Charles Grant in 1780 that ninety canoes went to Mackinac, Green Bay, and the Northwest every year.[15]

By this time the Indians were more sympathetic with the British, and the French-Canadians also were more friendly toward England than toward the American colonies. Despite Catholic persecution in the mother country at this time, the French-Canadian subjects of England (largely Catholic) had enjoyed for almost twenty years the religious freedom granted them by the treaty of 1763. These French-Canadian colonists were satisfied to remain under British jurisdiction. Most of them had made their living in Canada as *voyageurs,* clerks, or traders. They had learned the languages of the different Indian nations and many had taken wives among the tribes where they were stationed. The American colonists who might have won the allegiance of the French antagonized them by their religious intolerance.

A cherished military project of the British was undertaken in May, 1780. Prairie du Chien was used as a place of rendezvous for an expedition against the Americans at Cahokia and the Spanish at St. Louis. The man who was to lead this expedition, Captain Emmanuel Hesse, had a trading house at Prairie du Chien at least as early as 1777. Another one of the leaders was J. M. Ducharme who took charge of one group of Indians. Ducharme was accused of being one cause of the attack, desiring revenge on the Spanish for his arrest in 1773, and was also accused of being a traitor to the British during the attack. A third leader, Joseph Calvé, had his trading place lower down on the Mississippi.[16]

With this group of traders as a white border, a large horde of painted warriors of Sioux, Winnebago, Menominee, Sac, Foxes, Ottawa, Potawatomi, Kickapoo left Prairie du Chien May 2, 1780. Altogether there were seven hundred and fifty in the party: Indians, traders, servants, and leaders, with Machiquawish (Matchekewis), a well-known Chippewa chief, general of the Indian forces. They planned a surprise attack and came before Cahokia and St. Louis May 26. However, the Spanish and Americans had been informed of their coming and were prepared to defeat them at both places. The Indian loss fell on one tribe, the Winnebago, of whom one chief and three warriors were killed and four warriors wounded. There were no other casualties for the British. One American officer and four men were killed at Cahokia and at least seven about and near St. Louis, among them Jean Marie Cardinal. Those in the Spanish fort suffered, one officer dying of wounds he received. The Indians killed or drove off a large number of cattle and made good their retreat,—part returning by the Mississippi, part overland, and part by Chicago and the Illinois River. Major Montgomery's Americans pursued them, decisively defeated the Sauk at their village, and then continued up Rock River "four hundred miles," according to the account of James Aird.

A group of British traders had a storehouse at Prairie du Chien and it was arranged that Sgt. Phillips, who was accompanied by one John Long, a trader, should convoy to Mackinac all furs stored at Prairie du Chien. The success of American arms had begun to alarm the British, and they figured, rightly, that Prairie du Chien might be endangered by American forces in the event of the failure of the British attack on Cahokia and St. Louis. The main body of Americans likely followed the Indians only to the mouth of the Rock River, but it is possible that some of the soldiers did come up to Prairie du Chien. The trader Long wrote in his account of the Phillips expedition that "the Americans" arrived at Prairie du Chien five days after the convoy of furs left. All the pelts the party could carry—300 packs—were taken to Mackinac and the remainder—65 packs—were destroyed so that they would not come into possession of the enemy. Any plundering Americans who may have come must have found their journey fruitless.[17]

Prairie du Chien was not used again during the Revolution as a base for British military manoeuvres although a second expedition against St. Louis was planned for 1781, Wabasha to replace Matchekewis as general of the Indian forces. The success of the Americans was becoming more widespread and British control was seriously jeopardized in the West as well as in the American colonies proper.

CHAPTER SIX

The British Period (1780-1800)

THE INDIANS' ownership of the soil was practically ignored by the white men. Conquest, purchase, barter, and—year by year—the aggression of the whites drove the Indians farther and farther west. Until 1781, in spite of the actual residence of a number of traders, there was no formal claim to ownership of land at Prairie du Chien. Some crude farming was carried on, and at trading posts here and elsewhere potatoes and peas and melons were planted but in no instance did the French trader assume ownership of the soil. While men like Perrot took over whole sections of the North American continent in the name of the King of France, no individual ownership was asserted; nor did the French king permit any individuals to buy land directly from the Indians. The policy of French, English, and Americans was the same in this respect. Only the government dealt with the Indians for land. Consequently, when the settlers who had come from the Illinois country where land values were recognized used their influence to agitate for private ownership at Prairie du Chien, the British governor acceded to their request.

Formal possession of nine miles square of prairie above the mouth of the Wisconsin River was granted in 1781 at Mackinac. Pierre Antaya, Augustine Ange, and Basil Giard were the men to whom the grant was made by Governor Sinclair, commandant, who took it over from the Fox Indians in council. The Foxes had a village at the south end of the prairie at that time. The land was to come into possession of these Frenchmen and others whom they probably represented as a committee. This date is most frequently given as the beginning of the permanent settlement of Prairie du Chien. Pierre La Pointe[1] who acted as interpreter saw the price of the land paid in goods to the Fox Indians. None of the three Frenchmen ever realized gain from their holdings, although all understood the value of land. The final distribution of this land was arranged for by an agent of the United States Land Office in 1820.[2]

Basil Giard profited least, for in addition to losing the one lot he held in Prairie du Chien, he lost a large Spanish claim on the west side of the river.[3] Giard came with Ange from the Kaskaskia region (the American Bottoms) and was a trader and farmer here. His wife was a Sauk and their daughters married here.[4] Giard died in 1817. A large number of his descendants still live in this locality.

Of Augustine Ange not a great deal is known. He is supposed to have been a son of Jean Baptiste Lefevre and to have had some Indian blood. His lawsuits at Kaskaskia would indicate that he was not given to prosperity. There is no record of his ever having held title to land in Prairie du Chien, but he was living here as early as 1779 when Gratiot ordered a trader to furnish him with flour; and the first records of St. Gabriel's church show that he had daughters born here of Pelagia, a Sioux. He had two sons also.[5] His signature on the church records is in a fine, free hand. An Augustine Ange affixed a mark as his signature to a receipt for payment as boatman in 1816, which makes it doubtful whether it is this same Augustine. American troops going from here to St. Anthony's Falls in 1819 found on their way the body of a man identified merely as "A. Aunger." This may have been Augustine.[6]

Pierre Antaya, of the three, left the most permanent imprint on Prairie du Chien. His name is often and more correctly written Peltier or Pelletier although the descendants in this locality were called Antaya. Variations are Entaya, Antailla, Entailla. Pierre and his father Pierre were both engaged in Canadian trade. The younger Pierre came first with Marchesseau in 1762 and his name occurs repeatedly thereafter in Wisconsin trade. In 1776 he left the British and assisted the American cause; however, he must have become reconciled with the British again because in 1779 he was a small trader in one of the general store companies at Mackinac, in partnership with Hamelin.[7] As late as 1790 he received a consignment of goods from Pierre Grignon for trade.

His great grandson said that he was killed by the Indians while acting as a trader for Rolette, and his widow and seven daughters then moved into the Mill Coulee to live, perhaps on Indian land, some time before 1820. Pierre Antaya was probably related to Michel Antaya, but not a brother. Pierre Antaya's wife was a half-breed Fox, Catherine, and they had a large family, several of whom were baptized here.[8] Many French families in Prairie du Chien can trace descent from this early settler.

While the final battle of the Revolution was fought in 1781, the details of peace were not agreed upon until April 19, 1783, when the Treaty of Paris was signed, and the Indians were in an unsettled condition. Charles Langlade, signing himself Captain of the Indian Department, reported from Green Bay March 5, 1783, to Captain Robertson, British commanding officer at Mackinac: "to inform you that . . . according to what some Puants report when the Traders crossed the portage of the ouisconsin, Their nation wanted to Plunder them that in the confusion there was a Puant called Boeuf blanc killed and that to be revenged They took from Sieur Reilhe the Worth of five or six pieces of money in Drink and in other things, and as they were still drunk when Monsieur Blondeau passed he was obliged to give them also a great deal of Spoil in order to save his life."[9]

Anticipating the treaty of peace, of which he had no information at this time, the commanding officer at Mackinac April 26, 1783, ordered George McBeath, a trader, to "proceed to La Prairie de Chiens, the Rendezvous of the Western Indians, or to where you may meet them, and on your way thither you are to induce every nation or Band of Indians, to the Interests of His Majesty's Peace and Harmony among themselves, & in a particular manner recommend Hunting to them, and to keep at their Homes till called for.

"You are to smoke the Pipe of Peace with them, in the name of all their Fathers to the above purport, and give them as from me a proportion of what presents you have for that purpose."[10]

In accordance with these instructions, McBeath held a council with the Foxes, Sauk, Sioux, Winnebago, and Menominee May 24, 1783, at Prairie du Chien and returned to Mackinac by July 14. September 16 of the same year Blondeau was sent with a canoe of presents to arrange peace between the Sioux and the Chippewa. Because of the visit of these men only two chiefs of the Mississippi went to Mackinac in 1783 and none in 1784. Robertson himself sent McBeath without authority from higher officers and had some difficulty in getting the bills allowed but he made the argument that his action saved the government by preventing the Indians from coming to Mackinac for presents during these years.

As early as September, 1783, Washington called the attention of the Continental Congress to the lands north and west of the Ohio River. As the colonies had all given up their claims to lands in this territory, it became public domain and in April, 1784, Thomas Jefferson elaborated a plan to make out of it ten states with grandiloquent names. Under these arrangements, a territory was to be formed, bounded on the south by the forty-third degree of latitude, a line just below the southern limits of the present city of Prairie du Chien; but in May a new scheme was adopted and laws established for the government of this territory as it remained until 1787 when the Northwest Ordinance went into effect. Under this latter, five states were to be carved out of the land. The Treaty of Paris established the Mississippi as the west boundary between the colonies and Louisiana and the north boundary was to be a line drawn directly west from Lake of the Woods to the Mississippi River. It was found that the Mississippi did not reach that far north, but nothing further was done about that boundary line until after the War of 1812. Another provision, made in 1784, was for laying out townships. At first it was voted to make each seven miles square but finally—May 25, 1785—Congress voted to survey the Northwest Territory into townships six miles square. All this was under the direction of the Continental Congress of the colonies, for not until April, 1789, when Washington was inaugurated, did the present constitution of the United States go into effect.

Prairie du Chien was too far distant from the nation's capital to receive any consideration, and so whatever law and order prevailed at Prairie du Chien remained under the direction of the British traders. Charles Langlade, as captain in the British Indian Department, could have been called on perhaps to enforce any law that the British saw fit to enforce. Arthur St. Clair, the first governor of the Northwest Territory, called attention in 1790 to the fact that even in the time of the French possession of Canada there had been a settlement of considerable importance at Prairie du Chien.[11]

Of the size of Prairie du Chien in 1793 Robert Dickson wrote the following in a letter from Mackinac: ". . . about two leagues from where the Ouisconsin falls into the Mississippi there is a meadow of about three leagues in width called Prairie du Chien. Here a good number of families are settled. They have lately got cattle from Illinois and begin to raise wheat."[12]

Mackinac traders were going up and down the Mississippi by

way of Prairie du Chien at least as early as 1783. The time of the organization of the Mackinac Company is uncertain, but it was probably an outgrowth of one of the general stores at Mackinac. One member of the company, Murdoch Cameron, was trading British goods on Spanish territory in 1783 at a time when Mackinac traders had a large trading house at Cahokia.

Jean Baptiste Perrault came to Prairie du Chien with Marchesseau in 1783 and stayed two days before going down the river to Cahokia. The party also stopped at the Sauk village at Turkey River where Marchesseau had given credits. Arrived at Cahokia, they opened a store in the house of J. B. Saucier and disposed of their goods to Auguste Chouteau who smuggled these British goods from American territory into Spanish and traded them profitably up the Missouri River for furs. On the journey downstream, Marchesseau passed St. Louis in the night to prevent having the goods seized by the Spanish who never conceded the right of using the Mississippi to either British or Americans. Marchesseau's clerk, Perrault, did not return by this route. He took seventy-four packs of furs, five hundred Spanish dollars, and four hundred pounds of tobacco up the Illinois and by Chicago up Lake Michigan to Little Detroit, near Green Bay, where he waited for Marchesseau who did return by way of Prairie du Chien. The British insisted upon their right to trade in Illinois, whereas J. B. La Croix, one of the leading American merchants at Cahokia, tried to prevent it. The Americans claimed that the British were in unfair competition and that they were influencing the Indians against the American and Spanish traders who were then in friendly alliance to drive out the British. While Marchesseau himself did not apparently return to Cahokia, the Mackinac Company maintained a trade at least as late as 1790 when their agent Arundel complained that he was not sure what Governor St. Clair's regulations of the Indian trade were.[13]

Because the Indians were troublesome and were warring among themselves, making it difficult to carry on the fur trade, a number of Montreal merchants combined two years later to send Joseph Ainsse to Prairie du Chien and the Upper Mississippi with presents for the savages. The commanding officer at Mackinac furnished him with goods for the trip, and he left there in August, 1786, to make peace with the Indians at Green Bay and along his route to

Prairie du Chien and later to visit other tribes with whom the British had trade relations. Ainsse himself was a government interpreter, said to be well-versed in many Indian languages. However, on this occasion he was provided with other interpreters to aid him.*

Ainsse had difficulties enough on this expedition. He gave goods to Cardinal at the St. Croix River and thereby made Cardinal an unfair competitor of the legitimate traders already established there who had bought their goods through the regular channels. Because of this transaction Etienne Campion, a superintendent for the Montreal traders, was in some way involved with the Sioux who were about to take his life. Ainsse sold twelve government rifles of the seventy furnished him by Todd, a member of the Montreal society; and he sold goods to the value of seventy-nine pounds' sterling on credit to Antaya, a transaction which proved profitable. He granted an exorbitant demand for goods made by the daughter of a Yankton chief, the wife of Charles Jacques Fresniere. Also, he charged the government with goods which he bought from M. (Francois) Cardinal, Honore (Louis) Tesson, and Marchesseau. His greatest difficulty, however, was with Charles Patterson, a member of the Montreal organization. When Ainsse arrived at Prairie du Chien with the Indians he had assembled to take to Mackinac for a council, he found that Patterson was hostile in his attitude and had given the Indians liquor contrary to orders. Ainsse counciled with the Indians each of the four days of his stay at Prairie du Chien but found that on the last day Patterson held a secret council with the Sioux, telling them that he was the man who could furnish them with goods and that they should listen to him and not to Ainsse. As a result of this council, the greater number of the Sioux wanted to return home. Michel Labatte, a clerk for Patterson, told Ainsse of what passed at this council and Ainsse did what he could to repair matters. He left Prairie du Chien and camped three leagues south, from there sending presents to Red Wing, a principal chief of the Sioux, urging him to reconsider his withdrawal from the party. The following day Ainsse left for Mackinac.

* Dixon (probably Robert Dickson) who was a Chippewa interpreter in the Indian Department at Mackinac; and Francis Fresniere, C. J. Fresniere, Joseph Renville, and Joseph Laroque, all Sioux interpreters; Louis Berthe.

Despite his peculations, Ainsse felt that he had accomplished his mission of bringing peace among the Indians because one hundred ninety-six Indians accompanied him to Mackinac where peace was established among the assembled Indians at a council in July, 1787, at which the commanding officer (then Lt. Scott), John Dease, and others were present. The Indians had been induced to send representatives to this council by Ainsse who held minor councils on St. Peter's River in March and at other places during the winter and spring.

The dealings of Ainsse and John Dease, government storekeeper at Mackinac who aided him by manipulating the books of the store, brought the two men before a court martial. They were found guilty after a prolonged trial. The interest of this trial and of Ainsse's expedition lies largely in the fact that Ainsse produced in court a list of witnesses whose testimony showed all of the traders who were in the Prairie du Chien vicinity in the winter of 1786-87.[14]

From this testimony, the prominence of certain men at Prairie du Chien is evident. Hypolite (Hypolite Pierre?) Lariviere is one of these men. He was perhaps the uncle or perhaps the father of Pierre, a successful farmer, who settled at Prairie du Chien in 1785 and was the ancestor of the present-day Larivieres at Prairie du Chien.* Hypolite was a prominent trader on the Wisconsin from 1769 to 1790, having a partner some of the time. He was associated with Abbott, Giasson, and Durocher, among others.[15]

Joseph Laroque was important at this time and later. Julien Dubuque's name did not appear in the list, but he was here September 22, 1788, for at a council with the Fox Indians at Prairie du Chien he obtained a mining and trading concession on the west side of the Mississippi below Turkey River three leagues wide and nine leagues long. He made his home on this claim except for a brief period toward the close of his life. He purchased a Spanish claim of Francis Cayolle (Caihal) to land directly opposite Prairie du Chien on the west bank of the Mississippi.[16]

The name of his father, Augustin Dubuc, appeared among the traders in this locality in 1786-87, but he was not a witness at the court of inquiry at Mackinac in 1788, having died probably

* The original Julien Lariviere (Trottier) was an important outfitter in Montreal.

in 1787. Another witness who did not live to testify was Charles Patterson. Returning from Mackinac to Prairie du Chien in the fall of 1787 or in 1788 he was shipwrecked on Lake Michigan twenty-two leagues from Mackinac. There were ten other persons with him, including a female Panis slave. All the bodies were recovered and taken for burial by the soldiers to Mackinac. When Patterson's body was washed ashore, the slave girl was clinging to him. He had been advised that no boat could endure the storm, but when some of his men objected to going, he forced them. J. B. Perrault was promised an extra good wage to go as clerk to trade at Prairie du Chien that fall but he refused and thus escaped the terrible wreck that he saw when he and other traders picked up the bodies. The only survivor of the disaster was a large white dog given to Patterson by Ducharme upon his leaving Mackinac. The name Patterson's Point is still given to the place in Michigan at which his ship sank.[17]

In 1789 when Washington entered upon his first term as President, there was not a single American trader at Prairie du Chien. Before the French and Indian War, the French-Canadians had held the trade exclusively. Then had come the Spanish traders (up' the Mississippi) and the British (by the Canadian waterways) who were mainly represented by the Scotch, although there were also some men from the eastern colonies and some Jews. All of the British were more aggressive than the Canadians had been and they never understood the Indians as did the French. During the last fifteen years of the eighteenth century the trader population was a mixture of all these elements.

The first American trader to establish himself permanently at Prairie du Chien was Henry Monroe Fisher who came between 1790 and 1792 with Andrew Todd, a Scotchman trading for the Northwest Fur Company. However, Fisher soon became an independent trader with an outfitting place at Prairie du Chien which he operated for a long time.[18] His prominence in public affairs came after 1800. He was reputed to be a nephew of President Monroe and was connected by marriage with Charles Gautier and Michel Brisbois, a prominent contemporary at Prairie du Chien.

When Fisher came, Archibald Campbell and his ill-fated son John were here as were also the Crawford brothers, Louis and Redford. The Crawfords were associated with Robert Dickson.

In 1786 the latter seems to have been Chippewa interpreter for Ainsse. When the Americans captured Prairie du Chien in 1814, they found in some of Dickson's confiscated trunks records of trade back to 1786. Dickson was a near neighbor of Fisher.

Among the French Canadians were a La Pointe family, J. B. Faribault, Denis Courtois, Joseph Mercier, Claude Gagne, the Courvilles, Giards, and a number of Antayas. By 1798 Francis Gallerneau had come in as a blacksmith and practised his trade in competition with at least two other Frenchmen: Francis Duchouquette and Oliver Cherrier, the latter founder of a large and prominent family. We know of only one individual besides Parrant[19] engaged in Spanish trade who located at Prairie du Chien before 1800. This was Jean Baptiste Pauquette, whose son Pierre afterward became well known at Prairie du Chien and at Portage.

The security of life at Prairie du Chien and the other western settlements was determined by events which took place in other sections of the country. American settlers in the eastern part of the Northwest Territory were antagonized and resisted by the Indians, so the government sent out an army which was defeated but which was followed by a second expedition under General Anthony Wayne who signally defeated the Indians and compelled them to sue for peace. At the treaty of Greenville, Ohio, in 1795, the Indians acknowledged the supremacy of the United States and also agreed that the Indian title to lands occupied by French settlers in sixteen villages should be extinguished. Prairie du Chien was not mentioned as one of these, but the general statement preceding the enumeration would indicate that the title to lands at Prairie du Chien was also covered. Prairie du Chien was supposed to have had Indian title extinguished by the treaty that Sinclair made at Mackinac in 1781 with the Foxes then living on the prairie.

The same year Jay made a treaty with Great Britain for the Americans, which provided for American occupation of Mackinac. The British evacuation took place in October, 1796, and opened the way for actual American control of the Northwest Territory which had been practically governed by the British. No soldiers were sent farther west than Mackinac at this time. At Green Bay Charles Langlade was still reporting to the English officers in Canada as a captain in the British Indian Department and the

British maintained their trade position, claiming that Americans had no authority in this section which they recognized as Indian land.[20]

From 1783 on, the Spanish had a gunboat with about forty men plying the upper Mississippi to protect the Spanish trade and keep the British and American traders from Spanish territory. The instructions of the boatman in command were to confiscate goods of foreign traders and to divide such goods equally between the government and the crew. In 1797 the commanding officer of this boat was Don Carlos Howard, who planned an attack upon Prairie du Chien, counting on the Fox Indians who were friendly to the Spanish to help him make the assault, but when he arrived, he found the traders at Prairie du Chien were reinforced by Wabasha and his band and so, unable to capture the place, he withdrew without an attack.[21]

During the last year of the century the British were at war with Spain and greatly feared that the Spanish from Louisiana would attack Canada. There is nothing to show that Spain ever intended such an attack as the British feared. Perhaps the reason for the uneasiness of the British was the attack the Spanish made on St. Joseph in 1780 which was urged by Spain at the Treaty of Paris as giving her by right of conquest the part of the Northwest Territory west of Lake Michigan.

Because the way across American territory by the Wisconsin and Fox Rivers was wholly unprotected the British sent out messengers who were to bring in Indian chiefs to cement the friendship between the British and the Indians. These messengers were to remain in the different Indian villages for the purpose of watching Spanish manoeuvres and in case of an advance they were to instigate the Indians to attack the approaching Spaniards. As a result of this British activity, fifty Sac and Fox warriors from Prairie du Chien joined in council near Detroit in 1799 with Johnson, British superintendent of the Indian Department.[22] These Indians had never been seen before in this locality and were treated with exceptional consideration, Johnson being very liberal with presents to them. The Fox Indians remained friendly with the British until after the Black Hawk War.

Because three-fourths of the fur business was done at that time on American and Spanish territory, control of Mackinac was crucial to British trade. The loss of Mackinac was the beginning of the end of English domination of trade in the Northwest Territory, although it took another war to secure complete control for the Americans.

PART II

After 1800

CHAPTER SEVEN

The Fur Trade After 1800

So LONG as the independent French-Canadian traders purchased furs from the Indians directly, a large proportion of the population at Prairie du Chien was comprised of small traders and *voyageurs* who had left the trade. With the turn of the century a tendency toward monopolistic organization was already apparent. The history of the fur trade at Prairie du Chien after 1800 is the story of combination, restricted competition, and finally monopoly. Only the failure of the fur supply and the opening of new and more profitable fields to the West terminated the trade here.

By the end of the first decade of the nineteenth century there were three well-organized, well-financed, and well-equipped British fur companies competing in this locality: the Hudson's Bay Company; the Northwest Company; and the Mackinac Company, the latter organized by members of the Northwest Company to monopolize the business within the territories of the United States. The three companies had about six thousand French-Canadian *voyageurs* and clerks either wintering at the trading posts throughout the Northwest or going back and forth with furs and goods for the Indian trade. The Mackinac Company, as the name indicates, had its headquarters at Mackinac but had a subsidiary depot at Prairie du Chien, and while it did nearly all the business, there were also a number of the Northwest posts on the Upper Mississippi and a few Hudson's Bay posts. Every year at Montreal a quarter million dollars' worth of furs from the Northwest were bought, two-thirds of these coming from the territory of the United States.

With the new republic of the United States not a dozen years old, Prairie du Chien in 1800 was nominally under the Americans, but the nearest garrison was at Mackinac and as yet, since no civil government was set up, the traders' word was law. British traders had no restraint after 1790. They were carrying large quantities of liquor into the Indian country and exchanging it for furs, thus debauching the savages that they contacted. The Indians were entirely dependent upon and under the control of these traders who were expecting another war that would change the boundaries more to their taste and advantage.

Henry Monroe Fisher, the only American trader at Prairie du Chien in 1800, came, as we have seen, as an employee of the Northwest Company but later became an independent trader. There was no American market, so Fisher's dealings as an independent must have been with the British at Montreal or with the Spanish at St. Louis so long as Spain controlled this market.

With the inauguration of William Henry Harrison as governor of Indiana territory rules were made promptly concerning trade. A license form for Indian traders was adopted and one of the earliest of these licenses granted under the American rule in Wisconsin has been preserved and is here reproduced:

"Wayne County, the first day of
March, 1801
Territory of the US northwest of the Ohio

This certifies that Jacob Franks is authorized to vend merchandize within this territory for one year from the date hereof, the said Jacob Franks having this day paid to me Matt Ernest Treasurer of said County of Wayne the sum of ten Dollars, it being the annual tax imposed on Retailers of Merchandize by a law of this territory.

Matt Ernest, Treas. W.C."[1]

Because Franks was an outfitter at Green Bay, this license may have been for one of his men, perhaps Thomas G. Anderson who was trading for him that year.

Anderson had come through Prairie du Chien in 1800. That year he was bound for the Des Moines River as a clerk for Kinzie who sent out three canoes from Mackinac—two outfits under the Lagoterie Brothers, long residents of Prairie du Chien, besides the one under Anderson. The traders in opposition this winter were Joseph St. Jean, Maurice Blondeau, J. B. Berthelot, and J. B. Caron. Anderson was engaged by Franks to operate on the Des Moines River in 1801. That year his competitors were Denis Julien and his son Stephen.* For the next four years Anderson worked as Franks' trader at Milwaukee. In 1803 the opposition traders at Milwaukee were Antoine Leclair and Alexis Laframboise.[2]

* Denis Julien died at Prairie du Chien a number of years later.

At the time of the issue of the Indiana license reproduced above, Green Bay was in Wayne County; and Franks, although British, was taking no chance of having his goods vended illegally when he could obtain a license. Many traders at this time did not have the same view-point and so they flocked into the Mississippi Valley as before, heedless of its being Spanish on the west bank and American on the east. Even the threatened attack on Prairie du Chien a few years before because it was the rendezvous for illicit traders did not stop the illegal business.

Robert Dickson was one of the most intensely British of any of the traders at Prairie du Chien, despite the fact that he had been chosen by the governor of Indiana as one of the American agents of law and order. Dickson was associated with the Mackinac traders and was one of the most active of their number. A letter written by Dickson at Mackinac in 1804 stated that he was then departing for the Mississippi. His home was at Prairie du Chien where he continued to live and trade until after the war of 1812, when he retired to the Hudson's Bay settlement on the Red River.[3]

No man impressed his name on the settlement of Prairie du Chien more than Joseph Rolette. He came as a trader in 1804[4] and continued in the fur business until his death. Like Dickson, he was a member of the Mackinac Company. He and Dickson and James Fraser and Murdoch Cameron were partners, and it is said that they acquired a one-third interest in the Southwest Fur Company when it was organized by Astor and some of the British traders from Montreal.

John Campbell and James Aird were both resident traders at Prairie du Chien in 1800. Campbell was affiliated with the Mackinac group until 1806 when he became independent. His trading, begun as early as 1792, continued until his death. His father Archibald (Colin?) Campbell and his three half-brothers were all occupied in the trade. Their home was in Prairie du Chien and the sons continued in trade for many years, even after the father's death in 1808.

Murdoch Cameron, J. B. Berthelot, Jacques Giasson, Josiah Bleakley for many years carried on an active fur trade in the vicinity of Prairie du Chien. The latter's home was at Montreal and the other two were residents of Mackinac. Two other traders of whom Pike spoke when he visited Prairie du Chien in 1805 were a Mr. Woods and Allen Wilmot. There is nothing to show that any of these traders had been licensed by the United States or even paid duty on British goods imported for the Indian trade. This led Pike to say that the United States was defrauded of more than $26,000 annually by the traders on the upper Mississippi.[5]

Green Bay residents who traded on the Wisconsin and Upper Mississippi between 1800 and 1820 included Jacob Franks and his nephew John Lawe, eight Grignons, and Jacques Porlier.

About 1808 James MacFarlane, a Pennsylvanian, began trade at Prairie du Chien and made it his home until his death in 1826.

The early French traders at Prairie du Chien—Michel Labatte, Pierre Antaya, Basil Giard, Pierre Lapointe, Charles Lapointe, and Augustin Ange—were small traders and did very little business after 1800. There is a letter showing that Pierre Antaya was furnished by Pierre Grignon with a canoe to trade a few years before 1800, and a descendant of his said that he was killed by the Indians while clerking for Rolette.[6] Francois Bouthellier was a Prairie du Chien citizen at this time although later he was a trader and resident at Galena, where he died. Julien Dubuque also spent part of his time at Prairie du Chien.

The name of John Jacob Astor—who was to overshadow all the rest in the fur business—first appeared in operations at Mackinac in 1807 when he bought 17,500 muskrat skins from Robert Dickson & Co. through Gillespie who had been instructed by Astor's agent, Patterson, to buy them.[7] Astor was hampered in his trade, however, by the embargo act of December 22, 1807, which prevented the importation of British goods. Before this time, he had had large dealings with the Montreal fur traders and was well known there. The incorporation of the American Fur Company in New York April 6, 1808,[8] as a million-dollar corporation had no immediate effect upon the western trade although Astor was doing some business with the St. Louis merchants from 1800 on and during the years preceding the war of 1812 was in direct correspondence with Charles Gratiot from whom he purchased some furs.

After his return from Mackinac in 1808 Jean Baptiste Faribault decided to make his home at Prairie du Chien. He put up a house and suitable buildings, obtained goods from Rolette, and opened up trade. During the war of 1812 he suffered loss from the

Winnebago and in 1819 sold his holdings in Prairie du Chien and settled in Mendota on St. Peter's River where he and his family continued in the fur trade for many years.[9]

In 1810 eight British traders from Wisconsin—Robert Dickson, Allan Wilmot, James and George Aird, Jacob Franks, John Lawe, Thomas G. Anderson, and Joseph Rolette—ran the embargo, taking goods from the British headquarters on Drummond's Isle and passing the American fort at Mackinac unseen. When they reached Green Bay, they divided 10,000 pounds' worth of goods among them and proceeded to the wintering quarters assigned to each.[10]

This probably was not the only time British traders smuggled goods into the United States. The next year Robert Dickson avoided the embargo by bringing goods from Queenstown to Buffalo and by way of Ft. Pitt down the Ohio and up the Mississippi to St. Peter's where he disposed of them to the starving Indians at a total loss. In August, 1810, Astor's overland expedition to the Pacific passed by Prairie du Chien on the way to St. Louis. Wilson Price Hunt was leader and was accompanied from Montreal by Donald McKenzie and Alexander McKay; at Mackinac they picked up Ramsay Crooks.[11]

Before 1806 Murdoch Cameron, James Fraser, Robert Dickson, Joseph Rolette were associated with the firm of James & Andrew McGill & Co.* But that year they organized an independent company to be known as Dickson & Co.[12] The McGills finding the Mackinac Company unprofitable to them, in 1809 delegated to Porlier and Berthelot the power of attorney to act for the McGill interests in the general council. Evidently they sold the stock of their principals, for in 1810 two Northwest Company firms at Montreal—McTavish, McGillevray & Co. and Forsyth Richardson & Co.—took over the organization and called it the Montreal-Michilimackinac Company.

They then sent an agent to John Jacob Astor to make some arrangement to secure Astor's friendship and prevent competition with the American Fur Company.[13] January 28, 1811, the Montreal-Michilimackinac Company combined with Astor to form the Southwest Company. This contract was not signed by McGill

---

* This company included Francois Desrivieres whose mother married James McGill after the death of his father, Francois Amable Desrivieres, who was trading in Wisconsin at the end of the French and Indian War.

or by Cameron, Fraser, Dickson, or Rolette, although the latter four were reputed to have a one-third interest in the Southwest Company.

The main points in the contract organizing the Southwest Company were that it should last for five years, beginning April 1, 1811, and continuing until the end of the season in 1815, when proceeds were to be divided and that the two parties were to be equal partners unless the United States factory system should be discontinued, in which case the American Fur Company would have two-thirds interest instead of one-half but would also be obliged to stand two-thirds instead of one-half of the expense. Each company was to be represented by a clerk, the American Fur Company at New York and the British at Montreal, and these were to have assistants at Mackinac whom they were to visit yearly. No agent was to receive more than $2000 a year and actual expenses of travel. Although Astor was to have $2\frac{1}{2}\%$ commission on all sales at New York, the British were not to charge a commission. The company was to operate within the confines of the United States. After 1811 the Northwest Company promised to deliver to the new company every post or trading-house within the limits of the United States except west of the Great Divide.[14]

The passage of the Non-Intercourse Act by Congress March 1, 1811, prevented the goods furnished by the British partners and held at St. Joseph's from passing into American territory, where the Southwest Company was supposed to do all its business. The restriction resulted in a scarcity of supply at Mackinac, Astor's headquarters, so the Southwest Company was able to send only a small outfit into the Indian country this year. Returning furs met with the same difficulty, war having been declared June 18, 1812, by the United States against Great Britain, and Mackinac having been captured by the British the following month. By the terms of capitulation Astor's goods were saved, however, and later through his British partners at Montreal and through his influence with the President of the United States, he was enabled to remove his goods on a vessel bearing the flag of truce to Buffalo and then to New York. The war disrupted the trade of the Southwest Company and they had no well-organized force to carry it on.

The Northwest traders on the other hand, with Mackinac now in their hands, sent out numerous outfits and continued the trade in American territory much as they had done before.

During the war Astor really did considerable business. In 1813 he had goods that were shipped from Mackinac and St. Joseph's brought into the United States. All during the war Astor himself was buying through the merchants of St. Louis; Ramsay Crooks was busy along the lakes securing furs for Astor; and Robert Stuart, at this time independent, sold some of his furs to Astor. Both Crooks and Stuart had developed leadership through participation in Astor's overland expedition to the Columbia River, but neither was as yet a regularly employed agent of the American Fur Company.

One of the last acts of the Mackinac Company was a contract made through its Montreal agent with Charles St. Antoine *dit* Vacher of Maskinonge in the Province of Lower Canada, to make the voyage in a Company batteau and winter for three years in the dependencies of St. Joseph's, Mackinac, the Mississippi and Missouri Rivers and return at the end of the three years. His uncle, Joseph Saint Antoine de Vacher went his surety. The compensation was to be one 3-point blanket, three ells of cotton, one pair of shoes, one collar, and 48 livres in advance besides 24 livres on departure and 1200 livres or shillings ancient currency at the end of the three-year period.[15]

Another document of interest is a contract between Rolette and Dickson dated at St. Joseph's July 7, 1812—at a time when the war between Britain and the United States was already declared although the news may not have reached them. Rolette severed his connection with R. Dickson and Company, Dickson to give him the barge on which he came to Mackinac, to liquidate all debts against Rolette, and to pay him 2400 livres ancient Quebec currency in return for all Rolette's part of peltries, merchandise, and debts belonging to both.[16] At this time Rolette was not connected with Astor's company. Although Astor had an agent at Mackinac and began sending outfits into the Indian country in 1810, he probably did no business at Prairie du Chien until after the war.

There were other traders violating the American restrictions besides those mentioned, and Indian sympathy was largely with the British. In 1811 an American, Hunt, and his interpreter, Victor Lagoterie, had an establishment on the Rock River but they were attacked and driven off by the Winnebago; however, they escaped to Ft. Madison without personal harm. In 1812 Cabanné and Chenie, traders at St. Louis, were arrested by the Americans at Mackinac because they had violated the Non-Intercourse Act.

British traders and their Indian allies were active in aiding in the British capture of Mackinac. The Mackinac Company, as an organization, offered 100 Indians and all its traders with their outfits to assist the British despite the fact that their entire trade came from the territory of the United States.[17] We know they had a rendezvous at Prairie du Chien; Governor Howard of Missouri said the Hudson's Bay Company also had a post there;[18] and the Northwest traders did business up and down the Mississippi from Prairie du Chien.

After the capture of Mackinac British traders had free access to the northwest, the only danger being the American navy on the Great Lakes. The Indians, excited as always by war, made no hunt and neglected their cornfields so that they were on the brink of starvation when the British traders visited their western posts to make presents and buy any furs which might have been collected. The government paid for these presents.

Some individual traders were active—for example, Jacques Porlier who through Berthelot sold the agent of the Northwest Company 9644 livres of furs delivered at Mackinac July 4, 1814.[19]

When the Americans under General Andrew H. Holmes made an unsuccessful attempt to regain Mackinac the following month, Crooks used the protection of the army to journey for Astor from Detroit to Mackinac. Holmes captured a large amount of provisions on this trip but missed a large consignment of British peltries on their way from Sault Ste. Marie to Mackinac. After the repulse of the American forces Crooks returned with them to Detroit. Later in the year he secured passports and reached Mackinac.[20]

Conditions at Prairie du Chien were sufficiently alarming that Dickson, Superintendent of Western Indians under the actively functioning British agency, organized the inhabitants into a militia company under Francis Michel Dease as captain. The purpose was to protect the village against any hostile demonstration the Indians might make and to resist the Americans expected to come up the river from St. Louis. At the approach of the Americans Dease and his friends retreated and left the village in the hands of the Americans who established Ft. Shelby which was scarcely erected before it was attacked. Nearly all of the traders and their boatmen at Prairie du Chien took part with the British forces in the capture of the American fort July 20, 1814. Many of these men were active traders—among them Antoine and Michel Brisbois, Thomas G.

Anderson, Duncan Graham, Francis Michel Dease. The British commanding officer, William McKay, had himself been a trader in Wisconsin for many years.[21]

The fat years of the Northwest Fur Company were from 1794 to 1814, but with the end of the war the company was compelled to give up the fruitful trade in the territory of the United States, which had been the source of nearly two-thirds of its business. Yet despite the outcome of the war, individual British did not withdraw or cease to trade for many years.

In 1815 J. B. Berthelot sent goods to Jacques Porlier from Mackinac and said that they escaped paying duty to the United States because the army had not yet reached Mackinac. James Aird that year was reported as starving at his trading post on St. Peter's River.[22]

The amount of trade done by the British up and down the Mississippi and in the vicinity of Prairie du Chien can be surmised from the records of Jacques Porlier, only one of the many traders doing business in the American territory. May 15, 1816, Forsyth Richardson & Co. acknowledged payment on his account of 320 pounds sterling and recorded his balance due them as 400 pounds sterling. This was all British business, as Forsyth Richardson & Co. were members of the Northwest Company.

Under its original contract, the last outfit of the Southwest Company was to make its returns in the spring of 1815. However, February 6, 1815, the Montreal partners took in Pierre Rocheblave to share with them and soon after this Astor extended the contract for five years, provided that the United States did not pass laws that would interfere with the trade.[23] Astor's idea was that the British traders would be excluded soon, but he was not yet ready to take over the trade, as he had to have Canadian *voyageurs* and others in his employ. Besides, he did not want to enter into competition with the Northwest traders at that time.

By act of Congress April 29, 1816, the British traders were excluded from entering the Indian country within the territory of the United States.[24] The Green Bay traders—among others the Grignons and Jacques Porlier—were notified by J. B. Berthelot that no foreigner could get a license; yet, whether or not he had a license, Porlier wintered at St. Charles in 1816, and Lagoterie, trading with the Sac and Foxes, was hidden by these Indians and so protected from the Americans. The Hudson's Bay Company was in active competition as shown by the fact that they captured the entire outfit of the Southwest Company under James Grant, their trader in the Lake Superior country, who was accompanied by another trader, eight clerks, and thirty or forty Canadians. The outfit included Indian goods and seventy kegs of liquor; the latter, because illegal, Lord Selkirk probably figured could be seized with impunity. The outfit was a complete loss to the Southwest Company, although later the courts gave Grant a judgment for fifty thousand dollars. This and other losses made the year unprofitable for the Southwest Company.[25]

Nor was the trade without difficulties for the individual traders. Some of the British living in the territory of Wisconsin applied for American licenses; some were granted, some not granted, and some later canceled. Among those who were denied were several of the Grignon family and John Drew, who claimed to be an American. Porlier's license was granted and then revoked. Some of the men had their goods taken over by the Americans. Among these were Bouthellier, Brisbois, and Rolette at Prairie du Chien. The army took over not only the personal property of Francis Bouthellier but also the Mackinac Company property of which he was custodian. This property was converted to army use. So was the property—house, bakehouse, and several cords of wood—belonging to Michel Brisbois. Joseph Rolette's property, too, was commandeered, and he was banished from the village but later secured passports to return to his home and business.[26]

Pierre Grignon secured three licenses at Green Bay October 3, 1816, at fifty dollars apiece—two for Rolette and one for Bouthellier, in spite of the fact that the army looked upon these men as foreigners. James Aird, too, was licensed, but at Mackinac and not Green Bay. All three men protested the amount of the license. William Dickson, son of Robert Dickson, had a license to trade on St. Peter's River. J. B. Jacobs also had a license. September 16 marked the arrival at Prairie du Chien of James H. Lockwood, an American licensed that year, who spent the rest of his life as an active citizen at Prairie du Chien. The correspondent of all these traders was Jacob Franks who operated at Green Bay through his nephew John Lawe. Michel Dousman and Berthelot, and Bostwick as agent for David Stone, did business in Prairie du Chien in competition with the other individual traders and with the Astor interests.

There were no licenses for the American Fur Company in 1816, but the Astor interests were taken care of through licenses granted by Puthuff, Indian agent at Mackinac, to the Southwest Company and paid for by Joseph B. Varnum, one of Astor's agents.[27] As late as August 3, 1816, a bill of peltries for the Southwest Company reached Mackinac where Rocheblave was in charge.

Ramsay Crooks made contact in 1816 with Astor who had sent $150,000 worth of goods to Mackinac that year for the spring trade.[28] March 17, 1817, Crooks received a letter from Astor announcing that he had bought out the Montreal partners of the Southwest Fur Company and wished Crooks to take over their headquarters at Mackinac. Crooks was to have a four-year contract with salary fixed at $2000 annually plus expenses and some other consideration. The cost of the transfer to Astor was said to be $100,000, which did not include his agent's purchase April 8, 1817, of "a lot with two houses two stores and other dependencies thereon" at Mackinac for 400 pounds. These were evidently the dwellings Rocheblave had used for the Southwest Company.[29]

By August 4 Puthuff had licensed only three traders. Crooks protested the conditions in the licenses to Governor Cass who advised Puthuff to allow Astor consideration. Astor seems to have secured enough licenses for the necessary Canadian employees to enable the Southwest Fur Company outfits for 1816 to proceed to their several locations. Returns for the Southwest Company continued to come in until the end of the season of 1818 after which time there are no reports.

One of the first official acts of Crooks in 1816 was a visit to Prairie du Chien where he called on Colonel Morgan. He was appalled at the large business being done by the United States factory recently opened at Prairie du Chien at the old stand of the Mackinac Company. Antagonism to the United States factory system had before this been restricted to the British traders, but from this time forward the Astor interests were in open hostility and in 1818 Crooks wrote Astor that he had better withdraw from the fur business altogether unless the factories were discontinued. The American Fur Company maintained that the factory system was intended to drive out the British but that it was operating to hamper Americans in legitimate trade. It was not the number of the factories, however, which threatened private business, for there were never more than twelve at any one time and in 1816 there were just eight.

Before introducing the factory system at Prairie du Chien, it may be well to review the history of the factory idea. When Washington became President, he tried to devise some plan to treat the Indians as wards of the United States government. He wanted to make them friends of the United States by honest dealings, to bring them the arts of civilization, to teach them to cultivate the lands as well as hunt and fish and fight for a living, to furnish them with goods at cost, to remove them from the influence of the traders who even at that time were demoralizing the Indians in many ways but chiefly through the introduction of liquor among them. Washington had had a good knowledge of the Indians from his earliest boyhood and understood them quite as well as any of the men of his time. Also, he held an altruistic view of friendship with them. In the generous heart of Washington was the origin of the factory system.

Washington anticipated all the Indian troubles which came in the early years of the nation and hoped by dealing fairly with the Indians to alienate them from the British and win them to the American government, but the only action taken during his administration was the vote of Congress in 1795 to try the factory system and to appropriate $50,000 for that purpose.

Jefferson in 1802 induced Congress to pass a bill to revive the scheme and four factories were established—those at Ft. Wayne and Detroit for the northern tribes. With the purchase of Louisiana the system was extended there but discontinued at Detroit in favor of an establishment at Chicago. This was unfortunate, for the building was burned by the Indians in 1812 just before the second war with Great Britain. The factory at Ft. Wayne met the same fate. Even the British traders recognized the potential benefit to the Indians, a benefit counteracted by the Indians' desire to get immediate possession of their goods without the intervention of American regulations.

Indian trading houses were formally established by law April 21, 1806, and two years later John Mason, Superintendent of Indian Trade, sent out instructions to the men in charge of factories. These instructions clarify the government intention as to their function. In this statement Mason spoke of the purpose of the factories—to secure the friendship of Indians in a way most economical to the United States.[30]

Agents were to impress Indians favorably and inspire confidence by good faith and fair dealings; they were to be patient and conciliatory with the Indians on all occasions and to condemn fraud and deceit and prevent every form of trickery. Under no circumstances were they to pass imperfect goods upon them. Goods were to be sold at cost and furs sold without loss so that the factory would pay its ordinary expenses. The only white persons to receive goods through the system were the personnel of the factory and the army except in very exceptional cases. The factor was expected to be present at his post at all times and was to be provided with an interpreter. Every October the factor was to send the Indian Department a list of goods needed and to ship his furs as directed. Goods were to be ordered through the Indian Department and Prairie du Chien factory furs shipped to St. Louis to James Kennerley.[31]

Factories were to be established where there already existed an army post with at least two companies of infantry present. The commanding officer of the post was to furnish a guard and men to help in building but such men were to be entitled to ten cents a day and a gill of whiskey for such fatigue duty.

Following the war of 1812 Wisconsin was allotted two factories —one at Prairie du Chien and later one at Green Bay. Both the army detachment and John W. Johnson, an experienced factor newly appointed to the Prairie du Chien post, had orders to proceed to Prairie du Chien in 1815, but they were delayed until 1816, probably because the United States feared that the presence of troops might precipitate strife since the Indians who had opposed the United States in the war had not yet made a treaty.[32]

In the spring the troops were to convoy the factor and his goods and establish him in a building already existing or in one which they should construct. Johnson complained that he had to come to Prairie du Chien ahead of the army detachment and that the commanding officer did not furnish a guard or soldiers for fatigue duty. Receipted bills for civilian help show that the government was compelled to bear the expense of such labor. Johnson came from St. Louis to Prairie du Chien, arriving May 26, 1816, and made his first quarterly report June 30, 1816. This included several items of interest.

By this time he had spent $473.15 for the purchase of trade commodities. This included skins of 1000 muskrats ($250.00), 187 shaved deer, 134 raccoon, 12 otter, and 9 beaver. Frederick Dixon was paid $102.90—two-thirds for the purchase of a yoke of oxen and one-third for services driving them from St. Charles, Missouri, to Prairie du Chien. Immediately upon Johnson's arrival, the Mackinac Company was paid $23.40, 26 days' rent for storage space. Michel Brisbois was paid for baking and for storage of gunpowder in his magazine. Hyacinth St. Cyr received $3 transportation charges for hauling 24 cartloads from the river to the warehouse. Robert B. Belt received salary as assistant factor, John P. Gates wages as interpreter, and a number of boatmen wages for their services. The average pay of a boatman was $31 and the pay of patroons, $40. Other labor bills included payment made to mechanics (David Bowen, Theodore Lupein, Jean M. Cardinal for underpinning the buildings, Hypolite Thumbly, and others) for building services. Oliver Cherrier and Francis Gallerneau were paid for blacksmith services. $28.25 was paid Stephen Hempstead but the service was not specified. Laborers included Joseph Wallette (Ouillette), Jesse Holly, Pierre Penana, N. Gokey, Martin Jourdain, Pierre Boucher, Ben Michlen, and Solomon Juneau, "hireling for 3 months."[38]

Johnson had permission to sell goods at a 10% advance over cost and sold to many traders on this basis: Solomon Juneau, Antoine and Michel Brisbois, Louis Folbear, Charles LaPointe, M. Perriar, Scott Campbell, Duncan Campbell, A. P. Van Meter, William Belchers, Michel Trainer, Dr. E. Mendenhall, Francis Bouthellier, McNair & Owens, Rolette, J. B. Berthelot, Jesse W. Shull, Hazen Mooers, and others.

His customers were the Sauk, Foxes, Winnebago, Menominee, Iowa, Sioux, and sometimes Kickapoo and Potawatomi. In addition to his experience in factory trade and his suitable personality, Johnson had the advantage of having an Indian wife, a Sauk with whose tribe Johnson had dealt before the war, at Fort Madison on the Des Moines River. He had one handicap, however—deafness.

Johnson carried on a large business in lead and had several transportation bills to pay because of this item. He had accounts with the Quartermaster of the army, the hospital, the Indian agent, and the individual army officers. At times he had a clerk. Two men who served in this capacity were Robert R. Brower and Frederick

Barnard, the latter of whom made an effort to displace Johnson as factor.[34]

When Johnson came, he brought a negro boy who was a slave and a negro woman, also a slave, who was to do the cooking for the men. With the $3 a week allowed her by Johnson she bought her freedom and married a white man in 1824.[35]

In 1820 Johnson bought from Pelagie Lapierre 20 gallons of whiskey which he was to give the laborers and the Indians.

The appearance of Johnson was most unwelcome at Prairie du Chien. His boat was a large one—72 feet long and 12 feet wide manned by a number of men. It had cost $1000 to build and contained $25,000 worth of merchandise of wide variety ready to be sold at cost,—all the factor's wages, rents, and other expenses to be paid by the government. Nor was this all; he was to be in competition with the traders for the purchase of the products of the country—furs, feathers, maple sugar, lead, meats like bear, deer, and wild turkey. There were only two injunctions laid upon him by the government: that he sell no liquor to the Indians and that he sell no goods of any kind to the whites. Both he apparently disobeyed, often under plea of necessity.

Johnson's inventory in 1816 reveals the variety of stock considered necessary by the agent of a benevolent government dealing with its wards—guns, bullet molds, knives, 3½ barrels of whiskey, beaver and bear traps, tobacco, snuff, sugar, blankets and cloth as major items. Tools were included and utensils suited to the occupations of the people—iron kettles, fish hooks, cowbells, one box coffee mill, candlewick. For the women there were spices, looking glasses, white and colored cloth materials, "American patent" blankets, 617 yards of heavy furniture chintz, silver head bands, gorgets, ear wheels, ear bobs, gartering. Then, too, there were such alluring items as "callicoes," Prussian blue leather cockades and eagles for cockades, cloth blue gurrahs, spotted swan skin, one camboone, and pullicat handkerchiefs! Nine dozen Jew's harps found their place in his stock and one lone map of the United States and Lower Canada. The quantity of stock would indicate a large market for his wares and the presence of a considerable settlement at Prairie du Chien.

Johnson was successful from the first in spite of the competition of the hostile traders who erected their booths around the factory in such a fashion as to make access to it almost impossible. They belittled the American goods which were not always equal to English imported materials. They also gave presents to the Indians, sold some articles below cost, and—above all—supplied them with whiskey. Also, the British had the good will of the Indians, especially the old traders who had intermarried and many of whom had fought side by side with the Indians in the War of 1812. The Indians were instinctively unfriendly to the Americans whom they saw seizing their lands and, year by year, driving the Redmen farther West.

The traders resorted to every trick of competition. The Superintendent of the Indian Department suspected that somewhere along the line of transportation hi-jackers on one occasion substituted poor furs for the fine peltries sent to him by Johnson.

1818 was a good year for the factory. It made some money, but that year it met in the House of Representatives a defeat which caused its discontinuance four years later. From this time on it was under fire. Through the agency of the American Fur Company, Governor Cass, Senator Benton, and other members of Congress antagonized the factory system, and the Rev. Jedediah Morse was sent out in 1820 to investigate the feasibility of continuing the system. He visited Prairie du Chien, Green Bay and other places. One of the arguments he urged against the factories was that they were failures because they did not yield profits. Most of them did not yield profits, but the argument was fallacious because the original intention of the government was not the making of a profit but the fair treatment of the Indians in trade. The most that was expected of them financially was that they break even. The one at Prairie du Chien always paid its expense because it was well located and honestly and capably managed.

In spite of every effort of the Superintendent of the Indian Department, the unfavorable report of Morse and the influence of the American Fur Company resulted in the abolition of the factory system by Congress May 6, 1822. May 16 Crooks wrote that the factories "have at length received their *coup de grace*."[36]

One Donald Gant was sent to Prairie du Chien to close out the factory and instructed to sell the goods. He proceeded to do this without any particular effort to hurry about it. The American Fur Company objected to any sale of goods and also to the fact that Gant did not close out the stock promptly. Stuart, agent of Astor at Mackinac, wrote Crooks in 1822 quoting Rolette saying "that young man (Gant) who has been sent to close the factory concern, in place of doing so has opened it with as much éclat as ever."[37]

Stuart advised Astor to write to Grahame, acting Secretary of War, on the subject. If he did not cause it to be closed, Benton was to give him another rap. Crooks wrote Benton that these goods should be sent to trading posts to sell; in other words, the American Fur Company, which had destroyed the factory system, should inherit its goods. June 9, 1823, Gant received orders to turn over the lot and buildings held by the factory to the American Fur Company. The goods were consigned to Hone and Company of New York, a concern friendly to Astor, who sold them at auction at a very great loss. The inventory which Gant receipted to Johnson September 30, 1822, showed the extent to which the United States had been interested in the fur business at Prairie du Chien:

Merchandise	$25,478.06¼
Furs and peltries	616.00
Lead	81.20
Sugar	90.62½
Wild oats	8.35
Tallow	105.97½
Flour	119.15
Feathers	20.50
Mats	35.50
Wood	36.00
Cash	1,003.85
Debts	6,608.11¾
Buildings	4,598.00
Total	$38,801.33* [38]

The years succeeding the abolition of the factory system witnessed the gradual absorption of small corporations and of independent individuals by the American Fur Company which kept control of the fur business in the United States until Astor's retirement from it in 1834.

In 1817 Lockwood was licensed to trade for Franks at Prairie du Chien; Faribault was licensed for St. Peter's River; and J. B.

---

* The total shown in Johnson's first quarterly report—June 30, 1816—was $23,215.16.

Items here represented not a year's business but a quarter's since this inventory corresponded to a quarterly report.

Jacobs for the Buffalo River near the Mississippi. August 30, 1817, Lockwood reported to Lawe his arrival at Prairie du Chien.[39]

A number of clerks and *voyageurs* who were hired by one of Astor's agents, W. W. Mathews, left Montreal May 13, 1817, and a month later were at Mackinac. They were banded into nine outfits with a suitable allotment of goods provided each group of traders, interpreters, *voyageurs,* and clerks. These groups were sent out to various regions—Lake Superior, the Mississippi, the head of St. Peter's River, and the Missouri River. This year the American Fur Company employed from 1500 to 2000 persons; 240 boats were outfitted, each one carrying two traders and from four to six hands.[40]

A conflict between the American Fur Company and the military at Prairie du Chien began at this time. Two of Astor's traders, Darling and Farnham, were arrested at Prairie du Chien by the commanding officer of the fort, Colonel Chambers, because they had in their employ Edward Lagoterie and Joseph Saint John, two men who had been very obnoxious during the war. Colonel Chambers sent them to report with their two boats to William Clark, Governor of Missouri and General Indian Agent. They were ordered to stop on their way downstream at Fort Armstrong where they were to call on the commanding officer. They did this but announced at Fort Armstrong that they would continue to trade with the Indians in spite of Colonel Chambers. The commanding officer of Fort Armstrong thereupon sent Lt. Blair and a detachment to accompany them to St. Louis to wait upon General Clark. Because he ordered these licensed men of Astor to St. Louis, Colonel Chambers was sued for damages by the American Fur Company and a judgment of $5000 was entered against him. The jury decided that a license granted by any Indian agent was good in any part of the country until it was revoked, and both of these boats had been licensed by the agent at Mackinac.

Jacob Franks wrote John Lawe from Montreal March 11, 1818, some of the details of his business that year. He said he was taking two barges to Mackinac with as many winterers as he could procure, 300 beaver traps, 250 half axes, and other goods. Part of his merchandise was coming from Bostwick, Stone & Co. of Montreal. At this time he mentioned buying 30 pieces of stroud from them. He complained also of his accounts. William Dickson had sent only 1500 livres from Big Stone Lake and Franks wanted

Lawe to collect the balance of the account if Dickson should stop at Green Bay. He had not heard from Lockwood and so was uncertain whether he had secured an interpreter and reached the wintering grounds. Also, he was becoming anxious about Aird, for he wrote "It is time to close our account with Aird." Meanwhile Aird was writing Lawe from Prairie du Chien (April 17, 1818) that he and Lockwood had just arrived from St. Peter's after an unsuccessful season but he thought the loss he and Lockwood sustained would not amount to more than 500 pounds. Aird's letter mentioned Robert Dickson's visit to Prairie du Chien following a winter spent with the Hudson's Bay Company on Red River.[41]

Franks had plenty of trouble this year. He had to pay a duty of $280 on goods shipped in the year before. The United States government was slow in paying what it owed, and he was worried because Aird and William Dickson were behind in their accounts. Bostwick was introducing young Americans in the trade this year, sending them out in company with the experienced foreigners, their very presence, however, a gesture of conformity to the American law. They were not formidable competitors except insofar as they pointed to a policy later widely used.

Two rather remarkable papers appeared this year. July 30 Governor Cass gave Rolette a passport to return to Prairie du Chien to his family and business. At this time he was evidently regarded as a foreigner by the United States, although later he was an American citizen.[42] Ramsay Crooks and his companions also were given passports—to go to and return from St. Louis by way of Green Bay and Prairie du Chien. This was necessary since Crooks was not an American citizen[43] and he wished to avert arrest by the military. The suit of the American Fur Company against Colonel Chambers was still pending and Chambers was in no gentle mood. These passports did not give the men the right to trade.

However, the following year Crooks, acting for the American Fur Company, sent Russell Farnham to proceed up the Missouri River to trade and told him he need not fear arrest.

For the first and apparently the only time Lockwood was trading this year for the American Fur Company. He was driving a profitable trade, having with him as boatmen a number of traders and interpreters who were experienced in the business.* His license is

* The men authorized to go with him were Francois Fresniere, Duncan Camp-

here introduced: "Indian Agency Office Michilimackinac Ind (Territory) "Whereas the American Fur Company hath this day applied for a License in favor of James H. Lockwood a citizen of the United States of America to trade with the Indian Tribes on the Upper Mississippi, at and above Prairie du Chien, & its tributary waters. Now therefore (by special powers . . .) I do hereby authorize empower & License James H. Lockwood to trade with any Indian or Tribes of Indians on the Upper Mississippi at & above Prairie du Chien, and its tributary waters, in any article of Goods wares or Merchandise not prohibited by the Laws of the United States regulating Trade & Intercourse with Indian Tribes &c. &c. or Instructions of the President thereof prohibiting the sale of ardent spirits to Indians, until the Twenty seventh day of July in the year of our Lord One Thousand Eight hundred & Twenty. . . .

"Given under my hand at Michilimackinac this twenty seventh day of July In the year of our Lord One thousand Eight hundred & Nineteen.

"George Boyd
U.S.I. Agent Mackinac."[44]

There were complaints against Lockwood that he was vending liquor among the Indians at Prairie du Chien. The same charge was made against Rolette who that year was in partnership with Bouthellier at Galena where the LaPointes were also trading about this time.*

One of the trade practices of the British was to send out outfits with Americans technically in charge who were replaced by the British as soon as the outfits reached the Indian country. Sometimes a trader took actual command himself and sometimes acted in the

---

bell, Scott Campbell, Jean Bt. Mayrant, Hazen Mooers, Antoine Felix, Louis Froisir, Jean Bt. Jebon, Jean Bt. Taillir, Charles Mathew, Gabriel Metevier, David Swanson, Antoine Dabin, Jean Bt. Desormier, Pierre Bordeau, Jacques Lantier, Francois Mayatt, Antoine Goke, Jean B. Dorion (fils), Constant Relle, Alexis Gregoire, Louis Menard, Joseph Deneau, Pierre Ladebauche, Jean Bt. Allar, Charles Provost.

* Although Crooks's own traders were transporting liquor, he complained in 1822 that his traders from Mackinac and Lake Superior were having poor returns because of the competition of merchant traders from Prairie du Chien who used large quantities of liquor. A contract Rolette made this year gave the savages liquor to be paid for equally by Rolette and Grignon and Rouse, his partners by the agreement. This was, of course, contrary to the law. Whatever happened, at the end of the term Rolette threatened to sue his partners for damages.

capacity of interpreter or boatman. This stratagem was not always condemned. For example, when he secured his license from Cass, George Hunt, a Detroit trader, asked if John Lawe, a foreigner, could go with an outfit as interpreter and was told that there was no objection. However, Louis Grignon had his 1819 license revoked because he was a foreigner. This made it necessary for his partner John Lawe to secure an American to take over the outfit, so they engaged Roderick Laurence who overtook the party at Portage and opened up a trade on the Wisconsin River. Both Grignon and Laurence were sick a good deal of the winter and they hired a man named John Gunn to help them in the latter part of the season. The sale to Laurence was only a blind and so the loss from their very unsuccessful winter fell upon the partners Grignon and Lawe.

William Belcher when passing Laurence's camp somewhere near the bend of the Wisconsin (Helena) was looking for Louis Devotion in order to bring his goods to Prairie du Chien. For this purpose he had eight sleighs belonging to Rolette, commanded by Moreau. Louis Grignon, being sick, was expecting to go with him to see the doctor when Moreau should return to Prairie du Chien. After the delivery of these goods by Moreau, Devotion inquired of Lawe the probable cost of transporting to Prairie du Chien two boatloads of goods which he had left in Lawe's care at Green Bay. Lawe estimated the cost at eight hundred dollars. Devotion was interested because he had an opportunity to dispose of all his goods to Belcher.

Lawe's correspondence reveals the activities and troubles of the Green Bay traders on the Wisconsin River as well as in the vicinity of Green Bay. Besides the Grignons and Louis Devotion, Porlier and his son were carrying on an unprofitable business this winter. John Whelan, a Mackinac trader, Louis Rouse, Powell, and two Americans—Leepheart and Farnsworth—were in competition.

The licenses of Porlier and of Bernard Grignon were revoked; and George Ermatinger was refused a license, although he insisted he was an American. His outfit, evidently brought as far as Green Bay under Beaupré, was to be cared for by Lawe who was authorized to sell his boat to Rolette if the latter was passing. Lawe was notified from Detroit by Bostwick that the latter could not procure the sheep, turkeys, and pigeons that he asked for, but he was sending the whiskey![45]

The United States factory was busy in 1819 as is shown by the fact that it sold $1830.75 of peltries and furs. The following year more furs were sold, this time at auction at Georgetown, D.C. There is an interesting letter to Lawe written by Rolette at Prairie du Chien January 20, 1820, in answer to a letter brought by Mr. Moreau, then spending the winter with Rolette: "I drew from Lockwood all your papers and have notified Mr. Franks of it— everything in that way will be all right.

"As Mr. Brisbois Junr. [Joseph] by the most Stupid acts of any man left Four Bales Blankets with you which Has prevented me to Sell all my goods. . . . Had Mr. Moreau not assured me that Mr. Grignon was to bring them I certainly would have Sent for them last fall. . . . No News here everything is dull and it is impossible for us to Sell Christian goods with the Americans. Our Civil authority does all they can to do well and no one has a right to Complain. It is the first winter Since peace has taken place that we enjoy liberty and are dealt with as free men. It seems to me although they can be no returns it is a new World since that T. Chambers is no more here.

"Dancing and Frolicking goes on the usual rate everybody is on a good understanding and that because every man is independent."[46]

In spite of this complacent statement, a serious outburst did occur April 3, 1820, when the Sioux Indians burned the tent of Mr. Laurence where Augustin Grignon was trading on the Upper Mississippi River. Some of the baggage was burned and Grignon had his foot and arm injured. James G. Soulard of St. Louis who was trading at St. Peter's was a witness to the insult offered Grignon. Later when he was Indian agent at St. Peter's, he tried to get redress for Grignon. Mayrand had given liquor to the Indians, but Rolette's oufit near Laurence's was not molested, a circumstance arousing suspicion against Rolette.[47]

J. Bte. Mayrand made a good trade on the Upper Mississippi this winter and the returns of his partner, one Felix, were good, also, although he did not do so well as Mayrand. Louis Devotion, unsuccessful on the Wisconsin, went to trade on the St. Peter's and took his furs to St. Louis.

The long association of Joseph Rolette with the American Fur Company began in 1820, according to his daughter's statement verified by a letter in which Louis Grignon said that in 1821 Rolette told him he was agent for the American Fur Company. Up to this time Rolette had been the most successful trader at Prairie du Chien, and it was because of this that he was chosen by the American Fur Company as a partner.[48]

In the spring of 1820 Rolette sold 300 *minots* of wheat at three dollars a *minot*, besides 200 *minots* of oats and 30 *minots* of peas to William Laidlaw who had come from the Red River Valley as agent for Lord Selkirk. The grasshoppers had destroyed the wheat on Red River for two years, and Selkirk entrusted Laidlaw with the purchase of grain.*

This spring Lawe wrote Rolette that he was making him a boat, would buy him a horse, and had two pairs of wheels he would sell him.† Besides his real estate at Prairie du Chien, Rolette already had $10,000 in cash. This he must have invested with the American Fur Company as well as another eight thousand dollars or more in 1823, for there is a record of an eight-thousand-dollar mortgage given to Hypolite Rolette of St. Louis and redeemed within a year.[49]

The British Parliament in 1821 prohibited American traders from doing business on Canadian territory[50] and the two big British companies—Hudson's Bay and Northwest—united, taking the name of the former, probably because the company had been in active business from the time of its foundation in 1670. This year they withdrew all their posts on the American territory east of the Great Divide.

Some of the ablest of the clerks who were let out by reason of this combination organized a new company which they called the Columbia. Because they were foreigners, it was necessary for them to be licensed through an American group,—Telton and Company acting in that capacity. Active in the Columbia Company were Joseph Renville, William Laidlaw, Kenneth MacKenzie, Daniel Lamont. They had posts at Green Bay and Prairie du Chien and furnished active competition to the American Fur Company until 1827.

The American Fur Company made an arrangement with David

* Robert Dickson arrived with Laidlaw at Prairie du Chien March 10, expecting to meet Lord Selkirk's brother-in-law and to secure for himself from the United States government a return passport. Duncan Graham and Peter Powell were trading for the Hudson's Bay Company on Lake Traverse, and Amable Grignon, brother of the Green Bay family, was at Athabasca, while Jean Bapt. Jacobs had joined the Northwest Company.

† In this letter Lawe commented upon the recent return from Detroit of Rolette's brother, Laurent, who was a small trader at one time on the Wisconsin River at Muscoda and later at Portage.

Stone* & Company by means of which O. N. Bostwick, their agent, was taken over and their company agreed not to do business in the territory of the American Fur Company's Northern Department.

The American Fur Company's place at Prairie du Chien was originally located on the bank of the Mississippi, and likely comprised only temporary sheds. The property of Nicolas Boilvin was deeded in 1821 to O. N. Bostwick acting as agent for the American Fur Company.[52] However, because it was re-deeded the same year to Samuel Abbott, acting in his own person and not as agent for Astor, the transaction was probably a mortgage rather than a bona fide deed. Abbott may have befriended Boilvin, preventing the American Fur Company from securing title, for in 1826 Boilvin himself held a court of inquiry[53] in the Indian agency building on this lot and the following year Boilvin's successor had the commanding officer put in a partition for his use of the building as a dwelling.[54] In 1823 the American Fur Company took over the property just south of this, in which the United States factory had been located† and upon which the government had spent $3000 between 1816 and 1822. The United States buildings were wooden underpinned with rock walls[55] and were not rock buildings. This is the property which is today known as the American Fur Company property and upon which still stands the rock building known traditionally as the "Astor" building. Probably the buildings known as trading houses were used less for storing furs than for handling dry goods and groceries.

In October, 1821, Abbott was sent to St. Louis as agent for the Western Department of the American Fur Company where the corporation absorbed the most prominent fur traders of St. Louis—Bernard Pratte & Company.[56]

Rolette may have managed the company's affairs in Prairie du Chien from the time Abbott left until Hercules L. Dousman came as their agent. The American Fur Company at Prairie du Chien dealt in furs, cattle, feathers, lead, wheat, flour, meats, and ginseng; and later added a wholesale store.

In addition to his duties with the American Fur Company, Rolette was engaged in transportation in a small way. As we have seen, he had sent a train of sleighs to bring Devotion's goods to Prairie du Chien. Also he had furnished boats to transport troops

* Two years later Stone & Co. were entirely absorbed.[51]
† Main Village Lot No. 14.

from Prairie du Chien to Fort Snelling, and in 1825 he loaned his boat to General William Clark at St. Louis to bring Clark to Prairie du Chien for the Indian treaty. In 1821 Rolette sent a drove of cattle to the Red River by Alexis Bailly.

In 1821 Stuart advised the Green Bay traders to form a company and unite with Astor; this they did August 24. The same day the company was formed Augustin Grignon, one of the company, hired Francis Talard for a winterer. The salary was 700 livres ($116.75), "1 three-point Blanket, 1 2½ ditto, one of Cloth, 2 of Cotton Shirts, 4 livres of Tobacco and 2 of Soap."[57] The members of the Green Bay company were Augustin, Louis, and Pierre Grignon, John Lawe, and Jacques Porlier. The contract was to run for three years, and the next year Louis Rouse was taken in.

In spite of this contract, the American Fur Company sent their traders that year into the territory of the new company, and the Green Bay traders sustained heavy loss. They lost money each of the three years of the partnership. One difficulty was that they received a short supply of powder and were unable to furnish the Indians powder to make a hunt.

The factory at Green Bay in 1821 gave goods to William Jackson for trade on Rock River and to Jacques Vieau for trade at Milwaukee. Some of the Green Bay traders visited the places where they had traded the year before. The Grignons and Porlier had this year become American citizens.

In December Dan Whitney took a boatload of groceries and dry goods to Prairie du Chien to sell for cash, and about the same time Michel Dousman took two boatloads of the same kind of goods to Prairie du Chien on his way to the Red River of the North. This added to the competition of the American Fur Company at Prairie du Chien that winter. Further, the sutler of the United States army had a large store of goods for the local trade.* For some reason Tuttle, left at Prairie du Chien it would seem as agent for Whitney, incurred the displeasure of Major Fowle. Perhaps he too complained of the sutler's getting business among the citizens.†

In 1820 Michel Dousman had promised to send 200 head of

* The first sutlers at Prairie du Chien were located on Main Village Lot No. 12 but when the new fort was built, a sutler's store room was furnished within the barracks.

† Some of the former Wisconsin traders—Duncan Graham, Peter Powell, Amable Grignon, Louis Gravelle, Robert Dickson—were trading with the Hudson's Bay Company.

cattle to the Red River settlement and it is likely that he is the trader whose goods Selkirk threatened to confiscate and who was finally compelled to pay 5% import duties on them.

The independent trading of Michel Dousman at Mackinac and Prairie du Chien continued until 1823. "By the fall of 1823 the Green Bay Company seems to have pretty well gone under. Stuart wrote 'I have just returned . . . from Green Bay . . . I want to close our old concerns.' Money was not to be had but we are secured by mortgages on real estate for the most of what the people in that quarter owed us!"

Dousman and Lawe were the only Green Bay traders left in the fall of 1824. They formed a partnership to trade for the American Fur Company at Green Bay where Dousman was sent by the American Fur Company agent to aid Lawe.[58]

Traders who resided at Prairie du Chien and who got licenses to trade in 1823 included Harden Perkins on the Chippewa River, Etienne Dubois, and Pierre Pauquette at Portage; Edward Pizanne at St. Anthony; Antoine Brisbois at the Fromme River; Joseph Deschamps and Edward Ploudre on the Raccoon River; Hazen Mooers at Lake Traverse; and Joshua Palen, John Campbell, and Maurice Blondeau among the Sac and Fox.* [59]

The American Fur Company had 400 clerks and over 2000 *voyageurs* engaged in the fur trade at this time. They sent $37,500 worth of goods into the Upper Mississippi country. Robert Stuart was at Washington for the purpose of getting duty placed on nutria skins and coney and wool and Russian hares, etc., and he also wanted the duty lowered on strouds, Indian blankets, guns, etc.[60]

October 24, 1824, the American Fur Company in New York City had the greatest quantity of furs ever offered at auction in the city. There were 12,500 pounds of beaver, 120,000 muskrats, 72,000 raccoons, 60,000 hare and nutria, 10,000 buffalo robes. In 1827 Astor sold partly by auction and partly by private sale 550,000 muskrat skins at an average of 36¢ apiece. W. B. Astor, son of John Jacob, once estimated the annual income of the company at $500,000. It has been said that the Astor company in 10 years' business at St. Louis made over a million dollars. Altogether the

---

* Other licenses, obtained by Rolette, were for Alexis Bailly and Jean Baptiste Faribault, then on St. Peter's with headquarters at Mendota where Faribault had his home.

fur business netted Astor between one and two million dollars.[61]

May 25, 1824, Congress passed a bill requiring Indian agents to designate specifically such trading places with the Indians as they might deem suitable.[62] This law was to prevent traders from following up the Indian hunters and taking away from them their green furs, often in exchange for liquor. The common phrase for this practice was *courir la drouine*. It had been protested by the Indian chiefs as a serious abuse, for in this way the hunters brought no furs back to their villages. The traders were in the habit of going wherever they chose without being hampered. It was said that the American Fur Company kept out of the trade on the Columbia River because they were paid half a million dollars in 1824 by the Hudson's Bay Company.[63]

May 6, 1825, a protest against the law locating traders by the Indian agents came from Prairie du Chien and was signed by Joseph Rolette, Dennis Robinson, J. H. Lockwood, P. Hurtebise, Alexis Bailly, and Alexander Roc; and Astor had sent in the same kind of a protest against the law.[64] Also the same year the case of Astor against Chambers came up at St. Louis. Chambers was fined but was unable to pay. Taliaferro continued till 1840 as Indian agent at St. Peter's. For years the American Fur Company had tried to have him removed because he had consistently attempted to prevent the importation of liquor into the Indian country.

Gradually the competition of individuals and small companies was wiped out. Jean Brunet and his partner Jean Despouse came from St. Louis and in a small way entered into the trade at Prairie du Chien in 1820. William A. Aitkens and Truman Warren each had a contract in 1824 to get half their goods from Charles Ermatinger and half from the American Fur Company and to sell half their furs to each. The American Fur Company entered into a contract with Jacques Vieau of Milwaukee, who had then been trading in Milwaukee forty years.[65] Near Green Bay there was an independent trader named Farnsworth who used a great deal of liquor and reaped the harvest that should have gone to the members of the Green Bay company. Two of the younger Grignons entered the trade this year. They intended to trade with the Winne-

---

In 1824 Antoine Gauthier and Maurice Blondeau were given licenses to trade with the Fox and Sac on the Des Moines River. The latter was living on the Des Moines at this time, but Gauthier was still a resident of Prairie du Chien.

bago on Rock River. Antoine Gauthier was trading at Galena.

In 1825 M. Dousman seems to have supplanted Lawe as agent for Astor or to have joined the Green Bay company, for Stuart says, "Mr. Dousman is connected in your trade this season," and Dousman sent Henry McGulpin to Green Bay to assist Lawe.[66] In 1826 H. L. Dousman was sent to Prairie du Chien as agent for the American Fur Company, Rolette continuing as a partner. The year before Dousman had a small establishment at Shantytown (Green Bay).

In 1827 after long negotiations the American Fur Company absorbed the Columbia Company paying them $20,000 and assigning two of their ablest men—William Laidlaw and Kenneth Mac Kenzie—to establish a trading post near the mouth of the Yellowstone River at a place later known as Fort Union. They were called the U.M.O. (Upper Missouri Outfit). Renville, the leading spirit, retired and established himself at Lac-qui-parle.[67]

The American Fur Company had driven out practically all opposition of Prairie du Chien and the Northern Department with the exception of the sutler business of the United States army which was continued for many years by the garrison.

The volume of liquor trade increased yearly until in 1832 eight thousand seven hundred and seventy-six gallons of liquor were sent from Mackinac with outfits of the American Fur Company going into the Indian country.[68] At his post on the Upper Mississippi, Aitkens had been using annually from 400 to 500 gallons sent out by Ramsay Crooks from Mackinac. Since the liquor came through from Detroit, even some of it imported from Europe, it is not likely that Astor did not know of its shipment. Most of the liquor used in the Indian trade was diluted some—part of it as much as eight times. When this traffic was protested, Astor argued that he could not compete with the Hudson's Bay Company without the use of liquor.

The abuse was not new, of course. In 1802, 1822, and 1832 restrictions were placed by law to close loop-holes in former laws, but illicit traffic continued. As Indian agent, Boilvin permitted Bailly to transport liquor to St. Peter's on condition that he report to the commanding officer. He did, and the commanding officer seized the liquor and prosecuted him. On another occasion a subordinate officer from Ft. Snelling who seized liquor aboard an American Fur Company boat, was haled before the court for unlawful

seizure. Governor Cass was always very accommodating to the
American Fur Company in its violations of the law.

Astor in 1834 sold out his interests of the Northern Department
to Ramsay Crooks. In settling with Astor, the Green Bay traders
had to give mortgages to settle the bills owing him. Under fore-
closed mortgages Astor took over most of the lands upon which
Green Bay is located today. The Prairie du Chien traders, Aird and
Rolette, had the same experience. Both were reputed to be rich, but
Aird's estate as well as Rolette's was insolvent.[69]

In 1837, when the Winnebago sold their lands and arranged
to distribute $100,000 among the half-breeds of that nation, the
traders presented bills against the tribe that amounted to nearly
$200,000. Many of these were repudiated as not legal, and some
were paid only in part. The American Fur Company and their
traders had large bills most of which were allowed. Other traders
who had been among these Indians for many years were among
those who presented bills for goods.* [70]

The new American Fur Company was essentially an independent
concern and had few men interested directly in its stock. Rolette
still retained an interest; the two leading men were Hercules Dousman and Henry Sibley, the latter in charge of their holdings at
Mendota, Minnesota, and the former at Prairie du Chien. Sibley
had replaced Alexis Bailly who was in disgrace for having brought
liquor into the Indian country.

The new company had less opposition and their management
was under old and experienced traders; they had retained all the
good traders who worked for the old concern. Apparently, also,
they used as much liquor as the old company. The traders themselves, like Dousman and Sibley, enriched themselves. They had
not such experience in settling with Astor as the Green Bay traders.

Dousman and Sibley invested money in their home towns, while
Astor invested only in New York, far from the western country
where he made much of his fortune. When Astor sold out his
property at St. Louis to the St. Louis traders, his entire outfit as
valued by himself was worth less than ten thousand dollars, although it was scattered from St. Louis to the Pacific Ocean. The
main village lot that came into his hands in 1823 never cost him

* Francois LaBath, one of the successful young traders, a half-breed, put in a
claim as did Oliver Amelle, who lived with his Winnebago wife several years at
Prairie du Chien, later moving with the Indians to Long Prairie.

one penny; even the buildings were put up or repaired by the United States factor while the 200 acres of land he acquired from Rolette were by mortgage; he entered bills against the estates of both Aird and Rolette. All losses were charged to his traders while he always won because he sold goods at profit to them and sold their furs on a two and a half per cent commission.

The removal of the Indians after the Black Hawk War, and the final removal of the Winnebago and Menominee in 1848 brought the local fur trade to an end. In 1842 Rolette said his stone store building was rented to the American Fur Company. This new American Fur Company was able to continue its profitable business many years. When furs became scarce at Prairie du Chien, northern Minnesota furnished a large field for the fur dealers. Before 1838 the new company had established a large wholesale and retail store at Prairie du Chien and in addition was using Rolette's stone store building for storage and perhaps the lower story for actual sales. This building was commonly known as the Hudson's Bay Company building but never belonged to them at any time.*

After nearly forty years Dousman and his partner sold out in 1864 to a Mr. Hubbell of St. Paul and thus ended the company's activities at Prairie du Chien. Four years later Dousman died.

* On Main Village Lot No. 16 (just north of the present Glynn Hotel). It was built by Rolette in 1835.

CHAPTER EIGHT

Military Affairs After 1800
(Part One)

THE United States Army played an important role in the history of Prairie du Chien after 1800. To break up the influence of the British traders with the Indians, to stop Indian uprisings, and, later, to uphold the authority of the Indian agents and to aid the United States factors, detachments of soldiers were sent into the territory of the Upper Mississippi. While there were civil and militia officers appointed at Prairie du Chien in 1802, it was the army that kept order and insisted upon American law in the first years of the nineteenth century.

An exploratory expedition marked the first appearance of the American uniform, a sight which was very soon to become familiar throughout the Upper Mississippi region.

In 1805 Lieutenant Zebulon Montgomery Pike was ordered by General James Wilkinson, commander of the southwest division of the United States Army, to explore and report on the Mississippi River from St. Louis to its source, to select sites for military posts, treat with the Indians, make peace between the Sioux and the Chippewa, and find out what he could about the British traders who still occupied posts in the newly acquired territory of Louisiana.[1]

He left St. Louis at four o'clock in the afternoon on Friday, August 9, 1805, with one sergeant, two corporals, and seventeen privates in a keelboat seventy feet long, provisioned for four months. His roster is still preserved. Pike noted the rivers on both sides and islands in the Mississippi as he passed along and, as will be seen from the following extracts, made detailed comment on the traffic on the river. Also he spoke of the amount of wet weather they encountered. August 14 he met a Mr. Robedoux by whom he sent a letter to St. Louis. The next day he met a Mr. Kettletas of New York who gave him a letter of introduction to Mr. Fisher at Prairie du Chien. On the 16th he arrived at the house of a Frenchman on the west side of the river opposite Hurricane Island. The next day he passed three batteaux. On the 18th he passed an Indian camp on the east side of the river. He sent out a hunter on the 19th of August, and on the same day three canoes of Indians passed along the opposite shore. He passed the rapids of Des Moines without any difficulty on the 20th. The same day he met William Ewing, appointed to be an agent and farmer to the Sacs, who was accompanied by a French interpreter, four chiefs, and fifteen men of the Sac nation, bearing a flag of the United States. On the 23rd he met some Indians and made them a small present. Also he met three batteaux from Mackinac which were the property of Mr. Myers Michel. The following day two of the men were lost who went out to search for dogs belonging to Pike. On the 26th he met two paroques [pirogues] full of Indians, and on the 27th passed a paroque of Indians at the mouth of the Rock River. On the 28th he met James Aird, who was repairing his boat. The 29th he had breakfast at a Fox village.

September 1st Pike, who had been suffering from a dysentery, was taken with a violent attack of fever. Julien Dubuque saluted the party with a field gun and Pike, in spite of his illness, interviewed Dubuque about a report on the mines which Pike had been instructed to make. He also had dinner with Dubuque and listened to a speech by Raven, one of the Fox chiefs. While Pike was at Dubuque, Mr. Blondeau and two Indians arrived with Pike's two soldiers who had been lost. Through the kindness of Mr. Aird, they had received food, and the chief of the Fox village had given them corn and shoes and sent two Indians with Mr. Blondeau to return them. Pike paid the Indians and gave Mr. Blondeau passage to Prairie du Chien. September 2nd Pike saw several paroques of Indians opposite Turkey River, and on the 3rd also he saw paroques.

He arrived at Prairie du Chien at about 11 o'clock, September 4th, having eaten breakfast just below the Wisconsin River. At Prairie du Chien he took quarters at Fisher's, and was politely received by Mr. Fraser. The next morning at 10:30 he went in a Schenectady boat to the mouth of the Wisconsin in order to take the latitude—forty-three degrees, twenty-eight minutes, and eight seconds. Also he wished to look on the adjacent hills for the location of a military post. The party were accompanied by Mr. Fisher, Mr. Fraser, and Mr. Woods.

Pike ascended a hill on the west side of the Mississippi and made choice of a spot which he thought most eligible, "being level on the top, having a spring in the rear, and commanding a view of the country around. A shower of rain came on which completely wet us and we returned to the village without having ascended the Ouiscousing as we intended. Marked four trees with A, B, C, D, and squared the sides of one in the center. Wrote to the general." The location that Pike marked for a fort at the mouth of the Wisconsin River is still known as Pike's Hill and is now an Iowa state park. While there are some large trees that must have been there before Pike's time, and there are some with scars on them, it would be hard to locate the exact spot that he surveyed.

On the 6th he had a council with the Winnebago and Sioux chiefs and laid out a place for a post on a hill called *Petit Gris*, three miles above the mouth of the Wisconsin on the east side of the Mississippi and the north bank of the Wisconsin. He told of the difficulties he had with the interpreter; of Mr. Fisher's getting sick from drinking water out of the Wisconsin; and of his men beating all the villagers at jumping and hopping. He had changed his boat for two smaller ones, so on September 8th he set out at 11:30 with two batteaux to proceed up the Mississippi. He had two interpreters. One was Pierre Rousseau and the other Joseph Renville, the latter being the interpreter of Mr. Fraser, who was going as far as St. Anthony's Falls with them. Mr. Fraser was a young Vermonter, a clerk of Mr. Bleakley of Montreal.

The Indians on his way were friendly and were curious and excited because they had never before seen uniformed American soldiers. Some places he had seen them carrying the American flag, but as he went up the river, in many places the British traders who had posts had a British flag floating from the flagstaff. He had several councils with the Indians and from the Sioux obtained considerable grants of land along the Mississippi River upon which American forts could be built.

After spending the winter on the Upper Mississippi, he returned down the river, arrived at Prairie du Chien at two o'clock on the afternoon of April 18, 1806, and was met by large crowds on the bank of the river. He took up his quarters with Mr. Fisher. Mr. Campbell, justice of peace, as well as Mr. Fisher, made presents of meat and bread to the soldiers. Mr. Jarrot from Cahokia was leaving the next day for St. Louis, and Pike was sending a letter to Gen. Wilkinson by him. Sac and Fox chiefs of the Des Moines River called upon him. He received word that the Winnebago were going to deliver to him certain murderers. He got news from the States and Europe, news both civil and military. On April 19th he dined with Mr. Campbell in company with Messrs. Wilmot, Bleakley, Wood, Rolette, Fisher, Fraser, and Jarrot. Six canoes arrived that day with chiefs of the Yanktons. He took Renville into his employ as interpreter. In council he demanded the murderers from the Winnebago, who asked a day to consider. Also he talked with Wabasha, the Sioux chief. On this same day, Sunday, April 20th, there was a great game of *la crosse* on the prairie between the Sioux on one side and the Winnebago and Foxes on the other. On the 21st of April he had a long conversation with Wabasha, and also Red Thunder, a chief of the Yanktons, who complained of Murdoch Cameron selling rum to Indians in his village. Another council with the Winnebago was held and the evening spent with Mr. Wilmot of whom he spoke as "one of the best informed men of the place." The next day a council was held with the Sioux and Winnebago, the latter of whom delivered up the British medals and flags. On April 23rd at twelve-thirty he left Prairie du Chien. Just as he was leaving, he met a barge which delivered a letter from his wife,—"milady," as Pike wrote.

When American soldiers came again to Prairie du Chien it was to participate in an engagement of the War of 1812. In this vicinity there had been repeated and flagrant violation of the United States trade laws by British traders who were frank in their talk of a new war which would "restore" the country to England. The inhabitants of the village were divided in their allegiance. By 1811 it was feared war was inevitable, and Boilvin, the Indian agent, and Nicolas Jarrot, a Cahokia trader, issued a circular urging the inhabitants of the village to stand by the United States. Fisher, a relative of James Monroe, later President, so feared the war that he took his two oldest sons and a nephew, the eldest son of Michel Brisbois, to the distant Red River to get away from the conflict he foresaw at Prairie du Chien. Giard and Michel Brisbois probably remained neutral, although after the war Brisbois was sent to St. Louis as a traitor by the commanding officer at Fort Crawford. No proof of his being a rebel against the United States was advanced and he returned to Prairie du Chien. Giard was an old, delicate man, and the only charge made against him was that he gave powder to the British at one time while they occupied Fort McKay. He could hardly have done otherwise, and he received pay for it later. One reason it is likely Giard remained faithful to the United States is that nearly all the men who had come up the Mississippi from the Illinois country and become residents of Prairie du Chien were loyal Americans. Cardinal, whose father had been killed when the British attacked St. Louis in 1780, nearly lost his life by espousing the cause of the Americans. A letter written by Joseph Roc, dated at Prairie du Chien March 12, 1813, shows the conflicting views held by its citizens. Roc, also a resident of Prairie du Chien, was the hired American interpreter for Boilvin. While Roc vowed loyalty, it is a known fact that he was not playing the game fair, his sentiments being British.[2]

In 1812 Robert Dickson brought the news of the war to Prairie du Chien. He organized the people into a British militia and Boilvin, fearing for his life, fled. Francis Michel Dease[3] was captain and Dickson[4] himself was Superintendent of the Indian Affairs in the Northwest for the British, having brought goods for presents to the Indians so as to control them in the approaching war.

This was the state of affairs when in 1813 General Howard, commanding officer of the Western Department of the United States Army, at Belle Fontaine (St. Louis) got permission from the Secretary of War to establish an American fort at Prairie du Chien.[5]

An official report quoted later by Joseph Perkins, Lieutenant of the Twenty-fourth United States Regiment Infantry recorded his trip with General William Clark to Prairie du Chien for the purpose of building a fort at that place. General Clark left St. Louis May 1, 1814, with five barges. Besides the Regulars under Lt. Perkins, there were a group of volunteers under Captain Sullivan, who had enlisted for thirty days and were eager to return to St. Louis. After Sullivan's departure from Prairie du Chien, Yeiser was left in charge of the gunboat *General Clark* manned by thirty-two men. The British attacked this boat with their cannon. Because of damage done to the boat, it was compelled to retire lest it sink. They drifted down the river, taking supplies that would have been useful for the defense of the newly erected fort. The entire fort was built on a large Indian mound that stood back of the village, whose houses were scattered along the river bank. It was seventy feet wide and one hundred thirty feet long and was to be built in the triangular shape of a ravelin, with two bastions in front and one towards the river, very nearly in the shape of a triangle, with earthworks thrown up. This fort was named Fort Shelby in honor of Isaac Shelby, the first governor of Kentucky.[6]

The official report of Lieutenant Perkins dated August, 1814, is here given: "Sir: Having been ordered to this place on the recruiting service from St. Genevieve by Capt. Wilkinson of the 24th U. S. Infantry, on the 24th of April I reached this place and opened a recruiting rendezvous, on the 29th. I received an order from Major Z. Taylor of the U. S. Army, to take command of a detachment of sixty-one regular Troops of the 7th Infantry and ascend the Mississippi with Govr. Clarke and aid him in establishing a post at Prairie du Chien or any other place on the river he might think best for the protection of the frontiers. I accordingly obeyed the order and took command of the detachment entered on board of a Boat and on the 1st of May started in company with the Gun Boat Govr. Clarke and others to Prairie Du Chien, at which place we arrived on the 2nd of June. On our arrival the Govr. ordered me to land and take possession of the Mackinac Company's Houses, which order I promptly obeyed. On the 5th the Govr. fixed on a place for the Fort which was a small mound back of the Village and one of the most commanding spots about the place. On the 6th I commenced building the Fort under the order and directions of the Govr. who left us for St. Louis on the 7th. On the 19th I had the Fort so far advanced that I moved into it and mounted a six pounder in one Block house and a three in the other. I continued working on the Fort until the 17th of July when a large body of British and Indians made their appearance in the Prairie (about three miles distant from us) about twelve o'clock a flag arrived at the fort and demanded a surrender of it to his Majesty's forces unconditionally, which demand I refused, at ten minutes past one a fire commenced from the enemy's Gun (a Brass four) on the Gun Boat, which had been left by Govr. Clarke to aide and assist in the defence of the Post, would it be attacked, which was immediately answered from the fort and Gun Boat, about two hours after the action commenced the Govr. Clarke turned down stream and we in short time lost sight of her, but I had no idea that she had gone off and left us. The British, Indians and citizens kept up a constant fire on the fort until the evening of the 19th, finding the boat did not return and we had expended the most of the fixed ammunition for the six and three pounder, the water in the well had so far exhausted that we could scarcely get any to drink, and in attempting to sink, it caved in so that I had to give it over those circumstances together with the enemy's

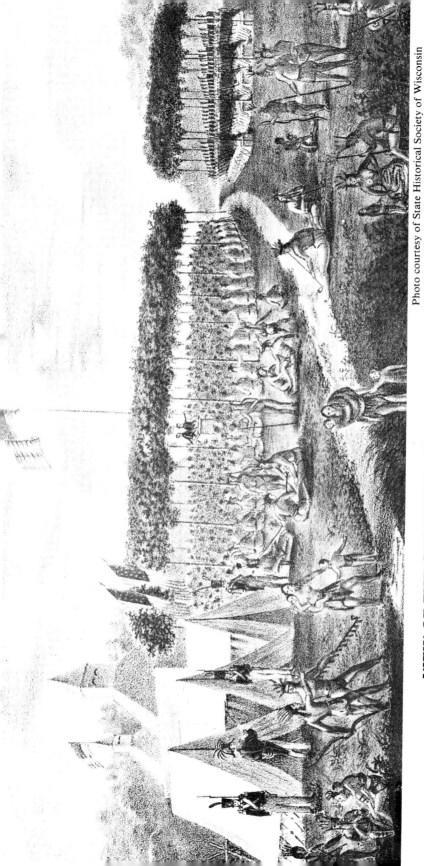

Photo courtesy of State Historical Society of Wisconsin

VIEW OF THE GREAT TREATY HELD AT PRAIRIE DU CHIEN

SEPTEMBER 1825

at which upward's of 5000 Indian Warriors of the CHIPPEWAYS, SIOUX, SACS & FOXES, WINNEBAGOES, POTTOWATTOMIES,

MENOMONIES, IOWAYS & OTTOWAS tribes were present

Gov. LEWIS CASS of Michigan and Wm. CLARK of Missouri, Commissioners on the part of the UNITED STATES

Marquette and Joliet

Early explorers of Prairie du Chien

Prairie du Chien, Wisconsin 1851

From drawing by Johann Baptist Wengler (1815-1899)

Captain Jonathan Carver
An early traveler and author who described Prairie du Chien in his writing

Photo courtesy of State Historical Society of Wisconsin

John Jacob Astor

New York businessman whose agents had a significant impact on Prairie du Chien

Hercules Louis Dousman

Agent for John Jacob Astor and Wisconsin's first millionaire

View of the Dousman House

Overlooking the Mississippi River, a popular hotel for river travelers

View of Blackhawk as a Young Warrior

Blackhawk, Celebrated Sac Chief
Painted from life by J.O. Lewis at Detroit 1833.

Jefferson Davis

Later President of the Confederacy, served the U.S. Army at Fort Crawford
in Prairie du Chien. Engraving by S. Hollyer.

View of the Surrender of Chief Blackhawk

At Fort Crawford from a drawing by Cal Peters.

Map of Prairie du Chien in the 1800's

Rendered by Gordon Peckham from a photocopy of the original map, artist unknown.

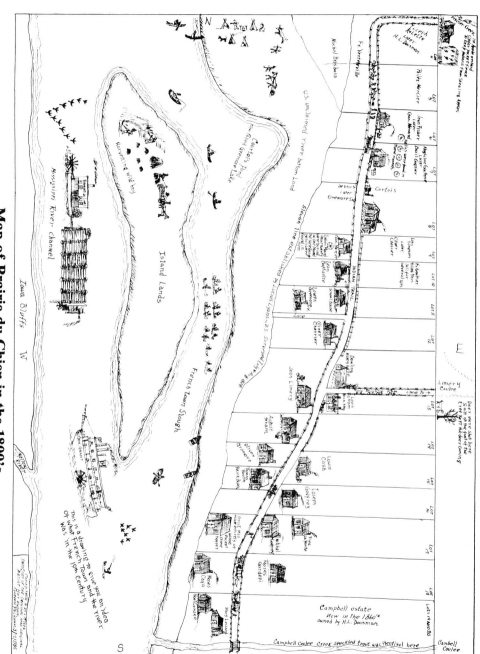

approaching us by undermining, I thought it best to capitulate on the best terms I could, and after consulting G. and J. Kennerly the former aid to the Govr. and the latter Lieut. of Militia, doing duty under me, the conclusion was to send out a flag which was borne by Mr. George Kennerly, and the following capitulations was entered into first the lives of the officers and soldiers to be protected from the Indian our private property respected, and to send us home as prisonners of War not to take up Arms against Great Britain or their Dependencies until regularly exchanged, during the three days and two nights engagement, I had five men wounded and no hospital stores, medicine, nor physician to give them relief; we surrendered at 8 oclock in the morning of the 20th though was permitted to stay in the Fort for our safety as the Puants had devised many plans to murder us; the Commanding officer finding them so much disposed to mischief was induced to place a strong guard of the Sioux and Cippaways around the fort to keep them off, we were kept in this situation for two or three days when they were sent off, after which time we could walk out without any kind of danger, On the 30th were all paroled except four men, two deserters from the British and two Canadians, who was claimed as their subjects, the Commanding officer furnished me with a Boat and Provisions for the Trip; I embarked my men at two oclock and set out for St. Louis accompanied by two British officers, a strong guard and a piece of artillery, who accompanied us as far as the mouth of the Rock river, where we landed on August 2nd. The comdr. of the Gun Boat went to the Village and after councilling with the Indians who were stated to be four or five hundred in number they agreed to let us pass, we set out about dark with one of the officers an interpreter and six soldiers who accompanied us as far as the lower Rapids where they left us and returned, we pushed on night and day and landed at this place on the morning of the 6th all is good health except the wounded who are like to recover . . . The force against us I think was about 1200 in all. J . . ."[7]

The archives have revealed the names of the men who were compelled to surrender at Fort Shelby.[8] Looking back for more than one hundred years we can hardly envisage the difficulties that surrounded the Americans in their rapidly erected wooden barracks, small and isolated, with five hundred miles of land filled with hostile Indians between them and civilization, forsaken by the gun boat that was relied upon to help them in the hour of need and

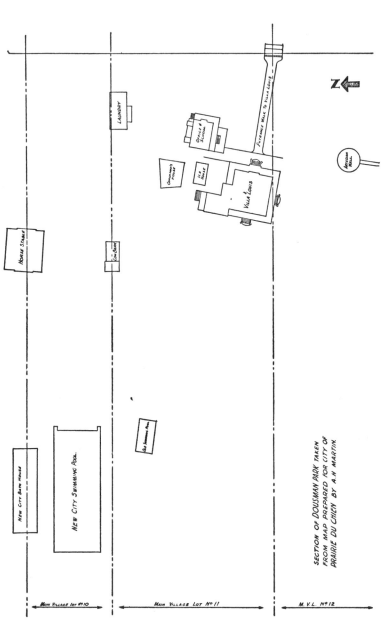

SECTION OF DOUSMAN PARK TAKEN
FROM MAP PREPARED FOR CITY OF
PRAIRIE DU CHIEN BY A. H. MARTIN.

MOUND ON WHICH VILLA LOUIS STANDS WAS THE SITE OF FORT SHELBY (LATER FORT McKAY) AND SUPPORTED

THE SOUTHEAST BASTION OF LOG FORT CRAWFORD

upon which many supplies badly needed within the fort were carried away. Time has justified the wisdom of the Americans in turning over the fort to the British, as no disaster—no loss of life, no loss of territory, or any charge of cowardice like that applied to Gen. Hull at Detroit—resulted. Under Colonel McKay, the British officer who captured Fort Shelby, were Joseph Rolette, a captain, prominent trader and citizen of Prairie du Chien; Capt. Duncan Graham, an old settler and British trader here; and Lt. Michel Brisbois, Jr., a half-breed son of Michel Brisbois, Sr.

For the remainder of 1814 and until May 25, 1815 the British held Prairie du Chien, using the same fort the Americans had built but changing its name from Shelby to McKay in honor of the British leader who had captured it. The feeble attempts of the Americans to relieve Prairie du Chien by American arms ended in disaster. Both Maj. Zachary Taylor and Capt. Campbell were defeated severely on the Mississippi near Rock Island. At these encounters the British were present to aid the Foxes and Sac, using a small cannon successfully against the Americans. Those who are ready to belittle the powers of the Indian warriors might well read Gen. Jackson's statement that he would just as soon encounter six thousand British soldiers as the same number of Indians,—and he met both Indians and British successfully in battle.[9]

By the Treaty of Ghent December 14, 1814, the War of 1812 finally established for all time the boundaries between our locality and Canada. Reluctantly the British soldiers withdrew. They learned from St. Louis of the ending of the war, but not until they received definite orders from Col. McDouall at Mackinac to retire at once did they evacuate, taking the guns and valuables and burning the fort. Capt. Bulger had orders to send the cannon to St. Louis, but he excused himself by saying it could not be done that way. Just why the British should burn the fort before leaving it in peace time, it being at that instant American property, is inconceivable, unless we view it from the British standpoint that some day Prairie du Chien was again to be English territory. In fact, they led the Indians to believe by the treaty the Americans acknowledged Indian supremacy over the northwest. Many Indians remained loyal to the English until after the Black Hawk War.

During the winter of 1814-15 there was not always harmony at Fort McKay. Antoine Dubois, who was a nephew of Wabasha and a brother to Rolette's half-breed Indian wife, was sent with

Louis Champagney to get meat of a Sioux tribe, Les Gens de la Feuille Tire, and the two were murdered by an Indian of that tribe. Rolette was accused of sending powder, fuses, and ball to these Indians and in other ways creating disturbances; so at the request of Robert Dickson, who disclaimed any "personal pique," a court martial was ordered by Capt. Bulger to try Rolette January 5, 1815. The main charge at the trial was the use of seditious words. The testimony against him was weak, and he was acquitted. Many a private during the British control having incurred the displeasure of an officer found himself court martialed.

Bulger proclaimed martial law December 31, 1814, for Prairie du Chien and surrounding country by a proclamation: "Whereas, it is necessary from the disturbed state of the country that martial law should be declared, I do by virtue of the Power and authority vested in me hereby proclaim martial law to be in force throughout the country from the date hereof which all officers, civil and military, and all persons whatsoever are to take notice and goven themselves accordingly . . ."

January 7, 1815, a court martial was called which tried the Indian Chunksah, accused of killing Champagney and Dubois. They found him guilty and sentenced him, expressing the opinion that he "ought immediately to suffer death by being shot." The decision was confirmed and the execution was carried out immediately in the presence of the garrison and militia under arms.

"The whole country was under arms" at that execution, said Bulger, and it made such an impression on the citizens of Prairie du Chien that January 15, 1815, a large number signed a statement expressing their thanks for the protection afforded His Britannic Majesty's subjects. There were forty-four signers, twelve of whose names were handed down to us. It almost seemed the British soldiers would openly defy the officers and that was no doubt one reason for Bulger's declaring martial law and having the militia called. Some of the soldiers were flogged and confined to cells with bread and water. At this day and age we feel the British discipline was too severe.[10]

The Americans, awakened by a realization of how costly their slowness of action and indecision about establishing themselves at Prairie du Chien before the War of 1812 had been, hastened now to erect a large, more suitable, and better garrisoned fort on the site of the former one.

Gen. Thomas A. Smith, Brev. Brig. Gen. commanding the western department of the United States Army, went up the Mississippi, taking six companies of the rifle regiment.[11] The troops arrived June 20, 1816, and the muster roll first sent from Prairie du Chien was dated June 30, 1816.[12] Major S. Long said that Col. Wm. Sutherland Hamilton[13] began the erection of this new fort, which is known to us now as the Old Log Fort Crawford, July 3, 1816. In regard to the name, a British letter writer assumed that this fort and the county in which it was built were named after British traders by the name of Crawford* but William H. Crawford was then in the cabinet as Secretary of War, a man who had for some years been prominent in the United States government. There can be no doubt that the fort was named after this officer.[14]

The first reports from the seat of this fort came in an official way by Capt. Willoughby Morgan in a letter dated "Camp Le Prarie du Chien" 5th July, 1816.[15] It did not take long to build a fort and give it a name, for the muster roll of August 31 was dated at Fort Crawford and soon after Colonel Hamilton left on leave of absence; when we next hear of him he was assigned to duty in Tennessee, and some time in March, 1817, he left the army.

When Colonel William Sutherland Hamilton left Prairie du Chien, the senior officer, Brev. Maj. Willoughby Morgan, assumed command and held it off and on until the time of his death at the new rock Fort Crawford April 4, 1832, while he was overseeing its erection. It may be said that the years from 1816 to 1832 had their story coincident with the life of Colonel Morgan.[16]

Willoughby Morgan appears to have been a son of General Daniel Morgan of Frederick County, Virginia, and lived at Winchester where in 1812 he became captain of the first company raised for the war. He was wounded at Mackinac August 4, 1814 when Gen. Croghan and Maj. Holmes led the Americans unsuccessfully against the British. After the war, he entered the army and was made a captain of Company B rifle regiment. When Col. Anthony Butler was sent to take over Mackinac, which he did

---

* Louis and Redford Crawford, who killed the Indian agent, John Campbell, were the only prominent Crawfords in this region. While at Prairie du Chien, Redford Crawford was a partner of Robert Dickson who was decidedly British. It is assuming a great deal to say that an American fort was named after such a British subject as Redford Crawford. It is not likely that Colonel Hamilton had ever heard of him before coming to Prairie du Chien and here he would find out his unsavory record.

July 18, 1815, he left Capt. Morgan in command.[17] Morgan changed the name of the fort from Mackinac to Holmes in honor of Maj. Andrew H. Holmes who was killed in the engagement the year before.

When Gen. Smith came to Prairie du Chien with six companies of the rifle regiment, Captain Morgan of Company B was with him, and Col. Wm. Sutherland Hamilton was left as commanding officer. Hamilton left in August and Morgan, being senior captain, was made commanding officer of the log fort, the erection of which had been begun July 3. It was practically planned and built by Morgan and finished in October. In August, 1816, he was relieved of his command by Colonel Talbot Chambers. During a large part of 1817 Major Morgan was commanding officer at Fort Armstrong, Rock Island, Illinois. In 1819 he was on the Missouri River near where Fort Leavenworth now stands and for two years (1820-21) he was at Fort Harrison, Indiana. He returned to Prairie du Chien in 1822 and until August 31, 1826 was bona fide commanding officer at Fort Crawford. In 1827 he was in command at Fort Dearborn, and for a time in 1826, commanding officer at Fort Snelling. He returned to the command at Fort Crawford July, 1830, and remained there until his death April 4, 1832. He it was who built the largest part of the rock Fort Crawford and the rock hospital. Colonel Morgan's grave is marked with an old fashioned tombstone in the United States military cemetery, Prairie du Chien.

While Colonel Chambers was assigned to Fort Crawford in August, 1816, he did not arrive until April 22, 1817,[18] and in the interim the command fell upon Capt. W. L. Dufphrey, who was rated very highly as a military officer by Colonel Hamilton, his superior. Hamilton said of him, "Dufphrey is a very capable officer. His equal is hard to be found in activity, attention, enterprise and subordination."[19] It was well that he was such a character, for over him later was a man whose unreasonable domination made the lives of all those under him almost unbearable. Dufphrey signed muster rolls as late as June, 1817. While Major Stephen Long was in Prairie du Chien in 1817, he spoke of Capt. Dufphrey's being bitten by a rattle snake, but he recovered from the bite.

When Colonel Chambers arrived at Prairie du Chien, he showed himself very arbitrary and treated many of the Canadian-French as traitors;[20] in fact, the Americans were apt to be overbearing to the French-Canadians—at least that was true at Prairie du Chien.

He assumed powers he did not possess. When the troops came in 1816, they took over the property of the Mackinac trading company and the site of Fort Shelby without saying "may we" and when General Smith came to build the old log Fort Crawford, they took over the fur company's property after Francis Bouthillier had rented it to John W. Johnson, United States factor. The American Fur Company recovered the property, however, and received compensation as rent for the time the United States held it and also benefited by the buildings the government put upon that lot (Main Village, Lot No. 14).[21] The lots upon which the fort was built were No. 9 Main Village occupied at that time by Alexander La Chapelle; No. 10, by James McFarlane; and No. 11 by Bazil Giard. Not only were the property rights of the *habitants* ignored, but also their liberty.[22] Michel Brisbois suffered at the hands of Colonel Chambers, being sent under arrest to St. Louis charged with treason, and maybe justly so, for he had been commissioned in the militia of Prairie du Chien by the governor of Illinois in 1809 as a lieutenant. It is not certain, however, that he took any active part against the Americans in the War of 1812, although his brother Antoine Brisbois assisted and directed the British soldiery, while Michel Brisbois, Jr., half-breed son, was an officer in the British force that captured Fort Shelby. Rolette was also one of the captains who served under Col. McKay and yet he was tried by an English court martial at Prairie du Chien during the year 1815 because he was suspected of being in sympathy with the Americans. For some fancied breach of good morals Rolette was banished for the winter of 1816-17 to an island in the Mississippi above Prairie du Chien. The same commanding officer, Colonel Chambers, had Charles Menard whipped for selling liquor contrary to the law and had it not been for the son of Boilvin might have suffered harm. Chambers arrested the clerks of the American Fur Company, and sent them to St. Louis. His action brought displeasure upon Morgan who acted in accord with the orders of Chambers, who was at that time his superior officer.

Chambers insisted on a liberal supply of liquor for the garrison, and he evidently got his share, for in 1826 he was accused of being drunk for weeks while in active service with troops, was court martialed and cashiered.[23] He was a bold officer and had been cited for bravery in the War of 1812 but the inactivity and lonesomeness of garrison life far away from civilization were his undoing. It was during the years he was in command at Fort Crawford that Major Long made his first visit to Prairie du Chien. No Indian disturbances occurred during the time Chambers was commanding officer. He was a stormy petrel and often was in trouble for real or fancied wrongs. In his early military career he was cited for bravery and advanced rapidly, but his early record was marred by his expulsion from the army and by the fact that he went to Mexico and became an officer in the Mexican army, fighting against the Americans in the Mexican War.[24]

In June, 1818, Dufphrey's company became Hickman's.[25] It appears that the garrison had been reduced to one or two companies and by April 30, 1819, Hickman's company were the only soldiers at the post. Capt. Llewellyn Hickman was commanding officer until June 30, 1819, when Lt. Col. Henry Leavenworth with seven companies of the Fifth Infantry arrived on his way to build a fort at St. Anthony's Falls.[26] He assumed command, distributed his troops—some to Fort Armstrong, some to Fort Crawford—and ascended the Mississippi August 8, 1819. The command at Prairie du Chien then fell to Major Peter Muhlenberg who held it until he resigned from the army June 1, 1821.[27] Things had been so quiet during these years that a large force was not necessary and nothing of a striking character had happened. In 1819, however, the War Department sent one of its higher officers to see how the western posts were being conducted.

Inspector General A. P. Hayne visited Fort Crawford in October, 1819, and reported: "Ft. Crawford Praire des Chiens under Col. C. A. Chambers is an Indian work composed of strong oak logs of a square form with two block houses each containing a 12 and a 6 pounder. The curtain of the work is formed by the buildings with appropriate loop holes, partitioned and protected. The quarters are very neat and comfortable and capable of accommodating 400 men with the necessary store houses and comprised in the curtain of the work. Its local structure is on an extensive prairie surrounded by immense high hills but too distant to command the work. It is capable of defending itself against any combined Indian attack, although it is in the power of the Indians in 12 days to assemble 2000 warriors. But is not calculated to sustain an attack of artillery. The great difficulty is to obtain fuel. They have to go 6 miles for wood. It takes half of command 2 months every fall to get enough for winter and these men are exposed to Indian attacks (one to three months getting wood every fall). The place is healthy and if necessary could be supported by products of the surrounding country."[28] Why Gen. Hayne said Col. C. A. Chambers was in command is not clear. Chambers might have come up from St. Louis where he was stationed, or he might have been superior officer to Major Muhlenberg, who was surely in actual command at the time. The inspector-general has used the wrong initials for Chambers, which he might easily do if the latter was not present.

In 1817 Maj. Stephen H. Long measured Fort Crawford. "The work is a square of 340 feet on each side and is constructed entirely of wood as are all its buildings except the magazine which is of stone. The enclosure is faced principally by the quarters and other buildings of the garrison so that the amount of all the pallisade work does not exceed over 350 feet in extent. The faces of the work are flanked by two block houses, one of which is situated in the south east and the other in the north west corner of the fort. The block houses are two stories high with cupolas or turrets upon their tops. The quarters, storehouses, and so forth are ranged along the sides of the garrison, their rear walls constituting the faces of the work. The buildings are constructed with shed roofs, sloping inwards so that their outward walls are raised 20 feet from the ground. The buildings are all rough shingled, except the block houses which are covered with smooth shingles. The magazine is 24 x 12 feet in the clear, the walls four feet thick, and the arch above supported by a strong flooring of strong timbers."[29]

It was during Muhlenberg's administration that Crawford County was organized and the first elections took place. The conflict between the precision of military control and the laxity and crude inexperience of civil authority gave rise to serious problems of jurisdiction.

When Maj. Muhlenberg retired, Maj. John Fowle, Jr., became commanding officer at Fort Crawford.[30] He was succeeded April 26, 1822, by Col. Morgan, who previously had been in command. Morgan was destined to have a stormy time, as Indian troubles began. He had to send troops to Galena in 1822 to protect Col. James Johnson* who had a license to work the lead mines on Fever River.

* Johnson was a brother to Vice President R. M. Johnson and in addition to his mining license he had a contract for transporting military stores and troops on the Mississippi and Missouri Rivers. His price for doing this was so high that there was a long investigation in Congress in relation to it. His boats made many trips to Prairie du Chien.

The Indians were resisting the aggression of the whites, for at that time those were Indian lands. Hardly had that detachment been recalled than rumblings of Indian unrest were heard on every hand. Francis Depouse, a Frenchman; Joseph Barrette, a Canadian; John Findley; and another white man were killed near the mouth of the Chippewa River in 1824, by the Chippewa Indians.[31] Blame seems to fall on the white men. After consideration, it was decided that Morgan should not interfere in the Sioux and Chippewa feuds, although the lives of the whites were becoming more and more jeopardized. Indian massacres and threatened uprisings were more frequent and the Indians less amenable to restraint.

At the great treaty at Prairie du Chien in the summer of 1825 the council met in the presence of the army on the sandy prairie just north of the old log fort, and there was deliberate military display intended to impress the Indians with the power of the United States.

While Morgan was still in command—in August, 1826—Inspector General George Croghan, Jr., visited the fort and reported: "Messes good—bunks on floor which is uneven due to freshets . . . soldiers neat soldier-like, clothing well marked, books accurately and neatly kept, although not according to regulation; hospital well arranged but without a single patient—medical stores in sufficient amount—books of the hospital not brought up to the present date in consequence of the sickness of the surgeon and the incapacity of hospital steward. Sutler's store without the garrison several hundred yards. Major Vose reports that the sutler (Capt. Goodwin late of the army) conforms to his wishes so precisely that in no instance can he be accused of letting the soldiers have 'whiskey' under whatever pretense without a written permission.

". . . Discipline, good. I approve Maj. Vose's methods for discipline—due to the almost entire exclusion of whiskey from garrison—1 gill at a time drunk at sutler's counter is all a soldier is allowed of whiskey—as a ration—half a gill is dealt out just before breakfast—the remaining half at dinner in the mess hall.

"Instruction not very good. Too much time for fatigue duty, both men and officers. Two hours morning; two hours evening should be given to infantry drill. Service, regular; clothing, good; subsistence, plenty and good. Ordnance Dept. under the commandant of post—no proper inventory; arsenal stores well arranged, but no surplus. Only guns on carriages two six pounders and a cannon; magazine building best I have seen. Powder and ammunition in good condition. Magazine small but sufficiently large for all purposes of the post."[32]

Morgan's command was transferred the same month to Capt. Wilcox of the Fifth Infantry, and the last of September Wilcox and his soldiers acted upon orders to abandon Fort Crawford and proceed to Fort Snelling to reinforce the command there.[33] Col. Snelling was censured for urging that step, which augmented his own garrison at a severe cost to Prairie du Chien. The evacuation of Fort Crawford at a time of great unrest encouraged the Indians to believe that the Americans were afraid to remain.

In the spring of 1827 John Marsh, sub-Indian agent at Prairie du Chien, received through his wife, who was a half-breed Sioux, information that the Winnebago anticipated killing all the American residents of Prairie du Chien, but of all the inhabitants only Michel Brisbois was properly alarmed. The Indians had been incited because of the American activities in the mines at Galena and also of the traders who had brought a more aggressive system among them. The Methode murders of 1826, charged to the Winnebago but never proved, marked a new departure in relations between the whites and Indians.[34] In past outrages of this sort the Indian either of his own volition or subjected to force brought in killers of whites for punishment in order to escape tribal punishment or in order to acquire white men's favors; but now for the first time the Winnebago refused to aid in the conviction of the guilty ones. Whatever the reason for withholding their assistance, one thing was certain: there was a change in the attitude of the Indians toward the whites. There were rumors that the Winnebago prisoners accused in the Methode affair had been turned loose at Fort Snelling to be slaughtered by the Sioux. This unfortunate situation resulted in the Winnebago War of 1827.

Red Bird, a Winnebago chief, was well known at Prairie du Chien and well thought of. Formerly he had been a trusted Indian, but apparently his tribe insisted that he be the one to strike at the white settlement nearest to him. With three other Indians he came to Prairie du Chien and asked for whiskey, which was denied them by the sub-Indian agent but evidently obtained elsewhere in the town. The first place they entered with evil intent was the store and residence of Lockwood. Passing through the store, they entered the residence part of the building, terrifying the women. It was

Duncan Graham's presence which saved the Lockwoods, apparently, for he induced the Indians to leave, his word carrying weight because he had lived many years in the Indian country.

From there they crossed the prairie and came to the mouth of the McNair coulee. In the northwest corner of the entrance to McNair coulee there stood two houses on a ridge.* In the south one lived Registre Gagnier and his wife, children, and hired man.[35] The children were a son, Francois, two and a half years old, and a daughter, Marie Regis, less than one year old.[36] Red Bird was well-known to this family, and he was invited in to eat in accordance with the prevailing pioneer order. Hardly had the Indians come into the house and been seated—it was after eleven o'clock in the morning—before they sprang up, shot, and killed Gagnier. Then his hired man, Solomon Lipcap, an old retired soldier, who was staying there, was killed. The mother rushed out of the house and wrested a gun from one of the Indians; then, with her son, she made her escape to the village where she gave the alarm. The people came to the rescue, but the Indians had fled. The two dead men were found scalped, and the little girl was found scalped but alive. She recovered from her wound and lived many years at Prairie du Chien where she is still remembered by some of the older settlers. She was twice married and raised a large family, some of whose descendants are living today.

This affair took place about noon—June 28, 1827. This fact is confirmed by the church records of St. Gabriel's church and by an official report of John Marsh, the sub-Indian agent, who was on the spot. This is one of the two atrocities of what is known as the Winnebago War and is always spoken of as the Red Bird massacre. After the surrender of Red Bird and his associates, they were imprisoned with two others charged with the Methode murders and were held. Red Bird died February 17, 1828, and the others were tried in September of the same year. Two were found guilty and the others discharged. When the matter was brought to the attention of President Adams, the ones found guilty were pardoned December 26, 1828.[37]

The fact that the garrison had been taken away from Fort Crawford encouraged Red Bird to take scalps. At this distance it almost seems that an Indian war of some magnitude was threatened. The

* About 600 yards south and east of the point known as Sugar Loaf on a line between that point and the bridge on the present U. S. Highway 18.

second outrage was an attack by the Winnebago upon two keelboats, *Oliver Perry* and the *Gen. Ashley,* under the command of
Capt. Allen Lindsay and at that time on their return downstream
from Fort Snelling with supplies and freight. On the way up they
had been threatened by the Sioux and the danger seemed so real
that Colonel Snelling furnished the crew of thirty-two men with
arms and ammunition. After going below the Sioux villages, they
little thought that there was any danger. The Winnebago had
appeared friendly to the crew on their way up the Mississippi, but
at the mouth of the Bad Axe River thirty-seven Winnebago warriors
now fired on the *Oliver Perry* and killed one man, Steward; mortally wounded a negro boy; and severely wounded two other men.
This was June 30, 1827, two days after the Red Bird murders at
Prairie du Chien. John Marsh reported both events to Gen. Clark
June 30. "The day before yesterday Basil Gagnier and Solomon
Lipcap, citizens of this place and an infant child of the former
were murdered and scalped by four Winnebagoes." Again July 10
he reported: "On the 27th ult. about noon two men were murdered
and a child scalped. Three days after a keel boat returning from
St. Peters was attacked about forty miles above this place by about
one hundred and fifty Indians; after a desperate conflict, the savages
were repulsed with the loss of ten or twelve of their number—
two of the boats crew were killed and four wounded. Another boat
has since been attacked but no one wounded."[38]

A Winnebago council had been called at Butte des Morts on
the Fox River, but Governor Cass, hearing of the Red Bird massacre, pushed down the Wisconsin, arriving at Prairie du Chien
July 4.[39] After the massacre, the inhabitants of Prairie du Chien
had gathered and with Thomas McNair as captain occupied the old
log Fort Crawford. Cass commissioned McNair to command the
Prairie du Chien militia. He went down to Galena and a volunteer
company of militia was organized there under Capt. Abner Fields
with Lts. Smith and William Stephen Hamilton. The Prairie du
Chien and Galena militia were placed under the command of Capt.
Fields, and were inducted into the United States Army by Captain
Thomas of the U.S.A. who was at the time stationed at the lead
mines of Galena and who came up with Capt. Fields. In the meantime Duncan Graham, whose wife was a Sioux, was sent with Jean
Bte. Loyer across the Mississippi and on horseback to Fort Snelling
to notify Col. Snelling, who came to Prairie du Chien at once with

four companies of the Fifth Regiment of Infantry. He assumed command and because of some trouble with Capt. Fields and his officers dismissed them, but gave them neither provisions nor transportation home. One of the Galena officers, Lt. Smith, challenged Snelling to a duel. Had it not been for the generosity of Lockwood, the men would have had trouble getting back to Galena. The Prairie du Chien militia were not discharged until August, and they never received any pay.

General Atkinson came from Jefferson Barracks with his troops, arriving July 29, 1827 at Prairie du Chien, which he made headquarters for the northwestern army. He sent a messenger to Gov. Cass to learn the outcome of the Winnebago council at Butte des Morts and sent Col. Snelling back with provisions and with orders to send four other companies of the Fifth Regt. Infantry and light boats. Col. Snelling arrived at his post August 16, and Maj. John Fowle arrived at Prairie du Chien August 21 with two keel boats and nine Mackinac boats. Cass's messenger, who reached Prairie du Chien August 19, informed Atkinson that the Winnebago council had been concluded August 11, but the matter of the attack on the Lindsay boats had not been settled, nor had the Red Bird massacre. Upon Cass's advice to take his troops to Portage, Gen. Atkinson started up the Wisconsin River August 29, arriving at Portage three days after the surrender of Red Bird and his accomplices. Gen. Dodge, with mounted volunteers, scoured both sides of the Wisconsin and kept in touch with Atkinson all the way up. Atkinson and Dodge held a "convention" with the Winnebago September 9 and made them sign an agreement not to interfere with the mines at Galena or in Wisconsin. The Red Bird prisoners were turned over to Gen. Atkinson, and they returned to Prairie du Chien, where those accused of attack on the boat were also turned over to the commanding officer. September 22 Gen. Atkinson issued a peace proclamation, and thus ended the Winnebago War. Gen. Atkinson credited the presence of Reverend Francis Vincent Badin with protecting the village of Prairie du Chien from general slaughter.[40]

Besides the regulars under Maj. Whistler from Fort Howard, the troops from Fort Snelling, and those from Jefferson Barracks, the mounted volunteers under Gen. Dodge and the Prairie du Chien and Galena militia had engaged in this Winnebago War, which lasted officially from July 4, when Cass arrived at Prairie du Chien, until September 22, when Atkinson declared the war over. The few casualties do not seem to have warranted such a show of force, but there was fear of a general uprising of the Indians on the Upper Mississippi. Fort Crawford was ordered regarrisoned September 6, 1827,[41] but, as a matter of fact, it had been occupied continuously from July 4. For many years after this it was the main military post on the Upper Mississippi.

Maj. John Fowle, who was already installed at Fort Crawford with four companies of the Fifth Infantry, was selected as commanding officer. Notwithstanding the auguries of Gen. Street and others, Fowle had an uneventful time. He was succeeded by Col. John McNeil April 30, 1828.[42] There is scant mention of him. The most conspicuous thing he did was taking over the land in the Campbell coulee for a military garden. The original garden space east of the fort had proved unsatisfactory, since the sandy soil on Lots thirty-three and thirty-four was not productive and the fertile part nearest the bluffs was owned and farmed by private individuals.

During the fall of 1828—September 26—the first tragedy at the garrison occurred. Reneka, a sergeant, while drunk, shot and killed Lt. John McKenzie, who was officer of the day.[43] The young officer was buried near the old log Fort Crawford, but when the military cemetery was moved in 1829 to Farm Lot thirty-three, his remains were buried there. This burial place has been well preserved and enclosed, and in 1932 the government put up a bronze marker at its entrance. Old-fashioned tombstones mark the grave of Lt. McKenzie and other officers who are buried there.

The principal military inspections in any camp or fort are those which take place either daily or weekly in the companies but, lest a command should get stale, now and then inspection is made by officers of higher rank. In the same manner these frontier posts were occasionally visited by the Inspector General or his representative. The first visit of this kind to Fort Crawford was made, as we have seen, in 1819 and the second in 1826.

Brev. Maj. Gen. Edmund P. Gaines came to Fort Crawford September 28, 1827, and stayed until October 14. He made the last official report on the old log fort, a report quite different from the two preceding ones as excerpts will show:

Construction—block-houses and huts, all of wood—is much decayed, not fit to inhabit except extensive repairs are made. The floors and lower timbers are decayed, in part due to overflowing of river. Orders have been given to Major Fowle, commanding officer, to repair it. Ten thousand feet of plank was brought from Fort Snelling with requisite tools. The high water in barracks is as high as four feet at times. The present site of Fort Crawford and all the prairie is unhealthful in Sept. and Oct. The number of sick at this inspection was one officer and forty-four men out of one hundred and seventy-seven officers and men. Some women and children sick also. Maj. Fowle says he was previously stationed at Fort Crawford from June, 1819 to May, 1822. He recommended a place on the west side of the Mississippi for a fort. Pike's peak seems the best place for a post. There is no spot in Prairie but is claimed by some individual except a few acres where the fort stands.

Dr. R. M. Coleman, Asst. Surgeon, said: "This is an unhealthy place—soldiers, villagers, and Indians have much sickness. Remittent, intermittent fevers, dysenteries, and diarrhoeas are prevailing diseases."[44]

Major Stephen Watts Kearny, who later became the first military governor of California under United States possession, came to the command September 10, 1828. He was highly praised by Surgeon Beaumont, whose words were: "The healthfulness and efficiency of the troops at this Post are unprecedented within the limits of my recollection, and I cannot consistently with my own belief and in justice to the disposition and efforts of the commanding officer of the Post (Major Kearny) forbear to observe that the present extraordinary state of health and good condition of the troops of the garrison ought in a great measure to be attributed to a well-regulated system of company messing and the industry, good order and strict but salutary discipline, effectually introduced and maintained among the soldiers of the command for the last five or six months in consequence of which they have, with few exceptions, become clean, diligent and sober men inured to and cheerfully performing a regular routine of practical useful military duties and exercises and the no less necessary and healthy employment of daily garrison police and ordinary fatigues, one of the obvious good effects of which is, much less time is spent by the designing and disorderly disposed in studying plans of mischief and transgression and few opportunities are afforded to execute them with impunity."[45]

In the early thirties a wave of temperance passed over the United States,[46] and about this time the army discontinued liquor as a ration to the soldiers. Some of the officers, like Captain Mason, were so impressed with the necessity of temperance that they complained of Thomas P. Burnett, sub-Indian agent who defended men violating liquor laws at Prairie du Chien.

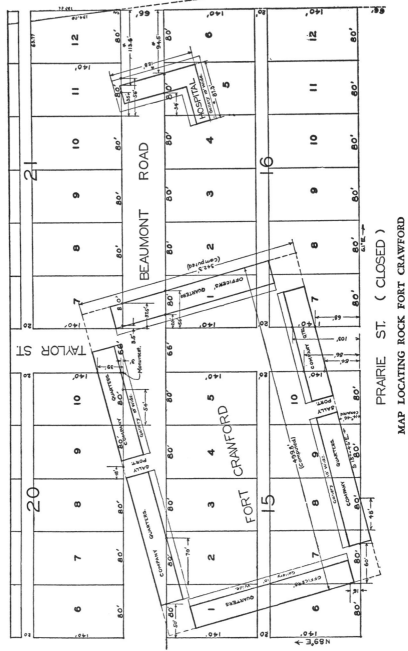

PRAIRIE ST. (CLOSED)

MAP LOCATING ROCK FORT CRAWFORD

CHAPTER NINE

Military Affairs After 1800
(Part Two)

WHEN IT WAS decided to retain the garrison at Prairie du Chien, agitation for a new fort arose. The high water of 1826 had driven the troops out of the fort for all of a month and done considerable damage to the entire buildings.[1] No sooner was the fort reoccupied in 1827 than an effort was made to secure a new one. In 1828 Major Kearny wanted to know whether the government was going to rebuild. April 2, 1829, Maj. Gen. Alexander McComb wrote to Kearny that it was decided to build a barracks at Prairie du Chien. While it was to be for eight companies, buildings for only four were contemplated that year. It was hoped that "harmony might prevail" despite overlapping of authority which led to some ill-feeling before the job was complete. Maj. John Garland, who had recently come as post quartermaster, was to superintend and pay out the moneys, and the commanding officer was to supervise the entire building.

Plans were prepared by Thomas S. Jessup, Quartermaster General of the United States Army, and sent to Fort Crawford for the approval of the commanding officer. These plans reached Prairie du Chien in June, 1829, but before they were received, Maj. Kearny had been ordered to secure a site upon which to build the new fort. He purchased from James H. Lockwood for $2000 Farm Lots Thirty-three and Thirty-four, Private Land Claims of Prairie du Chien, and in addition, Joseph Rolette sold the government for one dollar about six acres at the west end of Lot Thirty-five. This afforded the garrison a good landing-place on the Mississippi. This landing-place is now marked with a sentry post, sunk to within about nine inches of its top.[2]

It was decided to build the fort on the site of a group of Indian mounds, practically the same spot upon which Judge James Duane Doty wanted Crawford County to build the courthouse and upon the land which he had deeded to the county for such purpose. The fort was to be large enough for eight companies, with magazine, guardhouse, prison, hospital, storehouse, and a sutler's store, besides which afterwards were added blacksmith and carpenter shops, and outside and farther east the barns for the horses of the military. Plans proposed for the building of Fort Crawford do not seem to be accessible in the files of the Adjutant General's office in Washington. There is a drawing which is mentioned as a plan for the building of the barracks, but upon recent investigation no hospital plan could be found within the Quartermaster's department or the Engineer's department of the Adjutant General's Office.[3] It is difficult to say how much these barracks cost, because the appropriations were included with appropriations for forts being constructed in other parts of the United States, but in later years an officer of the United States Army—Major T. W. Sherman—estimated the buildings were worth $200,000.[4] They did not actually cost that much because the soldiers did the largest part of the work.

Major Kearny, knowing he was to be replaced as commanding officer, had refused to make any suggestions as to changes in the plans. In July, 1829, Lt. Col. Zachary Taylor[5] came to assume command. Gen. John McNeil who came with him had been advised by Gen. McComb of the Western Department that the commanding officer at Fort Crawford might make necessary or desirable changes in the plans for the new barracks.

It is not clear that the government intended to build a rock fort, and indeed it was suggested that the first story be of rock, half of it underground, and the second story of wood; but the nearness of the rock supply and the ease with which rock could be quarried decided them to build the entire structure of rock. Evidently the actual digging of cellar and laying of rock began in July, 1829, although as early as March 18 six carpenters from Maj. Kearny's command were assigned to the quartermaster, together with laborers for quarrying, burning lime, going into the timber, and preparing grounds for buildings.[6] Master mechanics were secured from St. Louis—masons, plasterers, and carpenters. Taylor on his arrival assigned one hundred men to aid Garland.

The rock was obtained "within a mile of the fort," most likely from a quarry situated at the mouth of the Mondell, then known as the Lariviere, coulee.[7] Apparently the rock on the Iowa side below McGregor, because a purer limestone, was used for burning lime,[8] and brick was burned extensively in Prairie du Chien, the clay along the bluffs being used for the purpose. A saw mill was built by the soldiers at the mouth of Yellow River, and the sawing of oak lumber began October 9, 1829.[9]

This year good headway was made upon the construction. It was said that there was rock enough on hand July 24, 1829, to put up half a block, and the saw mill had been commenced. August 31 Garland said that he had hired Isaac Harrison, an expert on pine lumber, to take charge of getting out lumber.[10] He also said at this date that ninety-one feet of the east barrack was commenced and forty-four feet of the north block. Again, October 9, he said: "One block officers' quarters 45 x 30, two stories will be done this fall and 200 x 30 feet of men's barracks, with 10 feet gallery will be done this fall." Besides this, he said eighty thousand brick were burned. November 20 Maj. Garland wrote that the frost prevented laying rock. While the two barracks referred to above had the rock work complete, they were not shingled and, as the river closed November 17, work had to cease except that February 14, 1830, twenty-four men were sent into the pineries on Chippewa River to get out lumber. Lt. Jefferson Davis was on this duty but left after the group and took a team of horses up to the camp. All returned early in May.

After about a year at Fort Crawford, all of which time he had been engaged in building the rock barracks, Col. Taylor went away July 5, 1830, on a six-months' leave of absence which was destined to be extended so as to keep him away from the post for more than two years. His wife was sick in Kentucky and he himself was sick. Before his return to Fort Crawford he was sent to New Orleans and other places on court martial duties, so he was away from Fort Crawford until the Black Hawk War began, when he met his command in the field.[11] Col. Willoughby Morgan succeeded Taylor as commanding officer at Fort Crawford.

Progress on the fort was not apparent during the summer of 1830. However, Garland said June 3 that four blocks of officers' quarters were up and the fifth commenced. These blocks were 46 x 30, three of them shingled and two floored. The one covered in the previous fall was now finished and occupied. He said that he had marked this in red in his plans. Each block had a gallery and was separated from others by six feet, although all were under the same roof. At this same time he said that the saw mill on Yellow River had been compelled to stop because the water of the Mississippi had backed up.

Indian troubles required the attention of the soldiers as late as August. The next report on the buildings was made December 9,

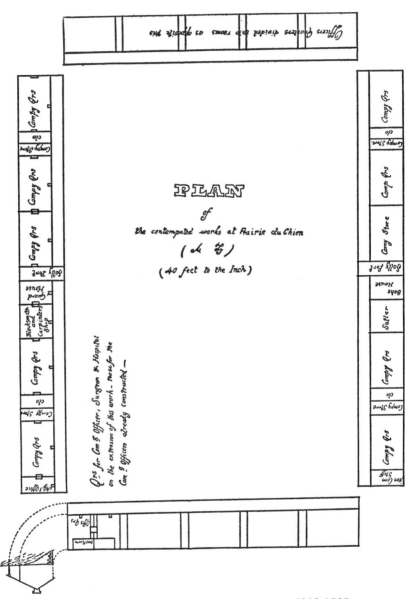

ROCK FORT CRAWFORD CONSTRUCTED 1829-1835

when teams were engaged in moving stores to the new barracks, not as yet named Fort Crawford but called by Col. Morgan in his report simply "New Barracks at Prairie du Chien." He evidently looked for a change in the name of the fort. On the date of this report Col. Morgan ordered Maj. Garland and Capt. Mason to make a survey of the barracks before occupying them, and December 16, 1830, the four companies present at the old log fort moved into their new quarters, leaving the sick and surgeon at the old fort, as the hospital was not finished.

January 10, 1831, Col. Morgan ordered Lt. Wilson to make a drawing of the new barracks, to be forwarded to the Quartermaster General, Jessup. January 20 Garland said there would be enough money to finish the hospital and put up the stone work contemplated. March 30 he mentioned two flagstaffs which were being brought down from the pinery. April 10 he asked for additional labor on barracks occupied and for flooring for piazza and for paving of basement floors. He gave July 1 as the date the hospital would be ready for occupancy.

Inspection of Fort Crawford was made by Inspector Gen. George Croghan July 20, 1831. "I have no review or inspection of this command, nor have I required any, for I found it so circumstanced that to have done so would have been attended with considerable delay as there were several distant working parties that must have been called in, besides the circumstances of its putting a complete stop for several days to the progress of the work going on here, that too, without affording to me any further information than is possessed by every one else—viz., that these companies which like all others of the Fifth Infantry were perhaps better drilled than any other companies in service, have lost much ground since they commenced service at Fort and Barracks building. I wish things would have been otherwise and that the 5th Infantry could have been permitted to confine itself to its more legitimate duties and thus have proven the high stand which it once occupied and which it anxiously desires to again attain." . . . "Since Aug. 15, 1830 (and to more distant date did I require a report) there has been at times not a man for duty and that even to include the winter months; the general average of men does not exceed one fourth of those on extra and daily duty; and farther that of these reported for duty a large proportion was during the working months detailed for the day in some extra service such as boating, etc., etc. Col.

Morgan has assured me that the only drills which he has had in his power to give to his command were during the nights last winter between the hours of retreat and tattoo whenever the weather would permit. . . .

"Hospital—Surgeon Beaumont. This year's supply of medicine has been received but it has since been lost owing to the falling of the shelves in consequence of the rottenness of the wall against which they were nailed. A return for an extra supply has, however, already gone forth on—" . . . "Of medical stores there is as much as can be consumed during the year." . . . "Sick in hospital 29 brought on principally by exposure during the recent excursion to Rock Island—cases of dysentery almost exclusively." . . . "The sick are not well accommodated, the rooms used as wards are in the old fort (July 20, 1831). They are of course uncomfortable. The bunks are bad and too few in number, some of the sick are consequently lodged upon the floors" . . . "It is expected shortly to get into the new hospital now about being finished, and it is therefore that for the time being this state of things is borne by Doctor Beaumont who although in feeble health himself, exerts himself to promote the comfort and convenience of the sick. . . .

"Books correctly kept. Col. Morgan and the council of administration differ widely on construction of 351st paragraph of Gen. Regulations. Subsistence—supply sufficient and good. The storehouse is in one of ranges of new buildings recently erected. The defect is joist of floor not strong enough to support the load. . . .

"Quartermaster's Department. Brevt. Major Garland—This department is amply provided and a regularity and order to prevail in forwarding the completion of the extensive buildings now in progress here, very highly creditable to all concerned. . . .

"Ordnance Department—4 pieces—2 12-pounders; 2 6-pounders badly mounted as carriages are out of repair—new ones ordered. The limbers are much needed in the construction to haul stone and other materials for the building. Of powder and fixed ammunition there is a tolerable supply. The old muskets in store will be sent to the arsenal at St. Louis—50 to be retained of best ones for emergency."[12]

October 10, 1831, Colonel Morgan wrote to Quartermaster Gen. Jessup that the quartters for eight companies would be under cover, besides storehouses for quartermaster—a sutler's store. An additional block of officers' quarters was to be put up the ensuing spring. "The hospital will be done in a few days. It will be one of the best I have seen at any place."[13] At this time six companies were occupying the barracks. A bill of October 14, 1831, shows items still needed for the hospital and surgeon's quarters:

3730	porch flooring @ 5¢ a foot................	$186.50
40	columns @ $4	160.00
373	yds. plaster @ 20¢ a yd..................	74.60
3	mantels @ $10	30.00
5	mantels @ $5	25.00
	Painting	50.00

$526.10

At the same time it was stated that $1028 was necessary to finish the officers' quarters excluding the south tier and $838 to finish the men's quarters. November 14, 1831, Morgan said he would keep the carpenters at work all winter.[14] Apparently the funds were exhausted and $10,000 more needed. He planned on finishing what was already under headway, letting additional range of officers' quarters on the south side rest until the next year, to be finished at his leisure. There is no statement about the hospital being done, so we may assume it was finished before this date and occupied by Dr. Beaumont and sick of the command.

The hospital consisted of a dispensary room about 15 x 20, a kitchen 15 x 20, a small ward 15 x 20, and a large ward 20 x 40 on the same floor. The surgeon's quarters attached and intended for medical officers consisted of four rooms on the same floor about 15 x 20 each, with a fireplace and separate doors for egress, and under all these quarters a good cellar.[15] The surgeon's quarters, which formed the north wing of the hospital building stood, for many years, in a state of dilapidation after they were abandoned until 1934 when this part was reconstructed, together with about fifty feet of the hospital proper. There is some discrepancy between the figures given above, taken from the Office of the Quartermaster General in Washington, and the ones usually given, but the measures given in different reports are frequently at variance.

October 15, 1833, General Croghan made a second report on Fort Crawford, Col. Taylor, commanding. "In 1831 I found it impossible to inspect troops—same condition today. Sooner than retard at this advanced season of the year, the completion of certain buildings that are much wanted, and that might besides be materially injured left uncovered during the winter months," he reported that, as in 1831, he did not inspect troops. "The barracks erected here are certainly the best in the country but they have been built at the cost of the best regiment that we ever had." The morning reports give only forty-nine non-commissioned officers and privates present of the five companies. Eighty-four on daily duty—extra duty—detached duty. Bunks, arm racks, both good. Messing, good; better than civilians have. Lt. Harris, Subsistence Department reports shortage on flour; Quartermaster Asst. Lt. A. M. Stockton reports stores sufficient for purpose of buildings now being erected. Stoves which have been furnished for officers' quarters are so small that few will be put up. Ordnance Dept. Serg. Melville reports amount of fixed ammunition is small. Col. Taylor will not make return until the magazine now being built will be ready to receive it. Hospital—Asst. Surgeon Wood. There are at present twenty-three N. C. and privates sick either in quarters or hospital, a larger number than can be properly accommodated in the hospital itself, which is far from being so convenient and roomy as its exterior appearance would indicate. It will be found necessary I apprehend to convert the rooms intended for the medical superintendent and now occupied by Doctor Wood into sick wards, and to give in exchange quarters within the fort if such it may be called."[16]

The fine morale and discipline of the garrison were broken down by making laborers instead of soldiers of the men. There was no time for drills and no inspections were possible, as the command was scattered getting material or helping the mechanics on the building. Even during the Black Hawk War very few of the First Infantry were considered serviceable for military duty, and after the war there was a lack of discipline and training. The troops left their fatigue duty April 30, 1832, to enter the Black Hawk War, but at the close of the war in August, they were to resume the building and construction of the fort.

Work was continued during the fall of 1832 and the year 1833. An appropriation was passed in the winter of 1833-34 to finish it. The last building was up in October, 1834, but it is not certain that the buildings were complete. At least two of them were given a second coat of paint in 1835. As late as July of that year bills were being presented.

The final report of Gen. Croghan on Fort Crawford was made October 11, 1836. At this time Col. Taylor was in command of seven companies of the First Infantry. "Hospital—The building as

I have before remarked is badly arranged but this malarrangement will not subject either the surgeon or his patients to any inconvenience so long as the post continues as healthy as it is at present. The supply of stores and medicines are abundant and order and neatness prevails throughout the establishment."

"Sutlers, Moore and Hamilton. They have large store at prices lower than in village of Prairie du Chien." Advises boats—Mackinac—sails, oars and tack at each post on river.

"Ordnance Dept.—No post whether on seacoast or the Interior is provided with better magazine and gun house than Fort Crawford. Powder and fixed ammunition in order and enough for present use. Wood could be furnished at 50% less cost by private persons."[17]

The construction of a fort was, of course, only an incidental duty accomplished with reluctance by regular army officers and men. The presence of the soldiers at Indian treaties, their services in the execution of justice and law, and their actual fighting in the Black Hawk War were their ordinary, legitimate duties.

To return to 1830,—Indian troubles were menacing and the army was called into service for the Winnebago treaty at Prairie du Chien in the summer of that year. Major Kearny was ordered to bring a detachment of soldiers from Jefferson Barracks to Prairie du Chien in order to strengthen the post and was ordered to place himself under the orders of the commanding officer at Fort Crawford.[18] He stopped at Dubuque on his way up the river to drive out the American miners who were intruding on the Fox lands. Leaving a few men at that place, he proceeded to Prairie du Chien according to orders. Since Colonel Morgan was serving as commissioner on the treaty, Maj. Kearny was ranking officer. No disturbance arose at the council, and the Indians were agreeable to valuable concessions. Because there was no outbreak, Major Kearny returned to Jefferson Barracks at the conclusion of the treaty, August 1.

Morgan felt called upon to keep detachments at Dubuque (usually under a sergeant) when orders were issued to arrest any and all persons found on the Indian lands after the publication of a general notice to all.[19] Unfortunately, Morgan's conformity to military orders carried him into the civil courts because of existing overlapping of authority and the unpopularity of the ruling he was ordered to enforce.

One Indian massacre in the vicinity of Prairie du Chien was

the one known as the Fox or "Kettle" massacre. Part of the report which Joseph M. Street, Indian agent, sent to Col. Clark, dated Prairie du Chien May 7, 1830, follows: "Sir: On an island in the Mississippi 15 miles below this place in the afternoon on the 5th of May of this instant, a party of Sioux and Menominee warriors of 118 men surprised 25 Fox Indians in their encampment and defeated the latter, killing 10 Foxes and taking all their canoes and several guns. The remainder swam to the western shore of the Mississippi and escaped into the woods. The Sioux lost one man killed and several wounded. Three of the wounded it is supposed will scarcely recover. The Menominees lost none and only one or two wounded."[20] This report is materially different from the account given in the *Wisconsin Historical Collections,* but, being official, is probably correct. However, when one reads the official correspondence of some of the Indian agents and finds the discrepancies in their different reports, he may find cause for exercising a little latitude in their interpretation.

It is not certain that the military took much notice of this massacre. At least so the Foxes complained. It is almost certain that Warner, the sub-Indian agent at Galena, and John Marsh, sub-Indian agent at Prairie du Chien, were much to blame for the occurrence. Warner had orders to notify the Fox not to come to Prairie du Chien, but, being drunk, went on to Galena and allowed the Indians to think all was well. John Marsh, who was partial to the Sioux, gave them notice that the Foxes were coming.[21]

1830 was significant because of the work of Dr. Beaumont, post surgeon at Fort Crawford, who performed most of his remarkable experiments on digestion during this year. He was alert also to malarial fevers, diarrhoeas, and dysenteries prevalent at Prairie du Chien.

The military establishment had its share of toils and troubles during 1831. June 27 the soldiers were summoned to Rock Island where General Atkinson felt the need of reinforcements. Black Hawk, who the year before had promised to remain on the western side of the Mississippi had crossed over and threatened the settlers near Rock Island. The show of a large military force was sufficient, however, at this time to convince him of his folly and after council he returned to the west side of the river. The troops were returned to Prairie du Chien July 5 and sent again into the woods and quarries and lime kilns to get the material needed to finish the fort.

Hardly had they scattered when the Sac and Foxes made an attack on the Menominee. This attack took place on Rousseau Island about a half mile above the old log Fort Crawford. It was revenge for the attack made by the Sioux and Menominee the year before. The report by Street, Indian agent, dated Prairie du Chien 7 A.M. August 1, 1831, follows: "Two or three hours before day on the morning of the 31st of July a party of 80 to 100 of Sac and Fox fell on the Menominees. Out of 40, 25 were killed and 7 or 8 wounded. They killed 8 men, 16 women, 11 children."[22] These twenty-five Indians were buried near the military landing-place of Fort Crawford.

There seems to have been little done about these affairs as it was the intention of the government to let the Indians settle their quarrels in their own way. However, the Menominee seemed very near to the fort and almost under the protection of the army; demands to punish the Foxes led to a show of force not used the year before and later an effort was made to take into custody some Fox who were accused of the deed. In September, 1832, a Fox Indian was held at Rock Island, but no one was punished for either massacre. The menace of the squatters at Dubuque mines was so great that a detachment of soldiers from Fort Crawford had to be maintained, and the Foxes were exasperated because of the whites' invasion of their lands and mines.

While the military authorities were endeavoring to obey the orders of higher authorities, they and the Indian agents were being double-crossed by the civil authorities, who maintained that too often officers exceeded their instructions. Chambers, Kearny and Street, Morgan, and Taylor had all been brought into court and some of them received heavy fines for carrying out orders of higher authorities.[23]

The keenness with which traders and miners and land seekers went after what they wanted—not always too particular about how they obtained their ends—led to many impositions upon the wards of our government who were supposed to be protected like children. When, at the outset of our government, President Washington urged the factory system for the Indian, it was deemed a failure because it did not yield financial returns, but Washington and its advocates considered it only in the light of an altruistic effort to uplift the Indian and convert him to Christian citizenship, an idealism that has never been realized in these United States.

The Black Hawk War was a series of skirmishes conducted

against an enemy who twice tried in vain to surrender. Black Hawk with some justice resented the encroachment of the Americans upon the ancient territory of his tribe; but when he crossed into Illinois a second time despite his agreement to remain on the Iowa side, United States soldiers went in pursuit. With him were the women and children of the Sacs, a thing most unusual among Indians bent upon warfare.

General Atkinson with the Sixth Infantry from Jefferson Barracks was following Black Hawk along Rock River when the men at Fort Crawford were called in as reinforcements. Col. Taylor, who had been on leave of absence for two years, returned to his command in May, 1832, and joined his infantrymen at their position on field duty.[24] He was given command of all the infantry, who, because regulars, were able to keep up with the mounted troops of Posey, Alexander, Henry, and Dodge who were under the direct command of General Atkinson. All these troops crossed the Wisconsin river above Helena July 27 and 28 and followed the Black Hawk trail. The morning report of July 31 shows that the mounted troops were encamped six miles east of the Kickapoo on the Ocooch Mts.[25] There is nothing to show where the infantry under Taylor encamped, but he must have been close at hand.

The defeat of Black Hawk was imminent. At the foot of the bluffs on the east side of the Mississippi near the mouth of the Bad Axe the soldiers overtook the Indians who were attempting to cross into Iowa. A slaughter ensued, nearly a hundred men, women, and children brought down under the raking fire of the regular army and the volunteers. Taylor's troops—Companies A, B, and G of the First Infantry and some companies of the Fifth and Sixth Infantry—occupied the center of the battle. With General Henry Atkinson, Taylor returned to Prairie du Chien August 4 and resumed command of Fort Crawford the following day.

Black Hawk and a few of his chiefs made good their escape and found a hiding place near the Dells of the Wisconsin River. Here they surrendered to the Winnebago, One-Eyed Decorah and Chetar, who brought them to Prairie du Chien and turned them over to General Street at the Indian agency August 27 at eleven o'clock in the morning.[26] Street in turn assigned them to Taylor, who kept them prisoners at the fort until they could be sent to Jefferson Barracks.

General Scott arrived at Prairie du Chien August 7[27] and received the report of Gen. Atkinson, an extract from which follows: "The troops crossed the Wisconsin July 27 and 28: regulars under Col. Taylor 400 in all; party of Henry's, Posey's, and Alexander's brigades, and Dodge's Battalion of mounted Volunteers came on main body of Indians August 2. We had 5 killed, 2 wounded of 6th Infantry; 2 wounded of 5th Infantry; 1 captain and 5 privates Dodge's Battalion; 1 Lt. 6 privates of Henry's; 1 private Alexander's; 1 private Posey's."[28] From this report one sees that the regulars sustained the heaviest loss.

In the absence of Col. Taylor and his infantry, Colonel Gustavus Loomis with forty men had garrisoned the fort at Prairie du Chien and sent a detachment under Lt. Joseph Ritner to Bridgeport to head off those of the Sac who were coming down the Wisconsin to escape the approach of Atkinson's forces.[29] He stationed a flat boat with a twelve-pounder at the mouth of the Wisconsin and had a Mackinac boat with twenty-five men on the Wisconsin River. Fifteen men were killed, and thirty-two women and four men captured by Lt. Ritner, and many of the Indians were drowned.

Meanwhile, a few escaped into Grant County and were captured by Col. Samuel C. Stambaugh who, with a few Menominee, pursued them. About eight miles from Cassville, August 10 [9?], he killed two and captured eight.[30] While Stambaugh was bringing his prisoners to Prairie du Chien, some Menominee squaws, remembering the Menominee massacre of the year before, concealed weapons and attempted to kill the prisoners. The *Galena Gazette* credited Capt. Elu Price of the Cassville volunteers with capturing these Indians, but he evidently had no hand in the capture or he would have said so in the report he sent from Cassville to Gen. Scott August 14.[31] In this he asked that he and his men be mustered out. He said that he had met the Menominee under Stambaugh who had killed two men and taken eight prisoners, all women except one boy, 17.

Another manoeuvre by water served a purpose at the battle of Bad Axe. Colonel Loomis sent a small detachment under Lts. Kingsbury and Holmes on the *Warrior* to the seat of the battle on the morning of August 2 to prevent the Sac from crossing the river.[32] After the battle this boat brought the officers and some of the soldiers to Prairie du Chien.

Those of Black Hawk's Indians who did succeed in crossing

the Mississippi near the Bad Axe were overtaken at Cedar River where two hundred were killed and twenty-two captured by the Sioux.[33] The captives were delivered to Taylor at Prairie du Chien September 4. As the Sioux were allied with the Americans against the Foxes and Sac, Marsh and Burnett, then sub-Indian agent, had invited the Sioux to attack those Indians who might attempt to cross the Mississippi. The Winnebago on the upper Mississippi, too, were kept from harm and also from aiding the Fox by an invitation from Gen. Street urging those of the tribe along the river from La Crosse to come down to Prairie du Chien where they were assured of safety. They accepted this invitation and so were concentrated away from the scene of the final battle.[34]

It was not the intention of the government to keep the prisoners of war at Prairie du Chien. Captain Robert Anderson, who later became famous because of his defense of Fort Sumter, S.C., at the beginning of the Civil War, was sent to bring Black Hawk to Jefferson Barracks, but cholera broke out at Galena, and, after two of the crew had died, the captain refused to bring the cholera to Prairie du Chien and so returned to Galena. September 3 Colonel Taylor sent a detachment from Fort Crawford under Lt. Jefferson Davis to conduct the prisoners to Jefferson Barracks. Davis formed quite a friendship for Black Hawk. When the *Winnebago* was passing Rock Island, the captain of the boat refused to stop or allow Gen. Winfield Scott to come on board.[35]

Two points on the service of Lt. Jefferson Davis and surgeon William Beaumont need to be cleared up. Davis was on leave of absence from March 26, 1832, until August 18, when he returned to his company at Fort Crawford. He was not in the Black Hawk War.* Dr. Beaumont stayed in his cozy home at the rock hospital

---

* The name of Jeff Davis is absent from the muster roll from March 26, 1832 to August 18, 1832, and he is marked here "on leave of absence." A furlough of 60 days "with permission to apply for an extension of 4 additional months" was granted January 15, to commence on the date on which he should leave his post. A second order dated July 21 granted him the additional four-month extension. The first was granted from Memphis by the commanding officer of the Western Department, Maj. Gen. Gaines and the second from Washington by Maj. Gen. Macomb, Adjutant General.

At the time of the Black Hawk War Davis was 2nd Lt. in Co. B of the 1st Infantry. During the war his place was filled by Brvt. 2nd Lt. Ogden and after his leave Davis did return to the position of 2nd Lt. in Co. B.

Extracts from a "private" letter dated Beauvoir, Harrison County, Mississippi, August 8, 1882, written to Honorable Geo. W. Jones, comments on his service in 1831 and 32. "I was sent there (Dubuque) by Col. W. Morgan in the fall of

all the time during the war; neither did he see any cholera cases at Prairie du Chien.*

For the second time in four years the garrison at Fort Crawford was shocked by the murder of an officer July 2, 1832, when Sergeant John Coffin was shot and killed by a soldier—Mathew Beckwith—who was imprisoned but escaped for part of the year. He was found at the mines at Beetown, Grant County, where Lt. William L. Harris was searching for deserters. Beckwith was tried, found guilty, and executed in front of the old jail on the rear of Main Village Lot Seventeen.[38]

This murder occurred during the interim following the death of Colonel Morgan in April, 1832.† After Taylor's return, discipline was enforced rigidly, and many court martials held in the new fort were salutary in their influence.

While the Black Hawk War was on, arrangement to build a military road between Fort Crawford and Fort Howard was planned. In the autumn of 1832, Lt. J. A. Center and Judge James Duane Doty made survey.[40] Between Prairie du Chien and Green Bay the road was to pass Fort Winnebago at Portage. This road was not built, however, until 1835, when Col. Taylor sent three companies to open it up.[41] They began May 28 and were done by

---

that year (1831) to watch the Indians who were semi-hostile, to prevent trespassing on Indian territory." . . . "I remained on duty there until the spring of 1832." . . . "I was relieved . . . by Lt. J. R. B. Gardener as private matters required me to go to Mississippi, my home." . . . "After the campaign of 1832 Lt. George Wilson with a few soldiers were sent to Dubuque. He reported his inability to keep out the trespassers to the commanding officer and a larger force was dispatched." . . . "Lt. J. J. Abercrombie and I were the officers of this reinforcement." This letter accounts for his detached duty before and after the Black Hawk War but no record or assignment to detached duty or other duty appears for the period of his leave.[36]

* The first case of cholera that appeared among the volunteers of the Black Hawk War or any of the regular army who were in the West occurred at Rock Island August 27, 1832, when two men belonging to Ford's Co. were taken sick. There is no record in the muster rolls of Fort Crawford indicating such sickness or any death resulting therefrom among the soldiers of the garrison. Even had it occurred, Dr. Beaumont left Prairie du Chien on leave of absence August 23 before it broke out among the soldiers at Rock Island. He would not have been allowed to leave Prairie du Chien if there was cholera among the troops at the post because his services would have been too badly needed as there was only one surgeon, Dr. Foot, his successor, present at the fort. The cholera came in the wake of Gen. Scott's troops from Fortress Monroe, Virginia, and broke out successively in Buffalo, Detroit, Chicago, and Rock Island.[37]

† Colonel Morgan had a sick spell in December, 1831, from which he apparently recovered but during the winter he failed and died April 4, 1832. He was buried in the Fort Crawford military cemetery.[39]

August 1, having built a hundred fifteen miles at a cost of about
$1200. This was the section to Portage, the part of the road as-
signed to Fort Crawford for completion. The roadway was thirty
feet wide and began at a rock post marked with the letters "U.S.R."
which was sunk at the landing place of the garrison and which can
be seen at the present time.* Beginning at this post, the road ran
in a straight line across the prairie to the mouth of the McNair
coulee. Following the south branch of this coulee it reached the
top of the bluff and kept east until it struck a ravine leading down
to the Wisconsin River. It crossed the Wisconsin at the present
site of Bridgeport, the south terminal in Grant County, a point
at the mouth of a slough about three hundred sixty rods west of
the present crossing.† The points were connected by a ferry and a
sort of storage house and hotel was built here for travelers who
might be unable to cross or were for some other reason detained.
The road went up Trout Creek, now known as Bridgeport Hollow,
to the left-hand valley known as the Hicklin Hollow which it
followed to the high ground on the "military ridge" now marked
by a boulder and bronze plate erected at that spot by the D.A.R.
From that point, the road kept the high ridge to Blue Mounds,
following approximately the course of the present Highway U. S.
18. After passing Blue Mounds, it turned northeast, then to Cross
Plains and Black Earth, going north and some east until it reached
the Wisconsin valley, and thence along that to Portage.[43]

This was not only a good road but it went through rich country
and was the earliest means of land travel and transportation for
the first settlers of Grant and adjoining counties.

When Wisconsin became a territory one of its first acts was the
organization of a militia.[44] At Prairie du Chien an open election
was held October 10, 1836, at which time field officers were elected
for the local militia. The candidates for colonel were James B.
Dallam, who received thirty-four votes and H. L. Dousman, thirty-
one; for Major, James Reed, who received sixty-one; Wm. Hul-
bert, three; and John R. Miller, one. Ten years later on July 4

* About one hundred yards west and south of the new C.M.St.P. station and
near the end of the railroad grading. This post marks two other important events,
previously referred to: the landing-place for the new fort and the burial-place
for the twenty-five Menominee Indians massacred in 1831.[42]

† In 1848 a bridge was built across this slough shortening the ferry to the
length of the main bridge where it continued to be until a wagon bridge was
built in 1857.

Dousman was appointed colonel of militia by Governor Dodge. He was active in his office* and very proud of this distinction.

July 31, 1837 after a long period as commanding officer, Col. Zachary Taylor with the entire regiment of the First Infantry started for the Seminole War in Florida.[45] His successor at Fort Crawford was Brev. Brig. Gen. George M. Brooke, who tore down the commandant's house and rebuilt it, making radical changes. That rebuilt residence is now the wooden part of the Prairie du Chien Sanitarium. Brooke also proposed to build two bastions on Fort Crawford and wrote to Gen. Charles Gratiot of the engineers' department for plans for the same, but no action was ever taken on this. In 1841 he induced the War Department to have the President set aside certain Indian lands across the Mississippi from Fort Crawford just north of Bloody Run, and known in Iowa as the military reservation, to be used as a garden for the fort. In 1842 the military built a road in Iowa from the old ferry landing about a mile above Bloody Run westward to Fort Atkinson. The east end of that road at the foot of the hill is marked with a bronze marker by the Iowa Historical Society.[46]

Officers who followed Gen. Brooke at Fort Crawford were mostly time servers. After the Mexican War, the post became obsolete. However, different military organizations used it as quarters. Among others were the Dodge Volunteers under Capt. Knowlton. Charles Brisbois, lieutenant whose death and military funeral were fittingly memorialized at that time, served under Capt. Wiram Knowlton.[47]

The last United States soldiers to be present at Fort Crawford left June 9, 1856, and because of the judgment Ira Brunson and B. W. Brisbois and Cyrus Woodman had obtained on the title of the land belonging to the United States, June 10 the property was seized in the name of these men. The sheriff, John H. Fonda of Crawford County, being refused admittance, broke into the enclosure and took possession. Mrs. Emilie Hooe, who at that time was caretaker and living in the commandant's house, protested this action, as did also a Mr. Prescott, who had some charge of the barracks, and a Mr. Chase.[48]

When the Civil War broke out, the fort was used as a rendezvous for the men recruited in this locality for Civil War service, but in

---

* An item in the *Prairie du Chien Patriot* June 29, 1847, on regimental orders gives account of complete districting of Crawford County.

the summer of 1862 Gov. Salomon said it was no longer needed for that purpose, and possession should be turned over to the men from whom they received the privilege of using it. However, in 1864 it was again headquarters—this time for the United States Provost Marshal of the third district of Wisconsin. When he was through with it, it was used the same year as the Swift Hospital for soldiers from the South. Capt. Emil Cutler had charge of the property during part of 1865.[49]

After that there was no further military possession. As late as 1862 Mrs. Hooe reported that the hospital was still intact, although many of the outbuildings and fences were either moved or destroyed. After that time it was allowed to go to ruin until the partial restoration made under the P.W.A. in 1934. Pictures beginning with one in 1864 trace its disintegration, but it is not easy to determine the dates of some of the pictures. The town is dotted with such relics as doors, windows, locks, sentry posts, and building rock, which gradually found their way into private hands. The site is now occupied by St. Mary's Academy, a private school for girls.

From the time Brunson, Brisbois, and Woodman were installed in possession of barracks by the sheriff in 1856, the day after the troops under Col. C. F. Smith left, until it was sold by the government in 1872, the barracks were under two claimants: the United States on the one side and Brunson and Brisbois on the other. A deed in the court house at Prairie du Chien indicates that after John Lawler bought the property from the United States in 1872 he made a settlement of the claims against it at considerable expense, no doubt to save a lawsuit.[50]

Besides the present military cemetery, used at first only for officers, there was one for the enlisted men about two blocks directly east of the fort. When Lawler bought this land, the bodies of these men were removed to Evergreen cemetery. Later some bodies were removed from there to the United States cemetery where they are marked with Civil War monuments as unknown soldiers.[51]

CONCLUSION

I take off my hat to the army. It is the right hand of the executive and represents the force needed to carry out the law. In the past it has been more than that. Our Revolutionary fathers wrested this country from tyranny and our Civil War veterans prevented the dismemberment of the nation. Both of these wars represent the

highest ideals. But in the development of this country in times of
peace there are great reasons to honor the men who have worn
Uncle Sam's uniform. To the unthinking man, a soldier is only a
bloodthirsty human being with killing as his main business. Let us
remember the men in the United States army are no hirelings—
they are our brothers; they do not love or seek carnage; they offer
their lives on their country's altar as a great patriotic duty.

Think of the men who came into this wilderness a hundred and
twenty years ago to maintain the integrity of the Northwest Territory. Their task was to protect this isolated settlement; to explore
the lands; to restrain the Indians; to make surveys; to build roads;
to protect the American trade and the American homes; and to blaze
trails over which your ancestors and mine trekked into this land of
milk and honey. Not only that—the officers, who were educated
men, many of them from West Point, and their wives, equally
intelligent, brought into this locality refinement and culture that
never would have reached here at so early a period otherwise. Suffering untold thirst, hunger, fatigue, cold, and wet, and savagery
around them at every turn, they remained at the expense of isola-
tion, homesickness, diseases of all kinds. These men surveyed and
made possible routes of travel, cutting roads through forests, over
streams, across swamps, on arid table-lands. They built barracks,
ignoring death-dealing reptiles and mighty grizzly bears, still the
terror of man. To cross some of the plains or highlands today is
enough to terrorize the timid. The howling wolf, the panther and
wild cat, the malarial mosquito—all were more numerous one
hundred years ago than today. The building of the Panama Canal
was made possible by the pioneer work of the army surgeon who
neutralized the ravages of the mosquito which caused pernicious
diseases like malaria and yellow fever. The fly that propagated
typhoid fever and cholera has been controlled. Typhoid has become nearly obsolete because of the inoculations used to prevent
it in the World War. The army was the empire builder in time
of peace. It endured all this that later you and I should enjoy the
blessing of a happy, prosperous country, and the least we can do
is show our gratitude towards these pioneers who were the strong
men of the country.

If any Christian man takes exception to my well-deserved ac-
claim of the army, I want him to know that the picture of Christ
that appeals to me most is the one where He lashes and drives the

"money-changers" out of the temple. Man's greed, selfishness, and criminality did not end after the temple was freed; many times since, Christ would have been called upon to chastise painfully and with force, as He did that once. There is enough of anarchy, insanity, and crime in our midst today to require restraint of a strong arm. That strong arm is the policeman on his beat and the soldier in his tent. Until the millenium comes, our strong arm must continue. No pacifist can control a mad man. Nothing but force and restraint will do that.

CHAPTER TEN

Indian Councils and Treaties

CAPTAIN PIKE'S expedition served, as we have seen, to introduce the power of the American government to the Indians along the course of the Upper Mississippi. His councils with the various tribes and bands were frequent but not attended with lasting success. There were many difficulties, and Pike was criticized later and his treaties unconfirmed.

The second day he was at Prairie du Chien, September 6, 1805, he held council with a small group of the Winnebago. There was no Puant (or Winnebago), interpreter present, so Pike talked with a Frenchman, the Frenchman with a Sioux, and the Sioux with a Winnebago. Perhaps the only thing he tried to impress upon them was that they were now under an American "father" and no longer one who was British. Pike's editor commented on the ambiguity of this "great American father," saying that the Indians were not themselves clear whether it was Pike, General Wilkinson, then commanding officer of the United States Army at St. Louis, or the President of the United States. Like other treaties he made, this one was so informal that no use was ever made of it.

For the laying out of fort sites in the vicinity of Prairie du Chien Pike did not see fit to ask permission of the savages because in a treaty at St. Louis in 1804 the Indians had already granted a parcel of their lands two miles square at the mouth of the Wisconsin for that purpose, the right or left bank to be chosen at the will of the government.[1] The arrangements he did make for a fort at the mouth of St. Peter's River did not seem satisfactory so that when Col. Leavenworth went up the Mississippi in 1819 he considered it necessary to secure from the Sioux the right to build a fort.

One naïve custom among the Indians was their practice of giving to the whites hostages for crimes committed by their tribesmen and then surrendering the guilty persons to the authority of the whites. During the months Pike was on the Mississippi above Prairie du Chien the Winnebago had killed three white men, all of whom lived near Prairie du Chien. Pike called a council April 21 upon his return to Prairie du Chien and asked the Winnebago to surrender the murderers. The chiefs replied that there was only one there at that time, but Pike was to take him and in twenty days they would bring the others to St. Louis for trial in the court there. A promise of this kind was to be depended upon. On the afternoon of the same day the Sioux went into council with Pike who made them promise to make peace with the Chippewa, to give up their British medals and flags, and to be loyal to the great American father.[2]

These councils illustrate the distinction between the terms *council* and *treaty*. Either party might ask a council when some problem of common interest demanded discussion or action. A treaty required the agreement of both parties present and in addition required the approval of the President and the ratification of the United States Senate. Treaties most frequently concerned the cession of land or rights.

Col. Leavenworth and three judges of Crawford County held the next council at Prairie du Chien June 11, 1820. This concerned the murder of three white men. Before the chiefs held as hostages were released, three Indians were brought in for trial. One of these was freed and the other two held for their crime. Col. Leavenworth was present when the civil authority was established at Prairie du Chien and he made use of the newly appointed county officers for this duty. The three judges may have been the three justices of the peace or perhaps the chief justice and his associates of the county court.[3]

A great gathering of all the tribes of the Upper Mississippi was convened at Prairie du Chien in 1825. Up to this time there had been no American council so large save the one held by General Wayne at Greenville, Ohio, in 1795. There were many tribes, a detachment of soldiers from Fort Crawford, and as many of the army officers as could be spared. The officers were present in their full dress uniforms to provide a proper setting for the meeting. At ten o'clock each morning one cannon shot was fired, and half an hour later the council opened. The chiefs and orators of each tribe were given time to speak before the assembled throng. Interpreters were on hand to translate the speeches and a secretary of the council recorded its proceedings.

This was a most significant treaty because it was called to make boundary lines between the tribes, a step preliminary to taking over the lands of each tribe separately at a later date,—a policy which Pontiac in his day had effectively opposed by creating a formidable confederacy of all the Indian nations. Tecumseh and his brother the Prophet had this idea, too, and like Pontiac fought unsuccessfully to maintain the solidarity of the Indians. At the treaty of Prairie du Chien there was very little open opposition experienced. However, a name significantly missing from the list of signers is that of Black Hawk, and there were very few Sauk present at the treaty. It is probable that Black Hawk resented the action of the American government. He was a British Indian all his life until after his defeat. Any idea that the mapping off of each Indian nation from its nearby tribe would bring peace could be entertained only in the mind of some man who did not understand the savages. One important provision of this treaty was the relinquishment by the Foxes and Sac of all lands east of the Mississippi, a point of controversy in the Black Hawk War. Another article of this treaty compelled the Indians to recognize the reservations at the mouth of St. Peter's River and at the mouth of the Wisconsin and also the "ancient settlements of Prairie du Chien and Green Bay" and the half-breed Fox reservation lying between the Des Moines and Mississippi Rivers.

Presents always played an important part in treaties. On this occasion boats containing presents left St. Louis for Prairie du Chien June 30, 1825. William Clark, General Superintendent of Indian Affairs, and John Biddle, who was to be secretary of the council, embarked at Clarksville July 9 and eight days later arrived at Fort Edwards where they found White Cloud and some of the principal men of the Iowa. A canoe belonging to the American Fur Company was borrowed and provisioned there and they started up the river. July 30 Clark and Biddle reached Prairie du Chien where Governor Cass had been waiting ten days for their appearance.

The council lasted from August 5 to August 19. A number of important men were present, among them: Henry Rowe Schoolcraft, Indian agent with the Chippewa from Sault Ste. Marie; Nicolas Boilvin with Winnebago, Foxes and Sac, Chippewa and Sioux and some Potawatomi and Ottawa; Lawrence Taliaferro from Fort Snelling with Sioux and some Chippewa; Thomas Forsyth from Rock Island with Sac, Foxes and some Winnebago. Clark and Cass were commissioners for this treaty and signed on behalf of the United States; for the Indians a great many prominent chiefs signed, among them: Wabasha, Little Crow, Sleepy Eyes, and

Red Wing for the Sioux; Decorah for the Winnebago; and Keokuk for the Sac. The names of witnesses include some twenty persons.[4]

For all their agreement to the treaty, the Winnebago were not inclined to friendship with the whites and the following year showed for the first time unwillingness to conform to their own custom of bringing in criminals for punishment. The Methode family—Francis, his wife, and three children—had recently come from Red River to settle at Prairie du Chien, where Mrs. Methode was reputed to be the most beautiful woman of the town. In March, 1826, they went to make maple sugar in Iowa on a little creek a mile and a half above the mouth of Yellow River just south of what is now known as Hanging Rock. On the north branch of this creek about three-quarters of a mile from its mouth, there was a grove of maple trees near which the Methodes occupied a log building. There were five or six camps of the Winnebago on this little stream, and they were the only Indians in the immediate neighborhood. Near the end of March, presumably the 26th, the whole family were killed and articles belonging to them strewn along the creek as far as the location of the Winnebago. Since it was the season when crossing the Mississippi was difficult, the ice partly out and partly broken up, and since passage along the swollen tributaries was also difficult, it seems that no other Indians could have perpetrated the deed, although there were one Sioux and one Menominee woman staying on Yellow River. Also living at Yellow River were Desilie, a man in the employ of Boilvin; the wife of Mr. Reed; and Prudent Langlois. The Winnebago did not bring in any of their tribe as the murderers.

When word of the murders was brought to Fort Crawford, Col. Morgan on the advice of Judge Doty sent a detachment of soldiers and arrested three camps of Winnebago living nearest to the site of the murders. After deliberation, Col. Morgan finally gave the tribe thirty days in which to bring in the guilty ones. On the last day allowed—July 4—eighty Winnebago came to Prairie du Chien and in the presence of Boilvin, justice of the peace and Indian agent, and Col. Morgan, a council was held in Boilvin's agency house. Witnesses were examined and the six Indian prisoners accused of the crime and held for trial were also examined, but all denied guilt. Interpreters were Mrs. La Chapelle, Louison Barthe, and J. P. Gates. Lt. Martin Scott had been told by a certain Pizanne that the Winnebago had violated the woman and asked that the inquiry call in as witnesses Mrs. La Chapelle, Mrs. Brisbois, Mrs. Pion, Mrs. Alexander Simpson, Mrs. Menard, and an Indian woman, Mrs. Kuttow. However, there is nothing to show that any of these were called. The whites did not seem to get anywhere with the inquiry because all charges were denied and the Winnebago chiefs who were in the habit of turning over their criminals refused to say who the guilty were. Evidence against the six held for trial seemed invulnerable, and yet no admissions were made by any of them. After the inquiry they were all returned to prison, but later four were dismissed. A persistent rumor spread among the Indians that the two remaining prisoners who were transferred to Fort Snelling when Fort Crawford was evacuated in 1826 had been murdered by the Sioux. This was not true. The prisoners were brought back to Prairie du Chien when the troops returned, and the two were tried before Judge Doty in September, 1828, and set free.[5]

The treaty of 1829, dealing directly for the cession of some eight million acres of farm and mineral land in Wisconsin and Illinois, was much more important than the treaty of 1825, although there were not nearly so many Indians present. There had been some attempt in 1828 to determine occupation rights but the Winnebago were not satisfied and put off settlement until a council should be called the following year. There were other tribes involved, too, and it was planned to have the council at Rock Island. General John McNeil and Colonel Pierre Menard were chosen as commissioners but after forty-nine days' disagreement "at every point" at St. Louis, a third commissioner was appointed—Caleb Atwater. He started out for Rock Island, but May 18 the place of meeting was changed to Prairie du Chien, and he came up the river with the other commissioners, leaving St. Louis June 30 and arriving at Prairie du Chien July 15. Charles Hempstead was made secretary of the council. Atwater said the next year that forty tons of goods were bought for the Indians to make good earlier promises of the whites.

Three hundred seventy-five men and six hundred forty women of the Winnebago and eighty members of other tribes were at Prairie du Chien awaiting the commission. This number was greatly augmented in the course of the treaty. A shade was erected near the fort by Gen. McNeil and his officers. Atwater's description of the scene is quite detailed: "Present at council Winnebago, Chippeway, Ottawa, Sioux, Fox, Sauk, Menomonee, and Potawattomie. Half-breeds, officers from the fort, Indian agents, sub-agents, interpreters and a great concourse of strangers from every city in the union and even Liverpool, London, and Paris were in attendance.

"The commission sat on a raised bench facing the Indian chiefs; on each side of them stood the officers of the army in full dress while the soldiers in their best attire appeared in bright array on the sides of the council shade. The ladies of the garrison and best families of Prairie du Chien were seated directly behind the commissioners where they could see all that passed and hear all that was said. Behind Indian chiefs sat their people by the thousands."[6]

Atwater was advised to go into the fort between sessions. McNeil did; and Menard, "being in ill health," went to Gen. Street's, five miles from the council house. Disregarding advice, Atwater remained with the Winnebago, where he was unharmed. By July 29 the first treaty arrangements were complete, and on this day the chiefs of Ottawa, Potawatomi, and Chippewa signed,[7] and August 1 the Winnebago chiefs signed a subsequent agreement.[8] The other tribes were merely interested spectators. Interpreters named were Pierre Pauquette, Jacques Mette, and Antoine Le Claire.

There were two distinct treaties for the reason that various tribes held claims not recognized by the Winnebago, who insisted that they alone could dispose of the land. By voiding the claims of the others the United States government was in a position to purchase from the Winnebago without fear of dispute or struggle. The land ceded by the Winnebago encompassed the entire lead region of Wisconsin and Illinois, including the Galena mines.[9]

That the Winnebago recognized the futility of resistance and the inevitable but unwelcome encroachment is apparent in two speeches at the treaty. Keokuk said that white persons had squatted on Indian lands, sold wood for steamboats, butter, eggs, poultry, etc., and also erected mills on Indian lands without any permission. Little Elk, too, spoke of the aggression of the Americans. "The first white man we knew was a Frenchman. He lived among us as we did. He painted himself, he smoked his pipe with us, sung and danced with us and married one of our squaws, but he wanted to buy no land of us. Then the red coat came . . . and next the blue coat who wanted to buy our lands."[10]

The lament of these two chiefs contrasts ironically with the joyous welcome the Indians had given the first white men. "How beautiful the sun is, O Frenchman, when thou comest to visit us! All our village awaits thee, and thou shalt enter all our Cabins in peace. . . . How good it is, My brothers, that you should visit us."[11] The Indians understood the "white brothers" better now!

For the valuable concessions of these treaties the United States made promise of payment immediately and in the future. The July 29 agreement with the Ottawa, Potawatomi and Chippewa called for $16,000 annually "forever"; $12,000 in goods as a present; 50 barrels of salt to be delivered to the Indians annually "forever" at Chicago; and the assignment of money and lands to particular Indians and half-breeds. The agreement of August 1 provided to the Winnebago $18,000 annually for thirty years, payable part at Prairie du Chien and part at Fort Winnebago in proportion to population centered about each place; $30,000 in goods as a present; 3,000 pounds of tobacco and 50 barrels of salt annually for thirty years, half at Prairie du Chien and half at Fort Winnebago; certain money ($23,532.28) to cancel Indian debts and obligations; assignment of land to certain Indians and half-breeds;[12] and to the widow of the murdered Registre Gagnier an annuity of $50 for fifteen years.

Bills were allowed a number of people for the expenses of this treaty. Some of the bills—for example, Jean Brunet's, $888.87½, for boarding commissioners and others—seem to be excessive. Gen. McNeil's pay as commissioner (exclusive of his regular army salary), amounted to $1417.60, or 45 days' service at $8 a day; Dr. Alexander Wolcott received $200 for services as Indian agent; Dr. William Beaumont for medicine and medical services, $200. Oliver Cherrier received $140 for services as blacksmith; Jean Fraser and Mrs. Catherine Myott, $104 for interpreters' services. Bills were presented for steamship accommodation (on the steamer *Josephine*), for express, storage, wampum (American Fur Company bill), and various personal services.

In addition to the signatures of the American commission and a number of Indian chiefs, including Whirling Thunder, Snake Skin, and Four Legs, the treaty was witnessed by forty persons.[13]

The final treaty at Prairie du Chien preceding the Black Hawk War was in July, 1830,—"the season of flowers."[14] The aspect of the Indians at that time was so threatening that Gen. Atkinson ordered Major Kearny to proceed from Jefferson Barracks to

Prairie du Chien with four companies of infantry. Gen. Clark, Superintendent of Indian Affairs in the West, was himself present at Prairie du Chien, but, since he and Col. Morgan, commanding officer at the fort, were both commissioners on the treaty, Major Kearny was ranking officer and as such had charge of the fort. It was expected that more than a show of force would be necessary on this occasion. Major Kearny was sent out to meet the Sioux and escort them to the treaty and prevent an attack upon them by the Foxes in retaliation for the Kettle massacre in May.

The Indians concerned in this treaty were rather those from west of the Mississippi than those from Wisconsin and Illinois. Lands ceded were west of the river, but the Winnebago were affected because they were later expected to remove themselves to a neutral tract established by this treaty between the Mississippi and Des Moines rivers in Iowa. This treaty also established a half-breed tract for the Sioux near Red Wing's village.

Three years after the Black Hawk War, Col. Taylor called a council to stop depredations on private property in the vicinity of Prairie du Chien. Taylor and Street met with the Indians and considered claims against the Winnebago for damages. Some were allowed and others denied.[15] At this time also Taylor tried to promote friendship between the Sac and Foxes and the Menominee and Sioux who were still hostile as a result of the massacres of 1830 and 1831.

The last important treaty at Prairie du Chien affecting cession of land was held September 10, 1836,[16] and extinguished Indian title to certain land along the Missouri River. Under the treaty of 1830 this land had been so ceded that it was within the power of the President to locate there any tribe of Indians he might designate, but now the citizens of Missouri wished it for white occupation. The right of Wabasha's Sioux in that tract was relinquished for a $400 present. Taylor, acting as Indian agent, represented the United States in this agreement and Wabasha and four other Indians signed. Witnesses were H. L. Dousman; W. R. Jouette, Capt. 1st Infantry; James Scott, Lt. 1st Infantry; George M. Pegram, Lt. 1st Infantry.

By the treaty of Washington city November 1, 1837, the Winnebago ceded all their lands east of the Mississippi River and the United States agreed to assume payment of recognized claims against the Winnebago to the amount of $200,000 and to distribute $100,000 to the half-breeds of the tribe.[17]

Gen. Simon Cameron of Pennsylvania and James Murray of Maryland were chosen to act on all claims under this treaty. The two men arrived at Prairie du Chien August 29, 1838. An accusation of fraud against them caused the Secretary of War to appoint another man, John Fleming, Jr., of Syracuse, New York, to review the work.

September 16, 1839, Fleming met the chiefs of the Winnebago in council at Prairie du Chien and explained to them that he was sent to carry out justly the terms of the treaty of Washington. They met a second time September 26 but refused to meet again. Hercules L. Dousman and John Rolf were interpreters; Mr. Lowry, Indian agent; and Ingersol, secretary of the Council. The list of half-breeds was submitted and the bills of traders and others were submitted to Fleming.[18] He evidently did not please the traders either, because they called a general meeting of protest for October 2 but thought better of it and called the meeting off. Daniel Whitney had been scheduled as chairman.

Pierre Pauquette had the largest bill ($19,133.98) and the American Fur Company, Rolette, and Michel Brisbois each about half of that amount. Some accounts were denied and most of them cut down. Charges were made and countercharges and a fraud which followed this netted one gentleman from Philadelphia ten per cent interest on money employed in purchase of half-breeds' lands and a five per cent commission on transactions, a fee exacted for his services. He paid out $40,000 for $80,000 worth of property but the United States government compelled him to return the money upon complaint that he was taking advantage of the poor and ignorant half-breeds.

In the 30's and 40's Iowa was being closed to the Indians and as they were pushed west and farther west, Prairie du Chien ceased to be a center of Indian gatherings. Such as took place after 1839 were of minor importance.

CHAPTER ELEVEN

Civilian Affairs After 1800
(Part One)

WITH THE opening of the nineteenth century, the American government became more aggressive in its control of the Northwest. July 4, 1800, Indiana began to function as an organized territory. The President appointed William Henry Harrison governor; and subordinate civil and military officers were appointed and commissioned by him. Prairie du Chien was a part of this new territory, located in St. Clair County, so named because formed by Gov. Arthur St. Clair in 1790 to include that part of the Northwest Territory lying along the east side of the Mississippi River north of the Ohio.

The first official census was taken April 1, 1801. By this census we become aware of the size of Prairie du Chien, which was credited with 550 inhabitants; however, this figure included scattered settlers along the Illinois River. The census was made preliminary to the naming of civil and other officers for the county at large and also for local government wherever a settlement existed. This was the first real attempt to establish American government all over the Northwest Territory.

Governor Harrison recognized Prairie du Chien by the appointment of civil officers August 19, 1802.[1] The appointees were John Campbell, justice of the peace, and Robert Dickson, justice of the peace. Both these men resided at Prairie du Chien. The great distance and the slow mode of travel separated this place from the seat of government, and, while a sheriff was appointed for St. Clair County, it was so widely spread out that the justice of the peace could hardly depend on the sheriff's office to function in such a remote place as Prairie du Chien. Perhaps for this reason the governor on the same day made military appointments: Henry Monroe Fisher, captain; Basil Gerard (Giard), Lieutenant; and Michael Labatte, ensign of militia of St. Clair County, all of these men residing at Prairie du Chien. Basil Giard was given a *dedimus* to swear these men into office. Since no justice of the peace or notary could be found at Prairie du Chien, the governor had the right to commission someone to administer an oath of office, and it is possible Giard may have been present or better known than the others. Probably these appointments remained only paper appointments, with law and order in the hands of the traders much as before.

In 1802 some of the people at Prairie du Chien began to fear that the Indian title to the village was not extinguished and emissaries sought the Fox chief at Cahokia. He gave them assurance that the Indians had no claims. The reception of Pike later and the Indians' permission to him to build an American fort further reassured the inhabitants of the security of their occupation of land.

In October, 1803, Governor Harrison issued the traders orders not to sell liquor to the Indians and about a month later—November 26—he again took notice of Prairie du Chien with a statement that he "appointed and commissioned . . . Henry Fisher . . . a Justice of General Quarter Sessions of the Peace for the county of St. Clair."* The same day he changed the list of militia officers for Prairie du Chien. He named Nicolas Labatte† lieutenant and Jean Marie Quere ensign. This seems to be the last time the governor of Indiana took any notice of Prairie du Chien; likely he knew that in 1805 we would become part of Michigan Territory and be cared for by some one else.

What kind of village was Prairie du Chien under this loosely organized control? Fortunately, we have several rather clear descriptions of it written by men who came here before the War of 1812.

The first real description of the little French village on what was then called "the Island" was made by Thomas Gummersall Anderson upon his arrival in 1800 on his first trading expedition to the Northwest. "Eighteen hours travel (from portage of the Wisconsin) sixty leagues, brought us to Prairie du Chien on the Mississippi. Here was a little village of perhaps ten or fifteen houses; and at the [distance] of three miles were three farmers. Except one framed one, the houses were all built of logs, plastered with mud, and covered either with cedar, elm, or black ash bark.‡ The people were nearly all Lower Canadians, carrying on, with small or larger stocks, the Indian trade. Without exception, they were kind and hospitable, and prided themselves on their honesty

---

* Charles Reaume of Green Bay was appointed to a like office the same day.
† A mistake? There is no record at Prairie du Chien of any Nicolas Labatte. Had Michel died this year? If so, was this his son, Francis?
‡ These varieties of tree are still prevalent.

and punctuality in paying their debts, and keeping their engagements. Very little money was in circulation. There were no lawyers
to excite strife. Notwithstanding all this fair appearance, there
were those among them, regarded as otherwise honorable, fair
and clever, who would defraud and overreach his neighbor, even
to despoiling him of his last copper."[2]

At that time apparently nearly all the houses were on the banks
of the Mississippi, west of the Marais St. Friole. There probably
was a population of 100 to 150 settlers here at that time, depend-
ing upon the fur trade for a living,—traders and their clerks, boatmen, Indian slaves, and servants.

Zebulon Pike wrote the next report. "There is a small pond or
marsh, which extends in the direction of the river; the town is in
front of the marsh." The town proper then (1805) consisted of
"eighteen dwelling-houses in two streets; sixteen in Front Street
and two in First Street. Some of them are framed and instead of
weather boarding, there are small logs let into the mortises made
in the uprights joined close together daubed on the outside with
clay and handsomely whitewashed within. The interior furniture
of their houses is decent and indeed in those of the most wealthy
display a degree of elegance and taste." These, with other houses,
"in the rear of the pond," and "scattered round the country, at the
distance of one, two, three and five miles," together with three
houses on the west side of the Mississippi, made "in the village
and vicinity, thirty-seven houses, which it will not be too much to
calculate at ten persons each, the population would be 370 souls;
but this calculation will not answer for the spring or autumn, as
there are then at least 500 or 600 white persons." . . . Pike said the
people "possess a spirit of generosity and hospitality in an eminent
degree." . . . "One half the inhabitants have Indian blood. Intermittent fevers occur spring and fall."[3]

Pike found the Americans—Fisher, Fraser, Wilmot, and Campbell—as well as Rolette and the other French very cordial, and
the Indians stood in respectful amazement because Pike's soldiers
were the first they had seen to wear the American uniform. The entire population came out to see the visitors and there were games at
which the soldiers defeated the citizens at jumping and running.
Pike saw the great game of *la crosse* played between the Sioux on
one side and the Winnebago and Foxes on the other.

He found British flags flying from trading posts, British medals given to the Indians, and bright uniforms being worn by Indian chiefs along the Upper Mississippi. In his councils with the Indians, he found British sentiment dominating the tribes. The traders, by presents, intermarriage with the Indians, and close association, maintained the British ascendancy. All over this section the traders' will was the only law. Even at Prairie du Chien, the home of the most prominent traders, the American law was unknown or ignored,—never enforced. Such military expeditions as those of Lewis and Clark to the mouth of the Columbia River and of Pike along the Upper Mississippi were the real beginning of American law and order in the Western domain.

In 1805 Prairie du Chien was transferred to Michigan Territory, but the appointments of Gov. Harrison seemed to be holding over at Prairie du Chien because Fisher and Campbell took depositions for Pike concerning Indian murders. Frequent disputes as to authority and frequent changes led to much confusion and difficulty. Mackinac, and not Prairie du Chien, received appointments for civil and militia officers, under the Michigan rule, because both Prairie du Chien and Green Bay were considered dependencies of Mackinac.* 1809 saw the assimilation of Prairie du Chien as part of the newly created Illinois territory.

The appointment of Indian agents was an early means of treating with the Indians and keeping them friendly. In 1806 Nicolas Boilvin of Ste. Genevieve was selected by the Secretary of War as sub-Indian agent among the Foxes and Sac along the Mississippi, with headquarters at the main Sac village; he was also expected to visit the Indians at Prairie du Chien† and along the Des Moines River. It is uncertain in whom appointment power was vested, as it was exercised in a conflicting manner by territorial governors‡ and by the Secretary of War. Boilvin's instructions from the War Department indicate the range of his responsibilities: ". . . You will make

* These officers resided at Mackinac but were well known at Prairie du Chien. Abbott and Michel Dousman were captains and Allan Wilmot lieutenant.

† That Boilvin did visit Prairie du Chien this early is shown in his testimony on the Basil Giard land claim in 1807. He swore to his personal knowledge of the ownership of that parcel of land on the west side of the Mississippi opposite Prairie du Chien then in question by the land commission.

‡ The governor of Missouri had charge of Indian agents at Prarie du Chien, although Prairie du Chien was never part of the Missouri territory. Territorial governors often had charge of Indian agents outside their own territory.

every exertion in your power to conciliate the friendship of the Indians, generally, towards the United States, and to encourage a peaceable and friendly disposition among themselves; to prevent any acts of hostility on red or white people, and to cause proper punishment to be inflicted on such individuals as may be guilty of any hostile acts. You will, by all the means in your power, prevent the use of ardent spirits among the Indians. No Trader should be allowed to sell or dispose of any ardent spirits among them; nor be allowed to have any at their trading stations.

"You will, by precept and example, teach the Indians such of the arts of agriculture and domestic manufactures, as your situation will admit. . . . You should early procure Garden seeds, peach and other fruit stones, and apple seeds. A Garden should be established for the most useful vegetables, and nurseries planted with fruit trees; for the purpose of distributing the most useful seeds and trees among such of the Chiefs as will take care to cultivate them. You should also instruct them in the art of cultivating and preserving the fruit trees and garden vegetables.

"The cultivation of Potatoes ought to be immediately introduced into your own Garden:—and the Indians should be encouraged to cultivate them, as an important article of food, and the substitute for bread.

"As soon as practicable, you will be furnished with a Blacksmith to make and mend the hoes and axes, and repair the Guns of the Natives. Ploughs should be introduced, as soon as any of the Chiefs will consent to use them."[4]

The War Department soon recognized the necessity for an Indian agent regularly appointed for Prairie du Chien, and December 7, 1807[5] John Campbell* was made Indian agent. Campbell was well known, for he had been an active trader as early as 1792. That year his name appeared in connection with the death of an Indian who was beaten at Mackinac by a *voyageur* and six traders, among them Campbell. After the death of this Indian, Campbell and the others were arrested but were never brought to trial. Campbell's father, Archibald, was a well-known trader and resident of Prairie du Chien as were his half-brothers. John Campbell lived with his family at Prairie du Chien where he held land in what is still known

* Archibald Campbell's son, John, was born in Ireland. By a Sioux wife, Archibald had three sons—Scott, Colin, and Duncan—and two daughters—Nancy and Pelagia (Margaret). The children of John Campbell included John, Duncan, and Nancy (who was cared for by John Johnson after her father's death).

as the Campbell coulee. Also, he owned property in Mackinac and with his sons ran a transportation business at the portage of the Wisconsin River for several years.

Campbell was Indian agent less than a year. In August, 1808,* he was mortally wounded in a duel with Redford Crawford at the Detour near Mackinac. Campbell's second is not named in the records, but Robert Dickson was second for his opponent. The men became engaged in a dispute which resulted in Crawford's challenge. It may be that the quarrel was fomented by British traders who resented Campbell's activity as Indian agent of the American government or it may have arisen from his activity as an independent American trader no longer associated with the trading company of which Crawford was a partner. Campbell lived two days after the duel.† His wound was cared for at St. Joseph by a British army surgeon. After his death, his body was conveyed by soldiers from St. Joseph to Mackinac, where he was buried. Suitable resolutions of respect and condolence were drawn up by the American officers, and each American was to wear crepe on his left arm for forty days. Dickson's part in the affair and his aspiring to the Indian agency made him extremely unpopular with the Americans, and fears were entertained that Crawford and Dickson would pay the price of their folly on their return to Prairie du Chien.[6]

Campbell apparently had requested Julien Dubuque to act as agent during his absence at Mackinac, and upon Campbell's death Dubuque was appointed agent by Gov. Meriwether Lewis of Louisiana. After serving one month and twenty-eight days, Dubuque asked to be succeeded by another man. He wrote a letter to the commanding officer at Mackinac, stating that he was too sick to attend to his duties and that the Indians were becoming threatening.

Nicolas Boilvin was then sent to Prairie du Chien by the governor of Louisiana and was an efficient agent up to his death in 1827. He arrived at Prairie du Chien November 28, 1808[7] and from this time made it his home, at first irregularly but after the War of 1812 permanently, living then on the north side of what is now called Boilvin Street. This appointment was eminently

* Probably August 11.
† A grand-nephew of Crawford later married a granddaughter of John Campbell.

satisfactory and was confirmed by the War Department, who commissioned him Indian agent in 1811. In addition to his agency duties, he received from the Governor of Illinois May 3, 1809, appointment as justice of the peace for St. Clair County,* a commission which was renewed when the portion of St. Clair county embracing Prairie du Chien became part of Madison county June 12, 1814.

Boilvin was well acquainted at Prairie du Chien even before his appointment. In 1811 he gave the Secretary of War a comprehensive report on Prairie du Chien, which would show that there was little change in the village from 1805 although the disturbed condition of the fur trade was much aggravated.

"Prairie des Chiens is an old Indian town which was sold by the Indians to the Canadian traders about thirty years ago, where they have ever since rendezvoused, and dispersed therein merchandise in various directions. The Indians also sold them at the same time a tract of land measuring six leagues up and down the river, and six leagues back of it. The village contains between thirty and forty houses, and on the tract just mentioned about thirty-two families, so that the whole settlement contains about 100 families. The men are generally French Canadians, who have mostly married Indian wives; perhaps not more than twelve white females are to be found in the settlement.

"These people attend to the cultivation of their lands, which are extremely fertile. They raise considerable quantities of surplus produce, particularly wheat and corn. They annually dispose of about eighty thousand weight of flour to the traders and Indians, besides great quantities of meal, and the quantity of surplus produce would be greatly increased if a suitable demand existed for it. All kinds of vegetables flourish in great perfection, and such is the beauty of the climate that the country begins to attract the attention of settlers. Different fruit trees have lately been planted and promise to grow well.

"Prairie des Chiens is surrounded by numerous Indian tribes, who wholly depend on it for their supplies. It is annually visited by at least six thousand Indians, and hitherto they have resorted to the Canadian traders for goods, because our own apprehended much danger in attempting to carry on a trade with them,

---

* At the same time Michel Brisbois was appointed Lieutenant and Jean Marie Cardinal ensign of Prairie du Chien militia.

particularly as the Canadians generally prevail on the Indians either to plunder them or to drive them away. Only one trader of our town returned into that quarter during the last year.

"Great danger, both to individuals and to the Government, is to be apprehended from the Canadian traders; they endeavor to incite the Indians against us; partly to monopolize their trade and partly to secure friendship in case a war should break out between us and England. They are constantly making large presents to the Indians, which the latter consider as a sign of approaching war, and under this impression frequently apply to me for advice on the subject. Hitherto I have been able to keep them friendly."[8]

Boilvin made two recommendations to stop this British trade: one, build a fort at Prairie du Chien with not less than two companies of soldiers; the other, put a United States factory here to supply the goods needed by the Indians. His vision saw fulfillment five years later, but not before a war had been fought between England and the United States in which the poor Indians were British pawns. Then it was decided to put in a factory and to accompany the goods and the person of the factor with a detachment sufficient to prevent an Indian attack.

The trade and military difficulties had increased from 1807. Boilvin was aware of many abuses which he was incapable of correcting. For example, he was aware of the illegal importation of British goods in 1810 despite the American embargo. Profits from a tremendous business in this year were garnered by British traders, most of whom lived at Prairie du Chien. Nor was this the only time the American government was openly defied. As early as 1805 Pike had estimated an annual loss of $26,000 duty due on English goods brought into the Indian country.[9] William Clark, Indian agent at St. Louis, called attention to the wholesale way in which traders took advantage of the government. The use of liquor in Indian trade was forbidden, but every British trader sold and gave it to the Indians whenever it suited his purpose to do so.

The traders were taking active part in the impending conflict between England and the United States. Citizens were aggressively partisan, most of them British.

In 1811 Robert Dickson brought his goods by way of Queenstown, Buffalo, and Fort Pitt, down the Ohio and up the Mississippi to St. Peter's and during the winter of 1811-12 distributed $10,000 worth of his own goods among the Indians on the Upper Missis-

sippi, who were starving.[10] On his way up the Wisconsin, the
following spring, Dickson was met by two runners with a confi-
dential message dated February 27, 1812, and signed by Capt. J.
B. Glegg of York saying "War may come" and asking if the
British could depend on the Indians.[11] June 18 he sent his reply
which was received at Fort George. On his way to Green Bay he
gathered 130 warriors of Sioux, Winnebago, Menominee and took
them to Mackinac. At Green Bay he held a council with Sac and
Fox and made Black Hawk leader, sending him against Chicago
and Detroit, but both cities had fallen before he arrived. These
Indians returned without seeing service, but the Indians who went
to Mackinac arrived in time to aid the British in its capture July 17.
The British at Mackinac had received news of the declaration of
war July 9, days before the Americans knew it. From Mackinac,
Dickson sent 5 canoes of presents to be distributed among Indians
at Green Bay, Prairie du Chien, and St. Peter's late in October
and then he went on to Montreal where January 1, 1813, he was
made "agent for the western Indians." He was to receive an annual
salary of 200 pounds sterling British money and in addition 1875
pounds to pay for presents he had given out of his own goods to
Indians the winter before. On his return West he had an Indian,
Amable Chevalier, for his lieutenant and interpreter. Setting out
from Montreal January 19, 1813, he stopped at Sandwich, Niagara,
Detroit, and St. Joseph, and March 22 he was at Chicago. During
the spring, as part of his British activity, he visited the tribes
at Prairie du Chien, arriving in April with Capt. Hamilton, and
later visited Indians on the Wisconsin. June 10, 1813, he arrived
at Mackinac with 600 warriors. This is likely the occasion on which
he organized the population of Prairie du Chien, about 200, mostly
hunters and trappers, into a local British militia.

The Americans at Prairie du Chien were terrorized by the British
traders and their Indian allies. In May, 1812, Boilvin left Prairie
du Chien and in December he wrote from St. Louis that he was
not expecting to return soon. However, letters were passing back
and forth between the two places. Boilvin had depended upon
Joseph Roc, the American interpreter,* who was deputized by him
to act in his absence. A letter from Roc dated at Prairie du Chien

* Roc later was rated Interpreter in British volunteers who captured Prairie
du Chien.

12th March, 1813, and sent in reply to one of Boilvin's entrusted to the Sioux chief Red Wing, shows Roc's state of mind.

"Prairie du Chien, the 12th. March, 1813

Sir:

I am yet alive, God has preserved me intill the present, to give you all the news. I could not write you by any other opportunity, being in great danger of my life, I am watched on all sides; I trusted to Mr. Faribeau to read the letters received from you, sent by the Sioux, Redwing. In my absence those letters were seen and Copies of them taken and sent to Mackinac by *Duncan Graham,* who left this a month since to bring forces which we expect every day to go and fight against the Americans of the Illinois. Mr. Boilwin you will be surprised, the letters that you had addressed here to Mr. Brisbois, Mr. Boutelling, Mr. Fisher, they have taken copies of your letters, and have sent an express to carry them to St. Peters River, to raise all the Nations to go to war against you and the Illinois. In short, Sir, I must tell you every thing is against you Americans, all Nations in general have given their word to the English.

The Traders together are setting them on against you all, that is all I can say for the present, and all the information I can give you.—

Sir:

The remaining of your property that you left here is all lost, even your cattle have been killed by the *fallavoins* [Menominee].

Mr. Boilvin, you must believe all that is in this letter.

I am, Sir, with the greatest friendship possible,

(Signed) Joseph Roc.[12]

Roc's mention of Red Wing as messenger may explain why the British branded Red Wing's band as American in sympathy. One of Red Wing's warriors was later made a chief by Gen. Clark because of his friendship and service to the Americans during the War of 1812. It is noticeable that it was the Menominee Indians who destroyed Boilvin's property and not the Winnebago. Boilvin was related to the latter by marriage. Roc seems to include Fisher as being one to help send copies of the Boilvin letters to the commanding officer at Mackinac.

Apparently J. B. Faribault was the American trusted to translate letters from Boilvin and no doubt also to write for Roc. It is now known that Faribault was personally acquainted with Gen. Wilkinson, and he is said to have been friendly to the Americans, having refused a commission in the British volunteers. This may account for the plundering of his possessions by the Winnebago in July, 1813.[13]

Faribault had a farm home on the prairie as well as a house and other buildings, including a store, in the village of Prairie du Chien where he had settled in 1806. He claimed a loss of $7680,—$5000 at Prairie du Chien and $2680 in lead and lead mineral taken at Dubuque mines. This loss was never made good. It is said in a sketch of his life in the Minnesota Historical Society records that after the war Faribault was made a lieutenant in local American militia, and we know that when he sold his property to Rolette in 1819 upon his removal to Mendota, he and his family, traveling overland, had charge of the transportation to Fort Snelling of the horses belonging to Col. Leavenworth's command.[14]

Joseph Rolette wrote February 10, 1813, to the British commandant at Mackinac, sending by Duncan Graham a confiscated letter of Boilvin. Rolette avowed himself a British subject and asked protection. Other names of signers of this petition for help are M. Brisbois, Capt. Berthelot, St. Jean *dit* La Perche, Fran. M. Dease, Duncan Graham, James Fraser,* Harry Monroe Fisher, Jn. Faribuilt, Denis Courtois, J. Bpt. Mayrand, Bazil Giard, F. Burke (La Chapelle), F. Bouthillier.[15] We would not expect to find the names of Fisher, Fraser, and Giard, or Michel Brisbois on the list, as they all held offices under the American government, but any kind of help would have been welcome to curb the Indians who were terrorizing the people of the village. The way the name Faribault is signed (Jn. rather than J. Bte. and spelled Faribuilt) might lead one to believe he did not sign it himself. Dickson's name was not on the list, as he was absent from Prairie du Chien; nor was he inclined to trouble himself further about the inhabitants, especially since he had a larger job on his hands.

In the fall—October 24, 1813—Dickson was dispatched from Mackinac to Green Bay with a detachment consisting of one subaltern, one sergeant, and 26 rank and file to establish a British post at Green Bay.[16] He arrived November 23 and established

---

* Fraser was lieutenant in the British army during the War of 1812. He never returned to Prairie du Chien, where he deserted his half-breed wife.

himself on what has since been known as Doty's island, where he remained until April 14, 1814. While there, he received letters sent out by Boilvin and Jarrot asking that the people of Prairie du Chien remain firm for the American cause and telling them that an American fort would soon be established at Prairie du Chien. These letters and other papers had been sent by messengers, De Manochell and Ribeau, who went first to Peoria and then on their way to Prairie du Chien were captured by the Sauk who turned them over as prisoners to the British to be sent to Mackinac. At Prairie du Chien, Brisbois and Rolette made fun of the contents of these letters and belittled their importance; what became of the prisoners, who said they received one hundred dollars for the journey, does not appear.

Dickson, having set out for Prairie du Chien in the spring of 1814, was at the portage of the Wisconsin April 24. He said he hoped to reach Prairie du Chien and return in nine days. Two versions of this trip come to us—one by a son of Capt. Bulger who says that Dickson was at Prairie du Chien when Gen. Clark arrived to establish an American fort, and the other that he left there three weeks before Clark arrived. Whichever way it was, Dickson was at Mackinac June 28 drilling and instructing officers for a contemplated attack on Fort Shelby.

Whether Boilvin had been at Prairie du Chien at any time from May, 1812, until he came with Gen. Clark in June, 1814, taking his family, does not appear, but his stay at this time was brief, for when the British made their attack July 17 he and his family went on board the gun-boat and returned to St. Louis. He did not return again until the summer or fall of the next year; and when, in 1816, he started to Prairie du Chien with his family, he was advised by Gen. Wm. Clark that it was a dangerous trip. However, Gov. Ninian Edwards of Illinois insisted upon his going and he did, returning to St. Louis in May, bringing 100 Sioux to the treaty held there that year.

From the time the British took possession of Prairie du Chien until they left, the record is only British—largely, the papers of Capt. Bulger and his son and a diary kept by Capt. Anderson. These sources divulge miscellaneous information. The civilians were under the military from the beginning of this period, but December 31, 1814, Capt. Bulger declared martial law. Dickson now accused Rolette of sedition and he was court-martialed January

5, 1815, but acquitted.[17] Two years before he had also been tried but the case dismissed. Indian councils were common. There were many causes for dissatisfaction. Food was scarce, and Duncan Graham complained of such as there was. Insubordination among the volunteers occurred almost daily. There was much drunkenness. The Indians killed much of the livestock at Prairie du Chien as well as at Green Bay. Capt. Bulger, Capt. Anderson, and Robert Dickson constituted a court of inquiry to decide upon claims for damage, and at Green Bay some awards were made but at Prairie du Chien only a few ever received compensation.*

After the war had ended, July 3, 1815, Thomas G. Anderson, who had been a captain at Fort McKay, was sent again to the Mississippi to make peace with the Indians and bring them presents;[18] for as yet the British traders did not realize that their control of Indian trade in United States territory was nearing its end. Finally Great Britain realized that the United States was a nation with rights to regulate its own trade and no further encroachment of American rights could be attempted. The war settled that for all time.

The year that elapsed between the evacuation of Fort McKay and the establishment of the American military fort was one of great anxiety for inhabitants. The first American government at Kaskaskia had not been of a character to make the people want a similar control at Prairie du Chien. The settlers had been a liberty-loving, free, easy-going class satisfied with their own kind of life and unprepared for the overbearing regulation which was introduced with American military occupation.

The intolerant attitude of many Americans is shown in a letter of Governor Ninian Edwards of Illinois written in March, 1816. In this he expressed the opinion that the inhabitants at Green Bay and Prairie du Chien should be driven off, as they had all assisted the British during the war. Since their aid had made the capture of Prairie du Chien possible, they should now be punished as disloyal intruders. This position, assumed also by the army, caused much distress and annoyance to the poor people who were indifferent as to who should rule them and were not above showing friendliness, as the Indians always did, to the victorious power.

* Later, through Indian treaties whereby the tribes agreed to pay for damages done, some Americans received damage claims. Boilvin received a large sum of money for his losses, as did Rolette and others.

The period was hectic for the Americans, too. Even the inter-marriages with the Indians did not bring absolute security and below on the Mississippi the Indians were said to have killed more settlers this year than at any period during the war. This warlike attitude of the Indians prevented the United States from sending an army up the Mississippi, as it might precipitate war if sent before many tribes had an opportunity to meet the United States commissioners in council and express their sentiments and receive satisfaction.

With the arrival of the American troops June 20, 1816, the inhabitants were in consternation.[19] Most of the people of the village had been arrayed against the Americans, even though the French-Canadians had not cared much who was ruling. They now feared reprisals, and the Americans treated all the inhabitants as squatters and aggressors to be driven out at will. They were secure, however, against the Indians. Another redeeming feature of the occupation was that the settlers found a market for their produce, furnishing wheat, corn, and fresh vegetables to the garrison. The commanding officer took over the property of the Mackinac (now the Southwest) Company buildings, for which their agent had made a contract a month before to rent to the United States factor, John W. Johnson. Michel Brisbois, as a lieutenant of the American militia, was arrested for treason and sent to St. Louis but permitted to return with the aid of his friends. His wood and his bake shop were confiscated, however, for use by the soldiers. Rolette was banished for the winter. Citizens had their houses moved off land required for military reservation, and the commanding officer assigned them other locations. They were whipped for very slight reasons, and as there was no civil officer there but Nicolas Boilvin, he was helpless to prevent this arbitrary rule which terrorized the inhabitants.

It is true that a large number of the people had been British sympathizers and volunteers in the war and so deserved the sus-picion of the American military. Men like Michel Brisbois and Basil Giard and H. M. Fisher, still holding commissions as Ameri-can officers, had been in a particularly delicate position during the war. Giard loaned powder to the British, but this could scarcely be interpreted as a friendly act, as it would have been seized had he refused the loan. Fisher left, taking Charles, the oldest son of Michel Brisbois, and his own two older sons, Alexander and

Henry, to the Red River country where he engaged with the Northwest Fur Company at first and later, after 1822, with the Hudson's Bay Company. Fisher's daughter Jane and one son George were left at Prairie du Chien with their uncle, Michel Brisbois, while his second wife and their daughter, only a baby, went to Mackinac to live. Fisher did not return until 1823, four years before his death. Charles Brisbois returned in 1843, while Henry Fisher, Junior, returned later and so far as we know Alexander never came back.

James H. Lockwood came to Prairie du Chien in 1816 and remained until his death. He was very active in public affairs and successful in his personal ventures. His first impressions are worthy of quotation: "On the 16th of September, 1816, I arrived at Prairie du Chien, a traders' village of between twenty-five and thirty houses, situated on the banks of the Mississippi on what in high water is an island. The houses were built by planting posts upright in the ground with grooves in them, so that the sides could be filled in with split timber or round poles, and then plastered over with clay and whitewashed with a white earth found in the vicinity and then covered with bark or clap-boards riven from oak. . . . There were on the Prairie about forty farms cultivated along under the bluffs where the soil was first rate, and enclosed in one common field, and the boundaries generally between them marked by a road that afforded them ingress and egress to their fields. . . . The owners did not generally live immediately on their farms but clustered together in little villages near their front. . . . There were a number of families of French extraction having no mixed blood. They were living in Arcadian simplicity. A great part of their time was spent in fishing, hunting, horse racing or trotting or in dancing or drinking. The only aristocracy among them was the traders who were a privileged class. Where settlers had Indian wives they were of many different tribes."[20]

About the middle of April, 1817, a Roman Catholic priest, Rev. Marie Joseph Dunand, a Trappist from St. Louis (Florissant), arrived at Prairie du Chien. He said that he had been invited to come. The monastery which had been located at Monks' Mounds, about seven miles east of St. Louis, had been abandoned and the monks sent East. Fr. Dunand, who had been prior, was allowed to remain and do missionary work in the locality of St.

Louis. Prairie du Chien was spoken of by Bishop Flaget of Bards-town, Kentucky, as being in his diocese in 1815, so he may have been instrumental in bringing about this visit. The invitation to come to Prairie du Chien may well have come from Jarrot, for many years a trader to Prairie du Chien, who had given the Monks' Mounds property to the Trappist order. Boilvin, too, and other men living in Prairie du Chien were well acquainted at St. Louis. Since the priest made his home with Boilvin, it seems likely that he used the Indian agency house of Boilvin for holding services. If so, the first place used as a church was located about where Boilvin and Front Streets now intersect. There is also a possibility, however, that he said Mass at the old Fort Crawford. Fr. Dunand organized the French-Canadians into the first congregation in Wisconsin, blessed a cemetery, baptized 135 children and adults, performed 14 marriage ceremonies, and spent thirty days in instruction and other religious activities. Since the days of the early missionaries, Prairie du Chien had not had the services of a priest, and he said all but three took advantage of his services. He even selected a site for a church building. He baptized the two daughters and a son of Robert Dickson, who was himself not a Catholic; a Jewish trader who had married a French woman, presented himself and his children for baptism. A complete record of this visit was left by Fr. Dunand; it remains intact except for the first six baptismal records, which have been lost in recent years. It was ten years before another priest came.[21]

In 1817 Major Stephen Long visited Prairie du Chien on his way to the headwaters of the St. Peter's River. Stephen Hempstead, a resident of Prairie du Chien for eight years, came with him from St. Louis as a French interpreter. Among others that he found on the way were two young men, one named King and one Gunn, who were grandsons of Carver and who were going to visit the Indians on the Upper Mississippi in regard to establishing a claim that Carver was said to have purchased from the Sioux when he visited the country in 1766. On his return trip Long arrived at Prairie du Chien a little after nine o'clock in the evening. He said that Wednesday, the 23rd of June, he and Doc. Pearson and Lieut. Armstrong took horses and rode about the neighborhood to discover a place better suited for a military post than the "present" position of Fort Crawford. He spoke of the ancient works of the Indian mounds that were numerous on the prairie and still more numerous upon the highlands just above the mouth of the Wisconsin. On Friday, the 25th, he spent the day in measuring and planning Fort Crawford and its buildings. We have his detailed description of the town and surroundings:

"The prairie is a handsome tract of low land situated on the east side of the Mississippi and immediately above its confluence with the Wisconsin. It is bounded on the east by the river bluffs which are intersected by ravines and valleys which afford access to the hilly country above. The village of Prairie du Chien was first settled by the French. The ground first occupied by these settlers was at a little distance below the present village. . . . Exclusive of stores, workshops and stables, the village at present contains only 15 dwelling houses occupied by families. These are situated on a street parallel with the river and about ½ mile in length. In the rear of the village at the distance of ¾ mile there are 4 others. Two and one half miles above are 5, and at the other end of the prairie, 5 miles from the village are 4 dwelling houses. Besides these there are several houses situated on the different parts of the prairie, in all not exceeding 7 or 8, so that the whole number of family dwellings now occupied does not exceed 38. The buildings are generally of logs, plastered with mud or clay, some of them comfortable habitations, but none of them exhibiting any display of elegance or taste. The inhabitants are principally of French and Indian extraction. About ½ mile back of the village is the Grand Farm, which is about 6 miles in length, and from ¼ to ½ mile in width, surrounded by a fence on one side and the river and bluffs on the other. Upon this farm, corn, wheat, potatoes, and so forth are cultivated. It would be possible to raise rye, barley and oats besides other vegetables. There are numerous Indian mounds on the prairie. Prairie du Chien, or the 'Prairie of the Dog' derived its name from a family of Indians formerly known as the dog Indians, headed by a chief called the 'dog.' The inhabitants of Prairie du Chien have lately caused 2 small schools to be opened, in one of which the English language is taught, and in the other the French."[22]

Besides these civilian schools there was usually a post school. The chaplain was often the person in charge, but in 1817 Sergeant Reeseden held this position.*

The French school to which Long refers seems to have been

---

* J. T. Mills, later circuit judge, was private tutor at the fort in the 30's.

taught by Charles Giasson, a French-Canadian who must have had some public support. The English school was taught by Willard Keyes, who was in the West temporarily and who had bought an interest in the Carver grant. In a letter dated at Prairie du Chien June 7, 1818, Keyes wrote: "On the 25th ultimo, I commenced a school in this village; have about 30 scholars mostly bright and active, at two dollars a month. . . . I have engaged for three months." In another letter, July 30, he said that he removed from Johnson's store to the "school house just finished. It stands 12 rods back of Main Street."[23]

James Aird donated ten dollars for the purpose of building a school house and a Crawford County record of 1820 orders that the "public school house" be repaired. We may infer that these references are to the school which Keyes taught in 1818.[24]

Constant Andrews was another close friend of the Carvers. He seems to have been a mill-wright and agreed May 18, 1818, to build a water-power mill guaranteed to grind 2 bu. an hour, located in what has since been called "Mill Coulee" near the upper end of the prairie. He also helped to build saw mills on Black River.[25]

The man who was most interested in the Carver claim was the Reverend Samuel Peters who was really the agent of the Carver interests.[26] He came to Prairie du Chien in 1817, but because the commanding officer would not let him go into the Indian country without the permission of the government he spent nearly a year at Prairie du Chien. Several marriages were performed by him during his residence, among others the marriage of Rolette and Jane Fisher in 1818. Nothing was accomplished by these five men who came to Prairie du Chien in the interests of the Carver claim, although Rev. Peters filed a copy of the Carver deed in the office of the Crawford County Register of Probate.[27]

Another distinguished visitor was Lord Selkirk, who came from his Red River settlement and called at Prairie du Chien October 18, 1817, on his way to Montreal.

The admission of Illinois as a state in 1818 caused Wisconsin to be assigned to Michigan Territory; that year marks the beginning of well-organized civil law at Prairie du Chien.

CHAPTER TWELVE

Civilian Affairs After 1800
(Part Two)

MICHIGAN TERRITORY was ruled under the county system of government, and what is now, roughly speaking, the state of Wisconsin was divided October 26, 1818, into two counties of Michigan —the eastern part, Brown; the western part, Crawford. Despite changes in county boundaries, Green Bay and Prairie du Chien have remained their respective county seats as then established.

Governor Cass sent commissions by Colonel Henry Leavenworth who arrived at Prairie du Chien June 30, 1819. Unfortunately, no official record of the proceedings at Prairie du Chien exists. We depend for information upon the narrative of Lockwood.[1] It is claimed that the commissions Leavenworth brought with him were blank, filled out at a meeting of citizens held in Boilvin's house to select the men who were to fill the civil offices. As the governor had the appointive power, it does not seem likely that he would allow the people to do more than suggest names. Two commissions are preserved, both dated at Detroit May 12, 1819. These were made out for John W. Johnson, chief justice, and Michel Brisbois, associate justice.[2] It has been claimed that Boilvin and not Brisbois was named associate justice at this time. Brisbois' name might not have suited Colonel Leavenworth because of his part in the War of 1812. The fact that Cass insisted on having the resignation of Boilvin before he would consider Rolette's application for judge in 1821 shows that Boilvin was acting then and leads to the opinion that he was the original appointee of the governor.

There are no records of other commissions so we are not sure how Crawford County officers were selected and inducted. Nicolas Boilvin, as justice of the peace for Madison County, Illinois, was instructed to swear in all the new officers. For a list we must draw upon Lockwood's account: John W. Johnson, Chief Justice of Crawford County Court; Francois Bouthillier, associate justice; Michel Brisbois (or Nicolas Boilvin), associate justice;[3] John Findley, clerk of court; Wilfred Owens, probate judge; John P. Gates, register in probate who acted also as register of deeds;

Thomas McNair, sheriff; and three justices of the peace: Nicolas Boilvin; John W. Johnson; and James H. Lockwood.

The first official record is for 1820 and is very incomplete. The office of coroner was filled June 10, 1821, by the appointment of a Mr. Bernard.*

Thus far, there was no provision for an election of officers by the people. At the time of the appointment of Bernard, Governor Cass wrote that he was sending a copy of the Michigan laws, its third code of laws. Also he wrote that, conforming to the wishes of the people, there would be only one session a year of the county court in Crawford County. Originally it had been ordered that court be held four times a year. Findley, it would seem, resigned as clerk and then changed his mind and, as his resignation was not accepted, continued in office until his death in 1824. The court functioned at least theoretically until it was stripped of civil and criminal jurisdiction by acts of the Michigan legislature June 18, 1828, and November 5, 1829, which lodged its powers in the circuit court.[4] Before this automatic end to the term of its members, Johnson had left Prairie du Chien in 1822 and Boilvin had left in the spring of 1827 and died soon after. Bouthillier continued to hold office and claimed Prairie du Chien as his home, although he was a trader in Galena from 1819 until his death in 1834.

The jurisdiction of the Crawford County Court was restored July 31, 1830, and Governor Cass appointed new officers: Joseph Rolette, chief justice; John Brunet, associate justice; and Alex Simpson, associate justice. No one was aware of these appointments until the commissions reached Prairie du Chien. As soon as Lockwood learned of the appointments, February 1, 1831, he asked for the removal of Rolette and complained of the other two men, saying Simpson was not at Prairie du Chien.[5] Rolette had his office taken away, and there is nothing to show but that Brunet and Simpson fared likewise. Soon afterward the court was comprised of Joseph M. Street, chief justice; James H. Lockwood, associate justice; and Hercules L. Dousman, associate justice.

In the fall of 1820 the United States sent Isaac Lee to Prairie du Chien to examine the private land claims. He first considered whether the Indian title had been extinguished and declared that

---

* A note in the *Michigan Pioneer* explains that name as Menard, but I see no reason to suggest this, as there was a Bernard at Prairie du Chien as early as this, I am sure.

it had. Pierre La Pointe, who said that he had acted as interpreter at the time of the purchase from the Indians in 1781, gave testimony of the agreement for nine miles square and said that he had himself seen the purchase price delivered in goods to the Indians at Prairie du Chien.

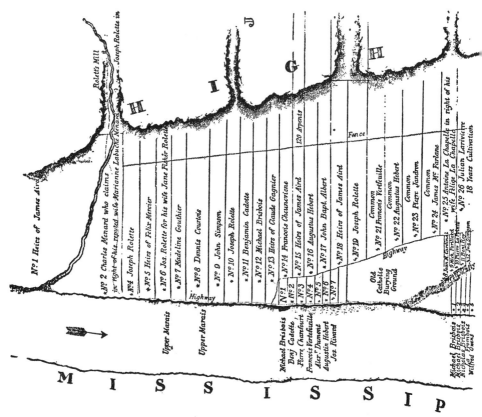

(SECTION ONE) 1820—LEE'S MAP OF PRIVATE LAND CLAIMS

Following this testimony, Lee took up the claim of each individual to a tract of land and called upon witnesses to tell what they knew about each case, and he either confirmed or rejected each claim examined. The testimony gives valuable information as to the settlement between 1796 and 1820. Lee's map is reproduced here to give a better idea of how the town was laid out by this first American land commissioner. It does not represent a scale.

When the actual survey was made, it was found that Farm Lot 38 on the schematic plan became Farm Lot 39 from the survey.[6]

To us Americans the French system of survey seems strange. It is the same that gives to the fields of Quebec their old-world

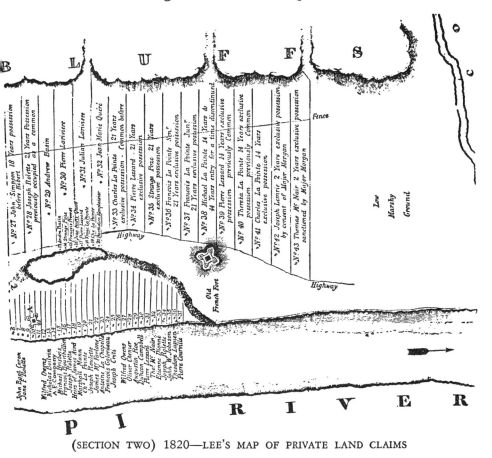

(SECTION TWO) 1820—LEE'S MAP OF PRIVATE LAND CLAIMS

character. The arpent (192.5 feet) was the unit of measurement and each parcel of land was a long, narrow strip extending from river to bluff. Seldom were any two lots the same width, but Lee's map indicates the width of each in arpents. He began numbering the farm lots at the north end of the prairie and continued south until forty-three claims were decided upon. In the same way he took up the settlement on the island, the Main Village. The lots here extended from the east channel of the Mississippi to a slough, the Marais St. Friole, a number of these lots included in the Fort Crawford reservation. Thirty-seven were laid off, many of which were not confirmed to the claimants at that time. A third group of lots known as the Upper Village or Village of St. Friole extended from the Marais St. Friole east to a thoroughfare extending north and south on what is now Beaumont Road. In this Upper Village there were twenty lots, beginning north of Frenchtown cemetery, running south as far as the site of the present Methodist church, and interrupted only by the Catholic cemetery. Lee allowed the Catholic church about sixty acres for a church and burial-place— from the site of old Frenchtown to a point known as Babin's, where the Marais St. Friole and a ravine meet.

Many of the lots assigned by Lee but unconfirmed were after- ward assigned to the claimants. His equitable distribution gave cause for but two disputes. The United States factor, Johnson, protested Astor's claim to Main Village Lot 14, but his protest was overruled in 1823. The other contest was between Nicolas Boilvin and the heirs of John Campbell, in what is known as the Campbell coulee. Not only were Campbell's heirs awarded the land he claimed, but twenty years later that claim was extended eastward to include about 400 additional acres.

Lots numbered 1 to 12 in the Main Village had been needed for military purposes in 1816 and all persons dwelling thereon had been removed. It was General Smith's intention at first to move all the French-Canadians as intruders, but Colonel Chambers decided to assign lots to all who were compelled to move and to such others as wanted lots for residence. The land south of Lot 21 was laid off and assigned by him. Since the basis of claims in all cases was occupation or cultivation continuous from 1796, the four-year tenure by which these last pieces were held was not sufficient to confirm them to the claimants. A petition sent by the inhabitants in 1821 resulted in the confirmation in 1823 of all except those which had been occupied by the military reservation of Fort Crawford; later these also went back to the original claimants.

These land claims show who were the first dealers in real estate. Denis Courtois, Pierre Lariviere, and Jean Marie Quere claimed in company the ownership of the land in Campbell coulee over which Campbell as purchaser had so much difficulty. Julien

Lariviere became a land dealer in a small way himself. Francois Chenvert began buying land early, but only for farm purposes. The first purchase he made was surrounded on all sides by Indian claims; even the house itself was supposed to be on Indian lands. By 1832 Chenvert was considered a prosperous farmer.[7]

As early as 1816 Joseph Rolette had begun to buy land and his holdings became so extensive that at one time he paid about seven-eighths of the real estate tax at Prairie du Chien. He bought both village and farm lots. His wife had considerable property, most of which he secured. Then later he bought land in partnership with Hercules L. Dousman, and by the time of the land boom in 1836 these two men had most of the desirable land in their possession.

The year Lee was in Prairie du Chien Governor Cass came here on his return from making a circle of Michigan territory. He stayed five days. In his party were James Duane Doty, for many years prominent in public affairs in Wisconsin, and Henry Schoolcraft, Indian agent.[8]

Three years later Doty returned. He had been newly appointed United States judge for Mackinac, Brown, and Crawford counties; and after holding one session of court at Mackinac proceeded to Prairie du Chien which he intended to make his home. Here he spent the winter and held court in November and participated in the election of 1823. A post office was established here that year, and Doty was appointed first postmaster. He bought two farm lots (33 and 34) and donated about eighteen acres of high ground to Crawford County to be used for a court house. He induced Governor Cass to select that particular spot as the capital of Crawford County.[9] This attempt to change the location of county affairs from the island on which most of the French-Canadians lived was opposed, particularly because the county jail was already built on the island on a lot deeded to the county by Rolette. Doty's land was never used for county purposes,* and he left Prairie du Chien after the May term of court in 1824. He went to hold a session of court at Green Bay where he made his home thereafter, coming to Prairie du Chien twice a year during his term as judge.

* In 1829 when these lots were selected for a military reservation Doty deeded this 18 acres to the United States because he said the county had not kept its part of the contract.

In 1853 the county attorney sold Doty's plot to Ira Brunson, B. W. Brisbois, and Woodman; this deed was one of the causes for suit over title.

Supplementing the county system of government was the establishment in 1821 of the Borough of Prairie du Chien, patterned after similar units in Connecticut and Ohio. Regulations conform to the laws of these states. The governor and judges of Michigan territory incorporated this "Borough of 'Prairie Des Chiens'" under an act of September 17, 1821. The boundaries of the incorporation were not given, but it was intended to cover all the inhabitants in this locality. Provision was made that the governor appoint the first officers and that election of officers take place at a town or borough meeting to be held the first Monday of the following January. Officers were to be a clerk (elected first in order that he might keep record of the rest of the meeting), a warden, two burgesses, a treasurer, and a marshal. No record other than the laws laid down by the articles of incorporation appears before March 20, 1822. At a meeting of this date minutes were signed by John W. Johnson, Warden, and M. Brisbois and Thomas McNair, Burgesses.* In the minutes it appears that Louis Crawford had been clerk but resigned and Richard Boyce been appointed clerk pro tem. That this was not the first meeting seems evident from the fact that Boyce was allowed $8 for copying sundry laws, etc., passed but not recorded by Louis Crawford, former clerk.† Perhaps Crawford kept no minutes for want of a record book.

May 6, 1822, another meeting was held, the minutes of this signed only by Boyce. These records do not give names of treasurer or marshal, but Judge Doty's records show that Charles Giasson was marshal and another source shows that Michel Brisbois was treasurer. Under the plan the clerk had the power to prosecute and the marshal had the same powers as a constable. The borough record does not show what took place at the first annual meeting in June, but there are records of meetings held December 7, 1822, and October 23 and November 20, 1823. These are signed by Joseph Rolette, Warden; Michel Brisbois, 1st Burgess; James H. Lockwood, 2nd Burgess. By order C. Giasson, Clerk. This would indicate the election of this group in June, 1822. No record is found for 1824, but for a meeting and enactments of January 17, 1825, only two signatures appear: Joseph Rolette, Warden; M. Brisbois, 1st Burgess.

* It may be because of his appointment as sheriff that McNair's name disappeared quickly as burgess.

† Little is known of Louis Crawford. He was a son of the British trader Louis Crawford and Pelagia LaPointe and a brother of Mrs. Antoine La Chapelle.

Many regulations were laid down in these years. A patrol on which every citizen was subject to service was organized to prevent conditions similar to those at Green Bay where there was much thievery and outlawry by the soldiers of the garrison. Since the military officers could not or did not control their men, the citizens of Green Bay were compelled to protect themselves by organizing the first patrol in Wisconsin.

Three streets were laid out, one north and south and two east and west. Main Street followed the line of the river and was 30 feet wide. Of the streets running east to the slough from Main, Street Number 1 between Lots 16 and 17 survives today as Fisher Street, and Street Number 2 between Lots 24 and 25 survives as a part of Black Hawk Avenue, the principal east and west street of the city.

Fire regulations required keeping chimneys clean and forbade straw-covered houses south of Fort Crawford. Horses were to be restrained on the streets; no one was permitted to drive faster than a trot. Planting of trees was subject to regulation, whether the trees were for ornament or merely utilitarian. The baker and his bread were both subject to inspection. Loaves were to be 1½ or 3 pound in size and prices were to be determined by the quality: into this the price of flour entered as an important factor. Two men— Oliver Cherrier and Francois Vertefeuille—were given positions as fence inspectors. A single fence enclosed all the cultivated land, and from April to October this fence had to be kept in repair by land owners.

The administration of these ordinances seems to have died out gradually, but in 1828 the township of St. Anthony was organized and the "borough" system was dropped. It probably did not function later than the last record. By the time Lockwood's name disappeared, he was county judge and no one filled his place as burgess. While the warden and burgesses signed themselves a court, it is not certain that they had judicial powers.

A map of this borough of Prairie du Chien is inserted because it shows the size and enclosure of the log Fort Crawford as also the location of the county jail, the American Fur Company's 600 feet of river frontage, and the location of certain other land-holders. The river frontage was not owned apparently by the American Fur Company but either occupied by tolerance of the United States which has riparian rights or occupied despite other

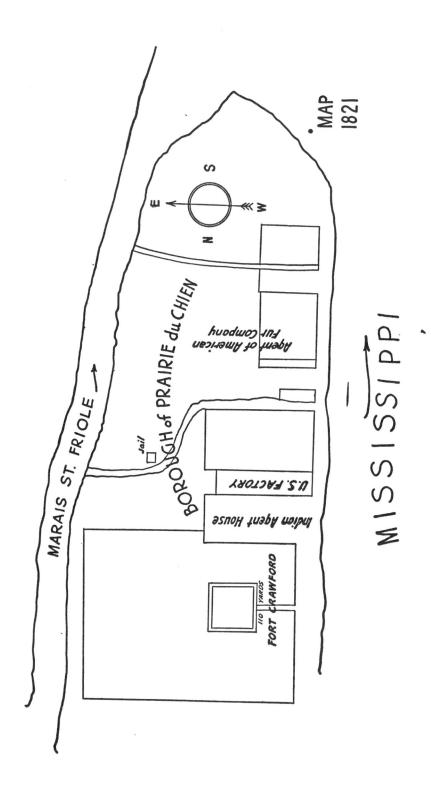

claims by reason of the impressive nature of the company's business.[10]

The introduction of the steamboat had the same revolutionizing effect upon transportation here as at other points on the Mississippi. The first steamboat to come to Prairie du Chien was the *Virginia* which touched port in 1823.[11] Before this time birch-bark canoes, piroques, batteaux, Mackinac boats, keelboats—all propelled by hand power or by sail or occasionally by animals, as on the canals and ferries—had carried passengers, furs, and cargoes of various kinds up and down the Mississippi. The use of steam made the previously dreaded upstream travel simple. Passengers enjoyed the novelty of the comfortable and comparatively rapid travel. Larger cargoes could be handled, and soon the steamboats or steam-propelled rafts and barges superseded the old means of transportation. Lumber and grain were the chief products for long-distance transportation. Rafting of logs became important at Prairie du Chien when Fort Crawford was being built, and the saw mills established by soldiers for this purpose were soon followed by the building of privately owned sawmills. At one time as many as twelve steamboats were at Prairie du Chien in one day. Towns which had good bays were popular—Wyalusing, for example—and then, of course, those places where wood could be easily secured. Such names as Reed's Landing, Red House Landing, York Landing are survivals of a time when the word had special significance to the boatmen.

The boats themselves contributed to the disappearance of timber along the river. At first crews tied up and cut their own wood for fuel, but gradually at convenient intervals there were regular landing places where the boats took on a supply of ready-cut fuel. Usually they took 20 cords at a time, and the men who sold piled it in two ranks of prescribed size. The captain measured it and gave his approval before the crew loaded it aboard. In contrast to the 2000 steamboats on the Mississippi in 1850, there were only 130 in 1826, all small, and only half of them in use for a seven-months season; yet in 1826 these boats consumed more than 450,000 cords of wood.[12] The amount of wood used later is almost incalculable. On the upper river there were often steamboat races and it is said the stokers threw hams into the fire to intensify the heat of the engine and make greater speed. Hickory and hard maple were desirable too, for they gave an extremely hot fire.

Pine lumber was abundant on the Kickapoo and Wisconsin rivers even on this side of Portage. The highlands and the valleys leading to them were covered with hickories and underbrush like hazelwood and here and there oak openings. The rest of this neighborhood and adjoining lands were covered with trees. In most places the tops of the bluffs were bare.

Between 1820 and 1828 marked changes had come in the make-up of Prairie du Chien. The Americans began to come in in the late 20's. The only Americans who had any land claims in 1820 were Thomas McNair, James McFarland, and Wilfred Owens. Fisher claims were assigned to his daughter because he was away at this time. Lockwood became a speculator in land, but his first purchase was not made until 1824. On part of the 200 acres pur-cased then he built what he said was the first "framed" house on the prairie. The fact that it was later used as the home of the commanding officer of Fort Crawford bespeaks its size and preeminence.

In his old age Lockwood was grieved when General Brooke tore it down and rebuilt. Lockwood's description of the building is of interest: "I sent men to the Black River, and got the timber for the frame and the shingles, and had the plank and boards sawed by hand, and brought them down to the Prairie. But then I had no carpenter or joiner, there being none at Prairie du Chien. I went on board of a keel boat that had landed, and enquired if there was a carpenter and joiner on board, on which a ragged, dirty looking man said that he professed to be such, and having before seen quite as unprepossessing fellows turn out much better than appearances indicated, I agreed with him at $1.50 per day and board. I built on the site near Fort Crawford, now occupied by what is called the commanding officer's house. My house was of the following description: a cellar-kitchen, 30 feet by 26 feet, with a frame on it of the same size, two stories high, with a wing 16 by 20, on the south side, one story, which I used for a retail store. There was a hall through the south end of the two-story part, the whole length of the house, with stairs from the cellar-kitchen up into the hall, and stairs from the hall to the upper story. The north end of the house was divided—the front part about 14 by 16 feet, into a parlor or sitting room; a chimney in the center of the north end, and a bed-room in the back part about 14 feet square; a door leading from the hall to the bed-room, and one to the sitting-room, and a door by the side of the chimney from the bed-room to the sitting-room, and a door from the hall into the wing or store. This house I afterwards sold to the Government, with the land on which the fort now stands. It was good enough for General Taylor and family while he commanded here; but as soon as General Brooke was in command, he got an appropriation from Congress to repair the house, and had it all torn down except a part of the cellar wall, and built the one which is there at present, at a cost of about $7,000."[13]

Doty's failure to secure cooperation on the location of a court-house site prevented for a time a shift of population from the island to what has since become the principal section of Prairie du Chien. Besides the homes and business buildings incident to the fur trade, the island was occupied by a sutler's store, the Indian agency house, the log fort, a boarding house run by J. B. Faribault, and, later, at the same location, a restaurant run by J. B. Pion. Charles LaPointe and Jean Brunet ran hotels here. The people in this part of town with a few exceptions were French-Canadians and some Indian mixed bloods. The buildings which we think of as old were not as yet erected.

There are a number of interesting pictures of early Prairie du Chien, some of them authentic and others drawn from memory or idealized by the artist. In one of these pictures—"Prairie du Chien in 1836"—the home of Rolette is shown as the most imposing dwelling on the river front. This coincides with the reports of travelers of the period. Caleb Atwater wrote in 1829 that this "old town" had seen better days, as was shown by the number of foundations and chimneys still standing.[14]

The great disadvantage of living here was the danger of flood. In times of high water cellars were filled, streets inundated, and often porches and ground floors flooded. In 1826 the water raise was 14 feet and that year the river was said to be nine miles wide at St. Louis.[15] In 1822, 1826, and 1828 the soldiers were compelled to leave the barracks because of high water and this unhealthful state of affairs was a factor determining the removal of Fort Crawford to higher ground.

The island was destined, however, to be chosen for the most luxurious home Prairie du Chien has ever seen. This was built in 1843 on the site of Fort Shelby by Hercules L. Dousman who established his home here and married Jane Fisher Rolette, his partner's widow, the following year. Twenty-eight years later, after Dousman's death, Mrs. Dousman rebuilt, preserving all those features of the house and grounds which had made it during his lifetime the mecca of distinguished and wealthy visitors to Prairie du Chien. A restoration of this home, the Villa Louis, in 1935, has made this the outstanding show-place of Prairie du Chien.*

Lee's report on the private land claims in 1820 had been tentative and so Lucius Lyon was sent out by the government in 1828 to make a survey, establishing the lines bounding the land of each claimant until practically the entire prairie was surveyed and each individual landholder knew exactly how much he had and where it lay. A few spots were not surveyed. His west line ran along the east margin of Water Street, leaving all west of that as government land, which had never been surveyed by the government and is still United States land. Also, there is on the east side of St. Friole a strip of land near the north extremity of the city of Prairie du Chien which was never surveyed and still belongs to the government. At that time the south line of the farm lots was the south line of Farm Lot 43, leaving some land between that and the Wisconsin River not surveyed. Lyon published maps following Lee's with some variation. Also, he left here his surveyor's notes, which explain a few historic points. For instance, he said at the time of the survey there was no building of any kind on Main Village Lot 16, despite the legend that a rock building known as the Hudson's Bay Company fur-trading post stood there. The building so designated was built much later by Rolette. The records of the Hudson's Bay Company show that there never was a post of theirs at Prairie du Chien.

In spite of the large tract of land west of the Indian trail indicated on Lee's map for Catholic church purposes, when Lyon made the survey he allotted less than an acre for a burial place, known today as the old Frenchtown cemetery.

A study of the Lyon map and of transfers which followed his survey answers many questions as to who lived where. The residence of Joseph M. Street, Indian agent, is of interest, since the surrender of Black Hawk was made to him at his house. Many visitors must have made his place headquarters as they did in the

---

* The property was deeded to the city by the Dousman heirs in 1935 and much of the original furnishings restored. Interiors were redecorated and extensive repairs made through the joint efforts of the Dousmans and the city of Prairie du Chien.

case of Boilvin, his predecessor. At first Street stayed in Boilvin's house, which he had had repaired. Then he moved to the mouth of the Mill Coulee (Farm Lot 3) where he was living in 1829. However, before the end of the Black Hawk war, he had induced a Galena man to build him a new house about three blocks north of the fort.* At first the government rented this but after Street's term ended it was purchased for agency purposes.

The sub-agents had to provide their own living quarters, although they were given subsistence allowance. John Marsh lived with his half-breed Sioux wife and two children on the island. Thomas P. Burnett, who succeeded Marsh in 1829, probably lived nearer the new fort. He did not marry for several years after coming here. Burnett came here from Kentucky—rather reluctantly, if we may believe his account of his disappointment at not receiving a better political appointment than a sub-agency in the wilderness. "The idea I had formed of the duties of an Indian agent," he wrote in a letter to Kentucky October 24, 1831, "I find by the light you have reflected upon the subject was by no means correct. I had thought my only duty was to sit behind a desk and issue out to the Indians their regular supply of whiskey, powder, lead and other articles which Uncle Sam covenants to furnish to the said Indians at an unusually low price; and in payment for said articles said Indians have ceded to Uncle Sam a certain tract or parcel of land known by certain boundaries, etc. Pretty tough work this, for a Kentucky lawyer especially. But it is not I find Uncle Sam's plan to hire laborers to work his farm and suffer them to sleep out their time in complete torpidity. No, they must be up and doing, must earn their wages by hard labor.

"It must certainly have been a queer kind of sight to have seen a Kentuckian, learned in all the lore of the law, holding a council with the red men of the forest. Like a young Mercury he arrives among them; deep thought and anxious expectations sit on every countenance. Now is the time; he arises, tells them in the most finished language of the most fertile imagination the object of the meeting, what Uncle Sam expects to do for them, and what they must do for him. As he warms with his subject his imagination expands; the earth, air, and sea are brought to his aid as comparative objects. He ceases and his audience knows not what he has said."[16]

* Upper Village Lot 20.

Many discharged soldiers made their home at Prairie du Chien and so were assimilated as civilians. However, officers and men at the garrison sometimes mingled with the civilians. It was said of the death of the post surgeon, Dr. Mendenhall, in 1823 that he died broken-hearted because he had been rejected by one of the quarter-breeds of the village. Dancing was a favorite recreation with all, and the color of the soldiery added zest to the balls. Mrs. Baird (Elizabeth Thérèse Fisher) speaks of one such occasion. "The officers gave a large dancing party at the fort in honor of Mrs. Rolette's visitors. There was as yet nothing but the walls up; the windows were not in, nor were the doors hung. But the floor was very smooth and offered a good surface for dancing. The party was a delightful one."[17]

Mrs. Baird spoke on this occasion of renewing acquaintance with Dr. and Mrs. Beaumont who were at the old fort. He was post surgeon, an ambitious young army officer with an active and inquiring mind, inclined toward the study of science. His great contribution to physiology resulted from his contact with Alexis St. Martin, a poor *voyageur*, whom he had treated at Mackinac in 1822 for a gun-shot wound. Contrary to the doctor's expectations, St. Martin recovered and during his convalescence the Beaumonts took him into their home at Mackinac. The man had been shot at close range, the charge entering his body on the left side in such a way as to carry away part of the sixth rib, part of the lower lung, and the left end of the stomach. After a lingering illness, the wound healed but left an opening into the stomach. This never closed. In 1825 Dr. Beaumont began experiments on digestion, using St. Martin as his subject. That year the two men were separated, and it was not until 1829 that Dr. Beaumont induced him to come to Prairie du Chien and return to his service. In December he began a series of experiments carried on for nearly two years, 50 of which are recorded in his now famous book *Experiments and Observations on the Gastric Juice and the Physiology of Digestion.* This was first published at Plattsburg, N.Y., in 1834 and later in England, France, and Germany. The medical profession were intensely interested because these were the first experiments on digestion conducted with a living human subject. Dr. Beaumont was a hard worker and his years at Prairie du Chien were busy ones. In addition to his experiment and his work at the fort, he practised among the civilians.

There was no civilian doctor at Prairie du Chien at the time. Dr. Beaumont's only competitor was Mrs. Charles Menard, the well-known Mary Ann LaBuche.* She was a good nurse and mid-wife and used herbs for treatment. It was she who attended most of the French. Much earlier there had been a Sioux woman, Marie, who served in the same capacity. An army officer mentioned her death in 1814 as a "great loss."[18]

In the early 30's many American families came and a "new town" sprang up to rival the old. The location of this was south of the rock fort. The building of Alfred Brunson's home occurred shortly before the American land boom. James Lockwood had moved to this section of the town and other families—Clarks, Tainters, Hunters, Lesters, Gilberts, Hills—had come in.[19] Many of these Americans left a decided impress on the town. They held practically all public offices under territorial organization and swung elections although they were not a majority. Some of the settlers in this "new town," however, were only speculators and their names dropped out in a few years.

The fever of land speculation hit Prairie du Chien in 1836 and 1837. Not only the local real estate enthusiasts but more particular-ly outsiders made efforts to enrich themselves and to attract settlers by booming the town. There was some legitimate trading, of course, but one company deliberately organized to entrap the gullible. Charles Van Dorn of Michigan bought 525 acres of land on the north side of the Wisconsin at its junction with the Mississippi and made 1050 shares to be sold at $200 each. He laid out a court house square, parks, and streets named after Presidents. Certificates of stock were issued and buyers were to share in the profits of the company in proportion to the number of shares they held. This land was a swamp at best, and in 1838 at a time of high water Feather-stonehaugh, a steamboat passenger, said he passed over this well laid out city; it was then 12 feet under water. When investors realized it was a swindle, Van Dorn left for parts unknown. Some stock certificates have shown up in the Kansas Historical Society in recent years.

Two other companies laid out certain other lands in and near Prairie du Chien and sold some lots in a projected addition to the settlement.[20] They have never been used except for farm purposes.

---

* She came to Prairie du Chien with Claude Gagnier, her second husband. She had previously married Duchouquette and later Charles Menard.

The men active in these companies were George Washington Pine, a New Yorker, and a number of hopeful citizens. Pine was also an officer in the Prairie du Chien Ferry Company, a banking concern which organized in 1836 and issued fiat money. The company did not last long, collapsing like the land schemes.

The local effects of speculation may be inferred from a letter written by H. L. Dousman. "August 7, 1836— ... "We are overrun here with land speculators, sharpers, etc. etc. They are buying up the whole country—they have got the people here perfectly *delirious*—there are two or three opposition towns in contemplation on the Prairie alone—I have lost at least 8 to 10 thousand dollars by selling out my land a few weeks ago—but I don't despair of making it out of them yet before they get rid of me."[21]

B. W. Brisbois' gift of a court house site on the mainland almost directly east of the island settlement caused a grouping of the Americans close by. William Wilson, who built the court house; Daniel Hopkins; and Richard Curtis were among this group. A nucleus of settlement here was one reason for the building of the first substantial bridge across the Marais St. Friole in 1839 at what is now Washington Street. It was built by Julien Lariviere who the same year built himself a large frame house at the west end of the street on the mainland. This house remained standing until 1936, continuously occupied by his descendants. It was not until 1857 that a bridge was built at what is now the principal crossing, on Black Hawk Avenue.

A second reason for building a bridge early at the Washington Street crossing was the location of St. Gabriel's Catholic church, two blocks north of the court house. The first priests to visit the congregation at Prairie du Chien had not used that site, but a donation of land for the building determined its location by Rev. Mazzuchelli.

Rev. Francis Vincent Badin was sent from Detroit to Prairie du Chien to minister to the Catholic population.* He arrived in May, 1827, and remained about three months, using the hall of the old hospital in the log Ft. Crawford, deserted at that time by the garrison, as his church. Here he gave religious instruction, administered the sacraments, and said Mass. He left a record of the

* He was a younger brother of Fr. Theodore Stephen Badin, the first priest ordained in the United States. For a time Fr. F. V. Badin was vicar general of Detroit under Bishop Rese. He later returned to France where he died.

baptisms, marriages, and burials he performed.* He commenced the building of a log church but this work was interrupted by the Red Bird massacre. He returned later—in the fall of 1828—and spent part of 1829 but did not return again.

Rev. Joseph Anthony Lutz was a priest of the Vincentian order who was sent as an Indian missioner to Prairie du Chien in the summer of 1831 and who was living in a tent on the prairie not far from Rousseau Island when the Menominee massacre occurred. He remained at least two weeks after that but returned to St. Louis (whence he came) never to visit Prairie du Chien again.[22]

The next year Prairie du Chien was visited by the well-known Dominican missionary, Rev. Samuel Mazzuchelli, who was born and educated in Italy and ordained in Cincinnati, Ohio. Under the bishop of Cincinnati he was sent to Mackinac and Green Bay and visited Prairie du Chien, spending 15 days here on this first visit in 1832. He is said to have been the parish priest of Prairie du Chien from 1832 to 1839.† Although he made his home at Galena where he was stationed from 1835 as pastor and as vicar general of Bishop Loras of Dubuque, he made many visits to Prairie du Chien during his pastorate and later.

Fr. Mazzuchelli is remembered for his exceptionally successful missionary work and for his teaching among the Indians. He organized a successful Indian school at Green Bay in 1831 and was more successful in teaching the Winnebago at Portage the next year than any missionary of his time among the western Indians. He published two Indian catechisms—one in Menominee and one in Winnebago. He was one of the most ardent advocates of temperance and organized temperance societies wherever he could at a period when liquor abuses were so flagrant as to have aroused the people to a need for action.

Fr. Mazzuchelli's priestly activity included the building of large and beautiful churches spread over a wide area in Wisconsin, Illinois, and Iowa. It was he who planned the rock building of St. Gabriel's church and he was here often during its construction to oversee the work. He himself worked in the quarries with the men who were getting out rock for the building. When the membership of the church here was probably not over 700, he laid the plans

* These records, lost for a time, were found in Montreal. Photostat copies are in possession of the Wisconsin Historical Library, Madison, Wisconsin.

† The pastoral records of Prairie du Chien can not be found but his own statement and the *Catholic Almanac* of those years are authorities on this point.

for a building 50 x 100 feet. This required a long effort for completion and even the aid of the Society for the Propagation of the Faith, but when finished, it was regarded as one of the finest churches in Wisconsin. It is still used and still a very beautiful church.

Joseph M. Street, Indian agent, proclaimed himself the first Protestant to profess his religion at Prairie du Chien. His affiliation with the Presbyterian church resulted in the choice of a Presbyterian minister, Reverend David Lowry, for the Indian School at Yellow River, an appointment which Fr. Mazzuchelli had expected to receive because of his experience at Green Bay and Portage. Rev. Lowry came in 1833, but his salary for the Indian school did not commence until January, 1834, and the school was not finished for another year.[23] Meantime he must have been acting chaplain at Fort Crawford and residing at Prairie du Chien. The Presbyterians had a following here until 1857 when they united with the Congregationalists and built a church which was known as the Congregational church and which is still standing although no longer used for church purposes. That this fusion was not agreeable to all parties is suggested by a letter here quoted.

"Prairie du Chien, Wisconsin, August 24, 1858 President James Buchanan, Dear Sir: The lands of Ft. Crawford in this city are no longer used by the government. I desire to purchase a site for a Presbyterian church. Will you have me informed how I must proceed to secure this object most readily.

Very truly, Your friend,
Nicholas Chevalier, Missionary of the General
Assembly Board Old School."[24]

The first Protestant minister to make his home at Prairie du Chien and work among the civilians and not as chaplain at the fort was Reverend Alfred Brunson, who came as superintendent of the Methodist Episcopal Mission of the Upper Mississippi and Lake Superior.[25] He was a Pennsylvanian who made his first trip from Meadville on horseback in 1835, returned to Pennsylvania for his family, and came again in 1836. The Brunsons came by boat down the Ohio and up the Mississippi, bringing their household goods and other belongings besides the material for their house which had been cut and fitted in Pennsylvania ready to be assembled here. It was some time before the house was built, but when finished it was a substantial building which stood and was occupied for more than eighty years. Reverend Brunson was active in public affairs, in education, and especially in the affairs of the Methodist church, of which he was made elder during his residence here. His congregation built a church in 1843, the second oldest church in Prairie du Chien.

As early as 1836 Rev. Richard Cadle, the chaplain at the fort, organized a group of Episcopalians.[26] It was some years before they built a church, although the name of the congregation, Trinity, dates from his time.

Other denominations came much later. In the 60's were built a Lutheran and a German Evangelical church, still in use.

What of education among the civilian population of the town?

From the time Keyes taught in the first school building in 1818, there has been at least one school in operation. Daniel Curtis, engaged by Rolette in 1824 as a tutor for his family, had some kind of a private school after he left the employ of Rolette. In 1832 a Cumberland Presbyterian divinity student taught school for six months. In 1836 practically all the residents of the town signed a memorial to Congress asking that the buildings of Ft. Crawford be converted to use as a university whenever the government should evacuate the fort. The same year a Miss Kirley taught a select "infant" school with 20 pupils, and at the same time another school boasted an attendance of 30. Henry Boyer, a French scholar who had taught at Mineral Point, kept a school at Prairie du Chien some time between 1840 and 1850.[27] There is a notation that there was an academy in 1840 which was run by nuns but there are no records to show this.

The territorial laws had been revised in 1839, requiring every town with not less than 10 families to become a school district and in 1840 a memorial was sent to Congress asking that a school system be established for Wisconsin. Efforts were made to establish a school to function as part of the town government in accordance with the intention of the law.

October 19, 1841, Alfred Brunson and William Cady, acting officially, set aside what was to be known as School District Number 1 of Crawford County. Plat was made and filed with the board of commissioners and a notice issued for a school meeting to be held November 1, 1841, at the Granite House.[28] Officers were elected but no further action was taken until March 25, 1843, when new trustees were elected. Lockwood agreed to convey to the trustees a lot* for a school house site in the section of the city familiarly known as Lowertown. There were 34 names on the tax roll at that time and the tax levy yielded $91.63 on a valuation of $36,650. Lockwood held more than one-seventh of the real estate.

The school building was to be 20 x 20 feet with a stove in the center. Contract to build was given April 6, 1843. The next meeting was held March 10, 1845. The school house was accepted and paid for May 20, 1846. Meanwhile, Brunson said, a Miss Ellen Overton taught for three months in 1846 in a rented room. She boarded with the children and was paid by the patrons of the school. Only eleven children attended. March 8, 1847, it was decided to buy a stove and put a fence around the school house. This year Miss Hannah Lockwood taught three months at $8 a month, and in 1848 Julia Barnum taught five months at $1.50 a week; $6.50 of her salary came from public funds and the rest of the $30 total was paid by pupils. Miss Elizabeth Rutan taught three months in 1849, and a Miss Gilman three months the same year for $2.50 a week.

Until we became a state, the funds from the sale of school lands were not available so up to this time schools were in their very nature private, as no other means (taxes assessed were negligible) except individual contributions either by pupils attending or by patrons were possible. Prompt conformity to state school laws was not expected. The Lowertown group were most persistent in maintaining a school and they continued to call themselves District Number 1 although it was not until 1850 that the formalities of legal organization were complied with. They were not considered a school district if we may accept an item from the local newspaper. "May 23, 1849—During the past winter there has not been a district school in any one of the nine districts of this town although their place has been in a manner supplied by select schools."[29]

The Lowertown school was taught three months in 1850 by Miss Nancy Fisher and four months by Fred Miller, the first man teacher. The school did not function in 1852 but was revived in 1853 when Miss Overton taught seven months at $8 a month in the summer and $10 in the winter.

As early as 1846 an advertisement for a private high school ap-

* Lot 4 in Block 8 of Lockwood's addition. This is diagonally across the street southwest from the frame part of Campion.

peared in the newspaper. "High school will open Monday December 28, 1846. Grammar, composition, general History including chronology, ancient and modern geography, algebra, geometry and rectilinear trigonometry with their applications to surveying and carpentry. Lectures on chemistry will be delivered by Dr. J. H. Day. A class of French will be heard every two days in the evening. $3.00 per quarter, paid in advance. Mr. Bouillat."[30]

May 2, 1849 the *Patriot* carried another ad: "A New School. We rejoice to announce to our friends that a Catholic Female School to be conducted by Miss P. McLeod under the patronage and inspection of the Rev. L. Galtier will commence on the 15th of this month. The discipline will be mild but strict; cleanliness is particularly desired. Reading, writing, arithmetic, English grammar, history, geography, plain sewing, marking and needle work will be equally taught to children according to their capacity.

"Terms will be moderate. Previous application for admission should be made immediately to either the Rev. L. Galtier or to Miss McLeod." (Notice dated May 1, 1849.)

A new high school advertisement appeared December 5, 1849, in the same paper. "High School. Mrs. Dwight would respectfully inform the public that she will open a select school on Wednesday in the brick building opposite the Prairie House. Instruction will be given in the various branches usually taught in high schools and no pains will be spared to render the advantages equal to those of any other schools in the country.

"That the course of instruction may be thorough and systematic the number of pupils will be limited to 20 during the present term.

"For reference apply to Rev. A. Brunson, Rev. E. Yocum, and E. W. and A. Pelton." (Notice dated November 14, 1849.)

By 1852 school news became more frequent in the paper— teachers' institute notice, advertisements of select schools by Mrs. Dwight and (April 19, 1853) Miss Irish. A school meeting notice is quoted: "September 22, 1852. Next Monday evening will be school meeting night. B. H. Johnson, Town Superintendent."[31] The signature of this notice recalls the fact that up to 1862 Wisconsin had town rather than county superintendents. The habit of local determination of school policies has resulted in the restriction of county superintendent's duties to control of the rural and village schools.

Records of the Department of State of Wisconsin show that a

Prairie du Chien Academy was incorporated in 1854 by H. L. Dousman, Alonzo Pelton, John Thomas, Ira B. Brunson, Hiram Wright, Samuel A. Clark, Hiram Knowlton, B. W. Brisbois, J. A. Howell, Buel E. Hutchinson, Isaac Perrit Gentil, Leander Leclerc, and Thomas A. Savage.

In 1857 the Dominican Sisters established a school which they continued for five years. In 1858 Lowertown built the rock school house still standing and in January, 1859, it was conducted by two teachers—a man and a woman.

Schools sponsored by groups prevented a public school system exclusively supported by taxpayers until 1875. Taxes were divided among Germans and French and Americans so that tuition was necessary for support.

The coming of the Americans had been the death knell for the waterways as arteries of commerce. These people had come from parts of the country above the fall lines of rivers and they had no sentiment for modes of travel which had meant so much to the ancestors of the French in the New World. Portages had been merely an annoyance to the French, but to the Americans it was the rivers which presented difficulties.

The earliest land travel in this region had been on foot or by the Indian pole method* or by horse or dog-drawn sledges or two-wheeled carts. On the ice, trains of sledges were moved by dogs or horses or oxen or even pulled by men.

Many Americans came on horseback and it was a favorite means of travel with them. The Indian trails were followed, or sometimes a man had to make his own trail, cutting his way through the timber and underbrush.

Major Long lost his course in 1823 when he came to Prairie du Chien on horseback, but his account makes light of his discomfort. "We encamped (June 18) at an early hour on a small stream which is a tributary of the Wisconsin and as we supposed at a distance of 12 miles from the place where we intended to cross that river. The next morning after a fatiguing ride over a rough and hilly country we reached the banks of the Wisconsin; as we could not ford it, we prepared a light raft, and sent Bemis across to obtain boats at Ft. Crawford. From the account of our guides we thought

* The Indian attached two poles, one on either side of the horse, fastened like a collar, and harness with the rear end of the poles resting upon the ground and the load resting on the two poles.

we were opposite to a point in the river . . . situated about 6 miles above the confluence of the Wisconsin and Mississippi rivers, but we afterward found that we were nine miles higher than our guides had reported us to be. The place where we encamped until means of transportation across the river could be procured, was in a wood at the foot of a high and steep bank. It was almost the only dry place in the vicinity of the river bank, above and below it being swampy. The river was about ⅓ mile wide and current very rapid.

"About sunset we observed two boats advancing up the river, in one of which was Colonel Morgan. . . . Although it was late, yet as the weather was fine, the party effected a crossing of the Wisconsin and having relieved their horses of all unnecessary baggage, the gentlemen proceeded under Col. Morgan's guidance towards the fort. It was 8 o'clock when they left the Wisconsin and about eleven when they reached the Mississippi. This ride at a late hour, was one of a most romantic character; the evening was fair and still; not a breath of wind interrupted the calmness of the scenery; the moon shone in her full, and there was pale light over the trackless course which we traveled. Our way lay across a beautiful country, where steep and romantic crags contrasted pleasantly with widely expanded prairies, which seen by the uncertain light of the moon, appeared to spread around like a sheet of water."[32]

When Caleb Atwater left Prairie du Chien after the treaty of 1829 he seems to have found travel cumbersome rather than romantic. "Henry Gratiot with a dandy wagon took me with him leaving Prairie du Chien. We had mats, blankets, cooking vessels, provisions and arms; crossed the river about 3 miles above its mouth in a ferry boat* and encamped on its south bank—Wisconsin shallow, full of sand bars and islands and a low stage of water; wild rice in bloom all along it. . . . After kindling our fire and cooking our breakfast and eating it, we started just after sunrise, making our way as well as we could, sometimes through thick-set and tall grass—sometimes through as impervious growth of bushes as I ever saw.

"By the aid of our knives we traveled up the river diverging gradually from it toward the southern point of the compass, until about midday. We succeeded in ascending the high hills and lofty

* Brunet had a license in 1831 for a ferry at Petit Gris. This must be the one referred to.

precipices of the Wisconsin basin on the south side. We were 4 or 5 miles south of river when we entered prairie. We supposed we had traveled 12 miles and ascended 1200 feet in elevation. Where it was prairie one went ahead and led the horses and one followed the wagon to lend a helping hand when an obstacle arose. Had to cut a road through bushes with knives and bend larger ones to get the horses and wagon over them. We came into the trace which Dr. Woolcott and his potawatomie had made on their journey home after the treaty. Finally turned to right where in ravine found a spring. . . . We passed two nights on way to Dodgeville getting soaked with rain the second night."[33]

Despite Atwater's difficulties, there was a wagon road which he should have been able to follow to the top of the ridge. This road was well defined when the military road was surveyed in 1832 and when it was built three years later, there were other connecting side roads. Carts drawn by horses or oxen, wagons, buckboards, democrat wagons, linchpin wagons, buggies—followed each other as the roads became better and the settlements more prosperous and more populated.

Bridges were not built early, and roads were often connected by means of ferries. The great immigration into Iowa by covered wagon after the Black Hawk War often followed a road below the Wisconsin River to a ferry from Wyalusing. Both the Wisconsin and Mississippi were crossed by ferry at numerous points.

There was a ferry at Bridgeport, one crossing to Millville, one to Walnut Eddy, and one between Woodman or Boscobel and Boydtown—all on the lower Wisconsin. First the ferry was poled over by men; then a tread power that used horses or even oxen to furnish the motion; but by 1840 steam displaced the horse power and so continued until it was displaced by gasoline.

On the Mississippi there were ferries from Wyalusing to the Iowa side, from Prairie du Chien to McGregor (1836), from Prairie du Chien to Neezeka, and also one to the military road for Ft. Atkinson. Other ferries were operated in the neighborhood, but they were of less importance. The Wisconsin river ferries lost most of their business with the building by a privately owned corporation of a covered toll bridge in 1857. The ferry distance at this point had been shortened in 1848 by the building of a bridge across the slough at the south end of the crossing. The ferry business across the Mississippi continued as late as 1934, two years after the building of a suspension toll bridge at this point.

In the 50's and 60's large quantities of wheat and other farm products were brought down the river. However, the era of the railroads was close at hand and that meant the transfer of commerce from water to land. The first train of the Milwaukee and Mississippi* railroad to reach Prairie du Chien came April 15, 1857. Depot and yards were built in Lowertown† and for a number of years this was the busiest part of the town.

The coming of the railroad brought a large group of Irish who established themselves here and soon exceeded in number the native Americans.‡

About this time the Bohemians began to arrive, and their number increased very rapidly for fifteen years or more. Since the days of the early French, no group of immigrants succeeded in impressing their nationality upon the village as the Bohemians have done. The Germans did not come early, but by 1864 they were numerous enough to establish a school self-supported where German was the only language taught. More of the French turned to farming in later years; and the center of their settlement moved farther north, one entire section of the town known as Frenchtown. For some reason they gradually decreased and lost their identity through intermarriage; and the easy-going habits—their dances and socials and New Year's calls and society picnics to honor St. John the Baptist, patron of Canada—all yielded to the changes in the times.

When the Civil War came, it found Prairie du Chien affected like other towns by the depletion of its male population, which began in 1861 and continued through the four years of the war. Like other towns, too, it saw a boom on land and on farm products which were being transported at this time of active market by both land and water. The Diamond Jo steamship line built a large warehouse on the island, and about the same time a five-story grain elevator was built south of this to care for transfer of grain from boat to train. The inhabitants of the island and of upper town, alarmed by the boom which the railroad had brought Lowertown, offered the inducement of money subscriptions as a subsidy for the transfer of the Chicago, Milwaukee, and St. Paul station to the island. This movement was unsuccessful at first, but continued agitation and the increase in both steamboat and railroad business

* Later known as the Chicago, Milwaukee, and St. Paul and now as the Chicago, Milwaukee, St. Paul, and Pacific.

† The west end of Farm Lot 36.

‡ In 1836 Patrick Quinn was the only Irishman, but some time in the 30's one of the Dunnes came and during the next years many of his relatives.

finally brought about the change. The Dousman Hotel was built by the railroad in 1863 to assure accommodations for its patrons. It stands empty today—too large and too poorly heated to be attractive for even the most optimistic of hotelkeepers. It commands a view of the river just south of the boatlanding.

At the close of the Civil War, Prairie du Chien was already supplanted in size and in commercial importance by St. Paul. After a century and a half of commercial interdependence, the settlement above St. Peter's River was finally to supersede the one above the Wisconsin.

CHAPTER THIRTEEN

Conclusion

After the Civil War changes came more slowly for a time, and the changes of the present are scarcely history as yet. Records are available on vital statistics, land transfers, legal papers; continuous newspaper files reflect the lives of the people in the last years. For this reason it is scarcely necessary to touch this period which is within the memory of so many living persons.

Interest in education was quickened by the establishment here of a public school system operating under the state law and by the establishment of three private colleges.

The Prairie du Chien College was instituted in the Brisbois Hotel soon after its evacuation as a hospital for convalescent soldiers of the Civil War and continued for three years, offering boys and girls alike a higher education. Efforts were made by the authorities of this school to secure its choice as a state normal school but Platteville was selected instead.

With the coming of the Christian Brothers to this school in 1871, it became a boys' school exclusively. Boarders and day pupils were accommodated then as they have been since under the Jesuit control. It was taken over by the Jesuits in 1880 and has operated continuously since under the names of Sacred Heart College, Campion College of the Sacred Heart, and Campion High School. At first it was a college and preparatory school but in recent years it has been a private high school for boys. The buildings and grounds of this school are remarkable in their completeness and beauty.

The girls' school was organized by the Notre Dame Sisters in 1872 under the patronage of John Lawler who donated the grounds for this school, as he had donated ground for some of the Campion buildings. Primarily a boarding school, day pupils were admitted and as the attendance grew, buildings were added and the surroundings developed. At first it was called St. Mary's Institute and later St. Mary's College, St. Mary's Academy, and now Diocesan Teachers' College. The college department in 1929 was transferred to newly constructed buildings at Milwaukee, where the school is known as Mount Mary College.

When the public high school was organized in 1875, several private schools were discontinued and the principal of the former German school became the first principal of the high school.

With changes of transportation elsewhere, Prairie du Chien has been fortunate in its place as a stopping-point for through trains on the Milwaukee road and on the Burlington, which came in in 1885. The transfer of cars across the river by ferries ended with the building of the pontoon bridge of the Milwuakee road, for which John Lawler secured the patent in 1874. The coming of the Burlington necessitated a railroad bridge across the Wisconsin.

Industries have been for the most part small. The button factories which were numerous forty years ago are gone; so are the cigar factories. The woolen mill holds position as the outstanding industry and has done so for thirty years. Artesian wells have added to the reputation of the town as a health resort, and a growing appreciation of its scenic beauty has brought many visitors to this spot.

Prairie du Chien is essentially, however, a city of homes and not a transients' town. Whether historic interest, scenic interest, business, domestic, or educational reasons have brought people here, they have remained as did the earliest of its settlers to leave their impress upon the locality.

Bibliography

PUBLISHED SOURCES

Annals of Iowa. A Historical Quarterly. 1893-1935. Iowa Department of History, Des Moines, Iowa.

Annals of the Society for the Propagation of the Faith. Earlier volumes in French: *Annales de l'association de la propagation de la foi, recueil periodique des lettres des évèques et des missionaires des missions des deux mondes, et de tous les documens relatifs aux missions et à l'association de la prop. de la foi. no. XIX, Janvier 1830. Paris. Volume IV.*

Appleton's Cyclopedia of American Biography.

Atwater, Caleb. *Remarks Made on a Tour to Prairie du Chien, Thence to Washington City in 1829.* Columbus, Ohio. Isaac N. Whiting, 1831.

Beaumont, William, M.D. *Experiments and Observations on the Gastric Juice and the Physiology of Digestion.* Plattsburg, N.Y. 1833.

Billon, Frederic Louis. *Annals of St. Louis in its Early Days under the French and Spanish Dominations; Compiled from Authentic Data.* St. Louis. 1886.

Black Hawk, Chief of the Sauk Indians 1767-1838. *Autobiography. . . .* Dictated by Himself. Antoine Leclair, United States Interpreter. J. B. Patterson, ed. and amanuensis. . . . St. Louis Press of the Continental Printing Company. 1882.

Blair, Emma Helen, ed. *The Indian Tribes of the Upper Mississippi Valley. . . .* translated, edited, annotated, and with bibliography and index by Emma Helen Blair. Cleveland, Ohio. The Arthur H. Clark Co. 1911-12. 2 vol.

Bryce, George. *Remarkable History of the Hudson's Bay Company Including That of the French Traders of Northwestern Canada and of the Northwest, XY and Astor Fur Companies.* Toronto. 1900.

Campbell, Thomas Joseph, S. J. *Pioneer Laymen of North America.* 1915-16. 2 vol.

Chittenden, Hiram Martin. *The American Fur Trade of the Far West.* N.Y. Francis P. Harper, 1902. 3 vol.

Cole, Cyrenus. *A History of the People of Iowa.* Cedar Rapids, Iowa. The Torch Press. 1921.

Coues, Elliott, ed. *Pike, Zebulon M. Expeditions to Headwaters of the Mississippi River during the Years 1805-06-07. 1895. Reprint from Original of 1810.*

Crawford County Courier, Prairie du Chien, Wisconsin.

Courier, Prairie du Chien, Wisconsin.

Durrie, Daniel S. *The Early Outposts of Wisconsin.* Annals of Prairie du Chien. Madison, Wisconsin. 1872 (?)

Featherstonehaugh, George William. *A Canoe Voyage up the Minny Sotor.* . . . London. R. Bentley. 1847.

Flandrau, Mrs. Grace C. (Hodgson). *Historic Northwest Adventureland.* 1926. n.p.

Folwell, William Watts. *A History of Minnesota.* St. Paul, Minnesota Historical Society. 1921-1930. 4 vols.

Galena Gazette, Galena, Illinois.

Gates, Charles M., ed. *Five Fur Traders of the Northwest.* University of Minnesota Press. 1933.

Hansen, Marcus Lee. *Old Fort Snelling 1819-1858.* Iowa City, Iowa State Historical Society. 1918. (In 1917 there was published a pamphlet of this title.)

History of Madison County, Illinois. Edwardsville, Illinois, 1882. W. R. Brink & Co.

Homans, Benjamin, ed. *Army and Navy Chronicle,* Washington, D.C. Vols. 1-13, 1835-1842.

Hoffmann, M. M. *Antique Dubuque 1673-1833.* Dubuque Telegraph-Herald Press. 1930.

Hosmer, James Kendall. *History of Louisiana Purchase.* New York. 1902. (Expansion of the Republic Series.)

Hosmer, James Kendall. *A Short History of the Mississippi Valley by James K. Hosmer.* Boston & New York. Houghton. 1901.

Houck, Louis. *A History of Missouri from the Earliest Explorations and Settlements until the Admission of the State into the Union, by Louis Houck.* Chicago. R. R. Donnelley & Sons Co. 1908.

Houck, Louis, ed. *The Spanish Regime in Missouri.* . . . Chicago. R. R. Donnelley & Sons Company. 1909.

Illinois Catholic Historical Society. *Mid-America, an Historical Review.* (Formerly *Illinois Catholic Historical Review*), Chicago. 1918-date. Vol. 1-17.

Illinois State Historical Library. *Collections.* Springfield 1903-1935. 25 vol.

Iowa Journal of Politics and History, editor, Benjamin F. Shambaugh, 1903-1936. State Historical Society of Iowa, Iowa City, Iowa.

Jacks, Leo Vincent. *La Salle.* New York. London. Scribner's. 1931.

Johnson, Ida Amanda. *The Michigan Fur Trade.* Lansing. Michigan Historical Commission. 1919.

Joutel, Henri. *Joutel's Journal of La Salle's Last Voyage* . . . Albany, N.Y. J. McDonough. 1906.

Kappler, Charles J. Ll.M., Clerk to the Senate Committee on Indian Affairs, ed. *Indian Affairs, Laws and Treaties.* Washington. Government Printing Office 1904. *Volume II: Treaties.* (In the Milwaukee Public Library this is indexed as Senate Document Vol. 39, 58th Congress 2nd Session, 1903-04.)

Keating, William H. *Narrative of an Expedition to the Source of St. Peter's River. . . . Performed in the Year 1823 . . . under the Command of Stephen H. Long.* Phila. H. C. Carey & I. Lea. 1824. 2 vol.

Kellogg, Louise Phelps. *The British Régime in Wisconsin and the Northwest.* Published by the State Historical Society of Wisconsin. Madison. 1935.

Kellogg, Louise Phelps, ed. *Early Narratives of the Northwest, 1634-1699.* N.Y. Scribner's 1917.

Kellogg, Louise Phelps. *The French Régime in Wisconsin and the Northwest.* Madison. State Historical Society of Wisconsin. 1925.

Le Page du Pratz. *The History of Louisiana. . . .* London. T. Becket & P. A. De Hondt. 1763.

Long, John. *Voyages and Travels of an Indian Interpreter and Trader.* London. 1791.

Long, (Major) Stephen H., Topographical Engineer United States Army. *Voyage in a Six-oared Skiff to the Falls of St. Anthony in 1817. . . .* Introduction by Edward D. Neill. pub. originally by Ashmead. Phila. 1860. (See Vol. II *Minnesota Historical Collections.* pub. 1889.)

Lyman, George D. *John Marsh, Pioneer, the Life Story of a Trail-Blazer on Six Frontiers.* New York. Scribner's. 1930.

Mahan, Bruce E. *Old Fort Crawford and the Frontier.* Published at Iowa City, Iowa, in 1926 by the State Historical Society of Iowa.

Marryatt, Frederick. *A Diary in America, with Remarks on its Institutions.* Phila. Carey and Hart. 1839. 2 vol.

Martin, Francis Xavier. *The History of Louisiana from the Earliest Period.* New Orleans. Lyman & Beardslee. 1827-29. 2 vol.

Myer, Jesse S. *Life and Letters of Dr. William Beaumont.* St. Louis. 1912.

Michigan Pioneer and Historical Society. *Historical Collections* 1874-1929. Lansing, Michigan. 40 vol.

Miller, William Snow. *William Beaumont, M.D., Pioneer in Physiology.* n.p. [1931]

Minnesota Historical Society. *Collections of the Minnesota Historical Society.* St. Paul. 1872-1920. 18 vol.

Mississippi Valley Historical Association. *Mississippi Valley Historical Review; Published Quarterly.* 1914-date. [Lincoln, Neb.]. *Proceedings.* Cedar Rapids, Iowa. The Torch Press.

Muldoon, Sylvan J. *Alexander Hamilton's Pioneer Son.* The Aurand Press. Harrisburg, Pa. 1930.

Neill, Edward Duffield. *The History of Minnesota: from the Earliest French Explorations to the Present Time.* By Edward Duffield Neill. Philadelphia. Lippincott. 1858.

Niles' Weekly Register. Baltimore, Md. 1811-1849. 75 vol.

North Dakota State Historical Society. *Collections.* 1906-1928. *North Dakota Historical Quarterly.* 1928-date. Bismarck, N.D.

Nute, Grace Lee. *The Voyageur.* N.Y. and London. Appleton. 1931.

Palimpsest, The. Issued Monthly by the State Historical Society of Iowa. Iowa City. 1920-date. 16 vol.

Porter, Kenneth Wiggins. *John Jacob Astor, Business Man.* Camb. 1931. (Harvard Studies in Business History, I) 2 vol.

Prairie du Chien Patriot, Prairie du Chien, Wisconsin.

Quaife, Milo Milton. *Chicago and the Old Northwest 1673-1835.* A Study of the Evolution of the Northwestern Frontier, together with a History of Fort Dearborn. Chicago. 1913.

Quebec. *Rapport de l'archiviste de la province de Quebec.* Redempti Paradis, Imprimeur de sa majeste le roi. 1929-30; 1930-31; 1931-32; 1932-33; 1921-22.

Richman, Irving Berdine. *Ioway to Iowa, the Genesis of a Corn and Bible Commonwealth,* by Irving Berdine Richman. Iowa City, Iowa. The State Historical Society of Iowa. 1931.

Salesianum. pub. quarterly at St. Francis Seminary, St. Francis, Wisconsin.

Scharf, John Thomas. *History of St. Louis City and County from the Earliest Periods to the Present Day:* Including Biographical Sketches of Representative Men. Philadelphia. L. H. Everts & Co. 1883. 2 vol.

Schlarman, J. H. *From Quebec to New Orleans, the Story of the French in America.* 1929. Buechler Publishing Co. Belleville, Illinois.

Shea, John Gilmary, ed. *Early Voyages up and down the Mississippi.* (1851). By Cavelier, St. Cosme, Le Sueur, Gravier, and Guignas. Albany. J. Munsell. 1861.

South Dakota Historical Collections. Aberdeen, S.D. 1902-34. 17 vol.

Steck, Francis Borgia, *The Jolliet-Marquette Expedition.* Washington, D.C. The Catholic University of America. 1927.

Stevens, Wayne Edson. *The Northwest Fur Trade 1763-1800.* Urbana. 1928. (Illinois, University of. Studies in the Social Sciences v. 14, no. 3.)

Stone, William Leete. *Life and Times of Sr. William Johnson, Bart.* Albany, 1865. 2 vol.

Tanguay, (L'Abbé) Cyprien. *Dictionnaire Genealogique des Familles Canadiennes depuis la Fondation de la Colonie jusqu' a nos Jours.* 1871. Quebec. 7 vol.

Thwaites, Reuben Gold, ed. *Early Western Travels 1748-1846.* . . .
Cleveland, O. The A. H. Clark Co. 1904-07. 3 vol.

Thwaites, Reuben Gold, ed. *The Jesuit Relations and Allied Documents.*
. . . *1610-1791* . . . Cleveland. The Burrows Brothers Company.
1896-1901.

Thwaites, Reuben Gold, ed. *Lahontan, Louis Armand de Lom d'Arce,
baron de 1666-1715 (?) New Voyages to North America* . . . Chicago. McClurg. 1905.

United States, Congress. *American State Papers: Public Lands Vol. V.*
pub. 1860 Washington by Gales and Seaton. (In Duff Green edition *Public Lands,* Vol. IV.

Wallace, William Stewart, ed. *Documents Relating to the Northwest
Company (Publications of the Champlain Society*—vol. 22) 1934.
Toronto.

Wisconsin State Historical Society. *Collections of the State Historical Society of Wisconsin.* Vol. 1-31 1854-1931. Madison, 1855-1931.
Proceedings of the Wisconsin State Historical Society. 1887-1932.
(1889-Turner: "Character and Influence of Fur Trade in Wisconsin.")

Wood, Edwin Orin. *Historic Mackinac* . . . New York. Macmillan. 1918.
2 vol.

Wrong, George McKinnon. *The Conquest of New France, a Chronicle
of the Colonial Wars.* New Haven. Yale University Press. 1918.
(Chronicles of America Series.)

UNPUBLISHED SOURCES

Bailly, Alexis. "Papers" in manuscript departments, Minnesota Historical Society and Wisconsin Historical Society.

Carver, Jonathan. "Journal." Manuscript copy, Minnesota Historical
Society.

Church Records: Dubuque, Iowa—St. Raphael's Church and Archdiocese of Dubuque
    Galena, Illinois—St. Michael's Church
    Prairie du Chien—St. Gabriel's Church
    Prairie du Rocher—St. Joseph's Church
    St. Louis, Missouri and Ste. Genevieve, Missouri—
    Jefferson Memorial Library, St. Louis, Missouri, and
    University of St. Louis.

County Records: Crawford County, Wisconsin. Records in Probate
    Court; Offices of County Clerk; Clerk of Court;
    Register of Deeds, Prairie du Chien, Wisconsin.
    Dubuque County, Iowa. Pertinent records (especially

marriages) in the office of Clerk of Court, Dubuque, Iowa.

Jo Daviess County, Illinois. Pertinent records (especially marriages) in the office of Clerk of Court, Galena, Illinois.

Dousman, Hercules L. "Papers." Minnesota Historical Society.

Gratiot, Charles. "Papers." Missouri Historical Society, St. Louis, Missouri; Wisconsin Historical Society, Madison, Wisconsin.

Hudson's Bay Company. Pertinent Records of Traders. Manuscript material used and "reproduced by permission of the Governor and Committee of the Hudson's Bay Company."

Letters. Specific references are given wherever these are used.

Sibley, Henry H. "Papers." Minnesota Historical Society.

United States. Washington, D.C. Records in the Interior Department; War Department, including Adjutant General's Office, Inspector General's Office, Judge Advocate General's Office, and Quartermaster Department.

Notes

1. Reuben Gold Thwaites, ed., *Jesuit Relations and Allied Documents*, LIX, 87-163; J. H. Schlarman, *From Quebec to New Orleans*, pp. 55-78; Francis B. Steck, *The Jolliet-Marquette Expedition*.

2. *Wisconsin Historical Collections*, XVI, 110.

3. Louise P. Kellogg, *The French Régime in Wisconsin and the Northwest*, pp. 207-225; Reuben Gold Thwaites, *Wisconsin in Three Centuries*, I, 230.

4. Kellogg, *French Régime*, pp. 240-260; *Wis. Hist. Colls.*, XVI, 143-160; V, 110-113.

5. Reuben Gold Thwaites, ed., *Lahontan's New Voyages to North America*.

6. *Wis. Hist. Colls.*, XVI, 173-199.

7. *Ibid.*, XVI, 208-210; Kellogg, *French Régime*, p. 273.

8. Schlarman, *From Quebec to New Orleans*, p. 118, footnote.

9. Kellogg, *French Régime*, p. 273.

10. See Appendix A for detailed information on these licenses.

11. *Rapport de l'archiviste de la province de Quebec*, 1929-30. In the index the name Messier, Rene *dit* Du Chesne is listed.

12. *Wis. Hist. Colls.*, XVII, 10-15.

13. *Ibid.*, XVII, 31-35.

14. *Ibid.*, XVII, 36-38.

15. *Ibid.*, XVII, 151.

16. *Rapport de l'archiviste de la province de Quebec*, 1929-30; *Wis. Hist. Colls.*, XVII, 230.

17. *Wis. Hist. Colls.*, XVII, 274.

1. See Appendix A for details of trade activity of the Marins and others.

2. Abbe Cyprien Tanguay, *Dictionnaire Genealogique des Familles Canadiennes* is the source of this and other information in this chapter on births, marriages, deaths.

3. Manuscript sketch of Paul Marin, based on Canadian Archives. This is in the possession of the Wisconsin Historical Library, Madison, Wisconsin.

4. Kellogg, *French Régime*, p. 296.

5. *Wis. Hist. Colls.*, XVII, 99, 143; V, 106-107. This is supported by a statement in a letter of Rev. Francis Vincent Badin in *Annals of the Society for the Propagation of the Faith*, IV, 537. [The Menomonis live on the banks of the Fox River at Butte des Morts] "ou le general Marin

detruisit presque toute la nation, il y a 60 ou 70 ans," [whence the place takes its name.]

6. *Wis. Hist. Colls.*, XVII, 364.
7. *Ibid.*, XVII, 446.
8. Manuscript sketch of Paul Marin.
9. *Wis. Hist. Colls.*, XVII, 451-455; XVIII, 7-10.
10. *Ibid.*, XVIII, 76-80, 85.
11. *Rapport de l'archiviste*, 1930-31.
12. *Wis. Hist. Colls.*, XVIII, 66.
13. *Ibid.*, XVIII, 193.
14. Schlarman, *From Quebec to New Orleans*, p. 295.
15. *Wis. Hist. Colls.*, XVII, 430.
16. *Ibid.*, XVIII, 158.
17. *Ibid.*, XVIII, 164-166.
18. *Ibid.*, XVIII, 196, footnote.
19. Kellogg, *French Régime*, pp. 425-426.
20. *Wis. Hist. Colls.*, XVIII, 167-195.
21. *Ibid.*, XVIII, 204.
22. *Ibid.*, XVIII, 206.

NOTES ON CHAPTER FOUR

1. This list is in the possession of the Wisconsin Historical Library.

2. *Michigan Pioneer and Historical Collections*, X, 480, 487; *History of Madison County, Illinois*, Chapter VII.

3. *Mich. Pion.*, IX, 548, ff.; *Wis. Hist. Colls.*, XII, 54-55. These accounts differ. Before the expedition started, a party of Sioux captured and confiscated a boatload of ammunition and provisions, carrying a Spanish license and intended for the trade at Prairie du Chien. It had 17 men, 50 tons of lead ore, and provisions. The account of Kay, owner of the boat, differs.

4. See Lee's map, p. 186.
5. *Wis. Hist. Colls.*, XII, 92.
6. *Ibid.*, IX, 291-292.
7. See Lee's map, p. 186.
8. *Wis. Hist. Colls.*, XVIII, 263.
9. Samuel Mazzuchelli, *Memoirs*, p. 163.
10. See page 68.
11. Frederic Louis Billon, *Annals of St. Louis under the French*, p. 227.

NOTES ON CHAPTER FIVE

1. *Mich. Pion.*, XIX, 630-631; X, 487.
2. *Wis. Hist. Colls.*, I, 25-48.
3. *Ibid.*, XVIII, 268.

4. *Ibid.*, XVIII, 263.

5. *Ibid.*, XII, 27-39; XVIII, 278, 279, footnote.

6. *Ibid.*, VI, 226.

7. *Ibid.*, XVIII, 292.

8. *Wis. Hist. Colls.*, XVIII, 339-341.

9. Charles M. Gates, ed., *Five Fur Traders of the Northwest*, p. 15.

10. *Wis. Hist. Colls.*, XVIII, 356.

11. *Ibid.*, XVIII, 370.

12. *Ibid.*, XI, 150.

13. *Ibid.*, XI, 105, footnote.

14. *Mich. Pion.*, X, 306.

First group: J. Sanguinet, M. Ange, Matheu Lessy and McCrae were to receive goods, serving as a committee while another group, a special committee, J. M. DuCharme, Henry Bostwick, Pierre Hurtebise and Ben Lyon were to outfit the traders but only by permission of the commanding officer. Robert Aird, Etienne Campion and L. DuCharme signed the agreement as a committee. Other names were: David McCrae & Co., J. B. Guillon (guion), W. Gosse, Ezekial Solomon, August Chabollois, John McNamara, A. Campion, Gamelin, George Cohn & Co., William Grant, J. G. Zanelius, P. Chabollier, Theodore Grahame, James Aird. Second group: 32 names of which these few are given here: Michel Ange, located Kalamazoo; Augustine Dubuque, Montreal; Francis Cardinal, La Pointe; Jean Bapt. Guillon, Montreal; Alexis Hamelin and P. Antaya, Mississippi River; Laurent DuCharme, Montreal; Pierre Grignon, Green Bay; Pierre Hurtebise, St. Joseph; Joseph Gravelle, Mississippi River.

15. *Mich. Pion.*, XIX, 508-509.

16. *Ibid.*, IX, 546-750. John Sayer, acting for Joseph Howard, Montreal merchant, presented a bill for supplies used by the Indians who went against Illinois. It was paid August 6, 1781. Items: flour, 5000 lbs.; tobacco, 600 lbs.; salt, 58 bu.; pork, 22 lbs.; galls taffia, 13½ gals.; fusils, 7; powder, 100 lbs.; shot, 50 lbs.; corn, 50 bags.

Also, *Wis. Hist. Colls.*, XI, 108-109, footnote; 154-157; 161-162.

17. *Wis. Hist. Colls.*, VII, 176; XVIII, 411; *Mich. Pion.*, IX, 558. Lt. Phillips was at "La Prairie du Chien" April 27, 1780 as is shown by a letter written by him to Lt. Clowes. He was reported by his commanding officer as being at Prairie du Chien June 4. These references are at variance with a statement in *Wis. Hist. Colls.*, XVIII, 411, but in accord with a statement in *Wis. Hist. Colls.*, XI, 148, here quoted: "Mr. Hesse is ordered not to move from his first stand until I send him instructions by Sgt. (J. F.) Phillips of the 8th Regt., who will set out from this (Mackinac) on the 10th of March with a very noted chief Machiquawish and his band of Indians."

Sinclair ordered Capt. Hesse to assemble his Indians at Portage to await Sgt. Phillips "who will set out from Mackinac March 10, 1780 with Matchekewis and unite with other Indians of Prairie du Chien for attack on St. Louis. (See *Mich. Pion.*, IX, 546.)

NOTES ON CHAPTER SIX

1. There were four distinct LaPointe families—I. (Old) *Pierre* Lapointe married a sister of Wabasha; he had two daughters: Pelagia who married 1) Louis Crawford, and had a son and a daughter; and 2) Alexis Lachapelle; and Victoria who married Edward Pizanne and had no children. II. Three brothers who came about 1795 and were distantly related to Pierre: *Charles* married 1) Pelagia LaPierre and had a son, Charles, Jr., who married Marie Larocque; 2) Suzanne Antaya (daughter of Michel Antaya); 3) Josette Antaya (daughter of Pierre Antaya); 4) Catherine Larocque; *Francois,* a farmer, who married Marie Antaya, daughter of Michel Antaya. He had a son, Barthelmy, who married twice, and a grandson, Frederick, who also married twice and whose descendants are living in Prairie du Chien; *Pierre* married Marie Antaya, daughter of Pierre Antaya. This man had no land claim and was perhaps a boatman or laborer. III. *Michel* who was not related to the others was adopted by John Simpson and married the widow of Francis Lapointe. IV. *Jean Baptiste* came from St. Louis about 1830 on the river boats. (Church records, St. Gabriel's Church, Prairie du Chien.)

2. *American State Papers:* IV, *Public Lands,* "Private Land Claims of Prairie du Chien," p. 867; see also map p. 186 and Chapter XII, pp. 185-188.

3. P. L. and Marian Scanlan, "Basil Giard and His Land Claim in Iowa," *Iowa Journal of Politics and History,* XXX, 219-247, gives a complete account of this.

4. "Records," St. Gabriel's Church; "Records," Register of Deeds Office, Prairie du Chien.

5. "Records," St. Gabriel's Church; letter of Mrs. Waldron to the author.

6. *Wis. Hist. Colls.,* VI, 201.

7. *Mich. Pion.,* IX, 658; Church records.

8. Church records.

9. *Wis. Hist. Colls.,* XI, 164; XVIII, 465.

10. *Ibid.,* XI, 164-166.

11. *Ibid.,* X, 339.

12. *Ibid.,* XII, 134-135.

13. *Mich. Pion.,* XXXVII, 508; *Wis. Hist. Colls.,* XIX, 301-303.

14. *Mich. Pion.,* XI, 514; XXIII, 633-642; *Wis. Hist. Colls.,* XII, 88. In addition to the interpreters, whose names have been given, a large number of traders and boatmen were in the region of Prairie du Chien.

Traders: Aird, James; Altinic *dit* La Violette, Gabriel; Antaya, Pierre; Blondeau, Nic; Cadotte, J. B.; Cameron, Murdoch; Campion, Etienne; Cardinal, Francois; Chaboillier, Louis; Dubuc, Augustine; Giasson, J.; Hamelin, Alex; Laframbois, Alex; Lagoterie, Ben; Lamarche, ?; La Motte, ?; Lapointe, Pierre; Lariviere, Hypolite; Larocque, Joseph; Marchesseau, Nicholas; Mitchell, ?; Muldrom, ?; Patterson, Allen; Patterson, Charles; Perrault, J. B.; Tesson, Louis Honore; Todd; Winter, ?. Boatmen: Barthelmy, ?; Cardine, Louis; Chevalier, Baptiste; Gigaire [Giguere], Antoine; Madore, ?; Plamandon, Tim; Steben, Jerry. Clerks: Debeau, Ambrose—for Aird; Le Bathe, Michel—for Patterson. Others: Ganot, ?; Reed, John; Tagolene, Ben.

15. "British Licenses," 1769-1790. Manuscript Department, Wisconsin Historical Library. See Appendix A for detailed information.

16. *American State Papers: IV, Public Lands.* There is a tradition that at one time Dubuque was the husband of a Prairie du Chien woman, Pelagia Lapierre. She was the first wife of Charles Lapointe, Senior, and the mother of Charles Lapointe, Junior, born in 1804. For detailed information on Julien Dubuque and Dubuque's Mines see M. M. Hoffmann, *Antique Dubuque.*

17. *Mich. Pion.,* XXXVII, 508.

18. Capt. Anderson ordered Michel Brisbois to fix up Fisher's building to store the supplies of the British army in 1814. *Wis. Hist. Colls.,* IX, 222.

19. See p. 58.

20. *Wis. Hist. Colls.,* XVIII, 463.

21. *Ibid.,* XVIII, 456-457.

22. *Ibid.,* XII, 106.

NOTES ON CHAPTER SEVEN

1. *Wis. Hist. Colls.,* XIX, 295.

2. *Ibid.,* IX, 137-206.

3. See p. 101.

4. *Wis. Hist. Colls.,* XX, 59-60.

5. Pike, *Expeditions,* p. 280.

6. Statement made to the author by Sam Barrette, Prairie du Chien, a great-grandson of Antaya; *Wis. Hist. Colls.,* XIX, 267-269.

7. Kenneth Porter, *John Jacob Astor, Business Man,* I, 60.

8. *Ibid.,* I, 167, 413; Hiram Martin Chittenden, *The American Fur Trade in the Far West,* I, 309: "Mr. Astor was the company and the incorporation was merely a fiction intended to broaden and facilitate its operations."

9. *Minnesota Historical Society Collections,* III, 168; "Dousman and Bailly Papers," Manuscript Department, Minnesota Historical Library.

10. *Wis. Hist. Colls.,* IX, 179.

11. Porter, *John Jacob Astor,* I, 182; Chittenden, *American Fur Trade,* I, 182-183.

12. Louise Phelps Kellogg, *The British Régime in Wisconsin and the Northwest,* p. 255.

13. Porter, *John Jacob Astor,* I, 461.

14. *Ibid.*

15. *Wis. Hist. Colls.,* XIX, 343-344.

16. *Ibid.,* XIX, 344-345.

17. *Mich. Pion.,* XV, 69.

18. This is not true. See p. 196.

19. *Wis. Hist. Colls.,* XIX, 355-357.

20. *Ibid.,* XIX, 355, footnote.

21. See p. 121.

22. *Wis. Hist. Colls.,* X, 129.

23. Porter, *John Jacob Astor,* II, 690.

24. *Ibid.,* II, 695; Chittenden, *American Fur Trade,* I, 310.

25. Porter, *John Jacob Astor,* II, 698; *Mich. Pion.,* XXXVII, 483.

26. See p. 101.

27. Porter, *John Jacob Astor,* II, 697; *Wis. Hist. Colls.,* XIX, 414.

28. Whether these goods were sent by both partners or by Astor alone is not clear. Porter, *John Jacob Astor,* II, 697.

29. Porter, *John Jacob Astor,* II, 699-700.

30. *Wis. Hist. Colls.,* XIX, 326.

31. *Ibid.,* XIX, 454.

32. *Ibid.,* XIX, 386.

33. "Indian Office, Unarranged," (four boxes), Manuscript Department, Library of Congress, Washington, D.C.

34. *Ibid.*

35. "Deeds," Book A, p. 229, Register of Deeds Office, Prairie du Chien; "Marriages," same office.

36. *Wis. Hist. Colls.,* XX, 256.

37. *Am. State Papers* (Gales and Seaton): Indian Affairs, Vol. II, p. 534.

38. The total shown in Johnson's first quarterly report—June 30, 1816—was $23,215.16. These items represented not a year's business but a quarter's, since this inventory corresponded to a quarterly report.

39. *Wis. Hist. Colls.,* XIX, 474.

40. Porter, *John Jacob Astor,* II, 701.

41. *Wis. Hist. Colls.,* XX, 42.

42. *Ibid.,* XX, 55, 59.

43. Porter, *John Jacob Astor,* II, 707.

44. *Wis. Hist. Colls.,* XX, 118.

45. *Ibid.,* XX, 125.

46. *Ibid.,* XX, 150-151.

47. *Ibid.*, XX, 162.
48. *Ibid.*, IX, 466.
49. "Deeds," Book A, Register of Deeds Office, Prairie du Chien.
50. Porter, *John Jacob Astor,* II, 716.
51. *Ibid.*, II, 734.
52. See map, p. 192. This shows the property of the American Fur Company as extending 600 feet north from the street now known as Black Hawk Avenue and fronting Main Village Lots 21 to 24 inclusive. Main Village Lot No. 13, two blocks north of Lots 21-24.
53. See p. 160.
54. See map, p. 187. The next transfer of this property (lot No. 13) was Abbott to Hercules L. Dousman in 1836.
55. See p. 96.
56. Porter, *John Jacob Astor,* II, 718.
57. *Wis. Hist. Colls.,* XX, 212.
58. Porter, *John Jacob Astor,* II, 736; *Wis. Hist. Colls.,* XX, 373.
59. Bills, Indian Files, Interior Department.
60. Porter, *John Jacob Astor,* II, 739.
61. *Ibid.*, II, 760; Chittenden, *American Fur Trade,* II, 823.
62. Porter, *John Jacob Astor,* II, 737.
63. *Ibid.*, II, 787-788, note 97.
64. Indian Files, 1825, Interior Department.
65. *Wis. Hist. Colls.,* XX, 360.
66. *Ibid.*, XX, 369.
67. Porter, *John Jacob Astor,* II, 746.
68. *Ibid.*, II, 807.
69. *Ibid.*, II, 779; 858-859. Mortgages given Astor by the Green Bay Company including Jacques Porlier, John Lawe, Augustin Grignon, Louis Grignon, and Louis Rouse, cost them about five thousand acres near Green Bay. A mortgage on 200 acres of Rolette's land was signed by Rolette and his wife August 29, 1836 to settle a note of Astor. Chittenden, *American Fur Trade,* I, 167, footnote: "W. W. Astor in a magazine article upon his illustrious ancestor says that this corporate body (the American Fur Company) was simply a 'fiction intended to broaden and facilitate his operations.' "
70. "Indian Files," Interior Department.

NOTES ON CHAPTER EIGHT

1. Elliott Coues, ed., *Zebulon M. Pike, Expeditions to Headwaters of the Mississippi River during the Years 1805-06-07,* I, 1, 8, 38, 83, 200; *Wis. Hist. Colls.,* IX, 172; XVIII, 440, footnote; XIX, 315; "History of Fort Crawford," manuscript in Adjutant General's Office, Washington, D.C.
2. *Wis. Hist. Colls.,* II, 128; IX, 218.

3. *Ibid.*, XI, 286, footnote.

4. *Ibid.*, XI, 278.

5. "History of Fort Crawford," AGO.

6. *Missouri Gazette*, June, 1814; *Wis. Hist. Colls.*, III, 274, footnote.

7. "Old Records," AGO. Photostatic copy of Perkins' report in the possession of the author.

8. "History of Fort Crawford," AGO. List follows. Names of officers: Joseph Perkins, Lt. 24 US Inf; George Kennerly, Capt. Militia; James Kennerly, Lt. Militia; John McKenzie, Serg. 7th Inf; Robert Morrison, Serg. 24th Inf; James Kearns, Serg. 7th Inf; Henry Hopkins, Corp., 7th Inf; Easton Nance, Corp., 7th Inf; Edmund Hollanno, Corp., 7th Inf; Lot Porter Fifer. Privates; 7th Infantry: John Bryarly; John Been; David Bigger; Anthony W. Byard; Edward Brunner; David Brown; Henry Brumer; William Bennet; Peter Benman; Henry Barnhart; Benj. Corp; Booker Davis; James Doherty; James Davourez; John Iford; James Johnson; Thomas M. Jefferson; Daniel Fink; Saml. McBride; James McBride; James Murphy; Lewis McCarys; John Martin; Thos. McClaine; Thomas Marshall; William Marsh; John Page; Pleasant Philips; Henry Reese; Epram Richardson; John Runnalds; James Robertson; Harmon Seers; Gustavus Smith; Elisha Trader; Hugh Tranner; Elijah Tuel; Thurston Vaughn; James Kennedy; Samuel Gray; John Gamblin; William Howell; William Heres; Henry Hall; John Hall; John Hall; Thomas Moore; Ely Anderson; Greenberry Baker; Ezekiel Gibs. Total—50 privates, 7th Infantry.

9. "Letters—Andrew Jackson," Indian Files, Interior Department, Washington, D.C.

10. *Wis. Hist. Colls.*, XIII, 1-162; "History of Fort Crawford," AGO.

11. "History of Fort Crawford," AGO.

12. "Muster Roll of Rifle Regiment, 1816," Old Records, AGO.

13. Sylvan J. Muldoon, *Alexander Hamilton's Pioneer Son.* So many have mistaken this Col. William Sutherland Hamilton, U.S.A., for Col. William Stephen Hamilton, son of Alexander Hamilton (first Secretary of the Treasury and killed in a duel with Aaron Burr), that this is a good place to correct any such impression. Alexander Hamilton's son, William Stephen, was at one time a cadet at West Point, but he early left school and sought his fortune in the West, arriving in Illinois in 1817; for a time he was assistant to a surveyor and later became Colonel of Illinois militia. He it was who formed the military escort of La Fayette when he visited St. Louis and Kaskaskia in 1825. He did not come to Fort Crawford as a regular army officer.

14. *South Dakota Historical Collections*, I, 126.

15. "Letter Files," AGO. Photostat copy of this letter in possession of the author.

16. "History of Fort Crawford," AGO; *Wis. Hist. Colls.*, XIX, 479; Letter from Virginia Historical Society to the author.

17. *Wis. Hist. Colls.*, XIX, 397, footnote.

18. Edgar Bruce Wesley, *Guarding the Frontier*, p. 138, footnote.

19. "Inspection Report of Lt. Col. Hamilton at Belle Fontaine, February 29, 1816," Letter File, AGO.

20. *Wis. Hist. Colls.* XI, 393, footnote.

21. "Letters," Letter of John Jacob Astor, May 26, 1826, Indian Files, Interior Department. For fort location, see maps on p. 136 and p. 140.

22. *Wis. Hist. Colls.*, II, 128-129.

23. "General Order Book," IV, 166, Testimony at court martial: "December 6, 1825, alarmed camp by discharge of firearms . . . had a fit November 17, 1825 . . . disturbed camp during night by discharging firearms, sounding the 'long roll' or 'to arms' upon the arms."

24. *Wis. Hist. Colls.*, II, 230.

25. "Regiment Returns," AGO: *Wis. Hist. Colls.*, VI, 263; II, 229; footnote.

26. "Regiment Returns," AGO: "Letters," Letter of Maj. Gen. McComb, August 30, 1819; *Wis. Hist. Colls.*, VI, 200-217.

27. "Regiment Returns," AGO.

28. "Inspection Reports," I, 110, Inspector General's Office, AGO.

29. *Minn. Hist. Colls.*, II, 9-83, Stephen H. Long, "Voyage in a Six-oared Skiff to the Falls of St. Anthony in 1817." Coues, ed. *Pike, Expedition*, I, 36, footnote, said he had a picture of this fort in his possession, but after his death his papers were sold and scattered. "Through the attentions of Wm. Hancock Clark of Detroit, Mich., I am in possession of a water-color picture of the fort roughly but tellingly done by his illustrious grandfather, William Clark, who with Governor Lewis Clark, effected the important treaty of Prairie du Chien, Aug. 19th, 1825. This measures 18 × 15 inches, and shows a part of the stockade straggling up to that one of the blockhouses which was on the hill or mound, as described by Long. The general effect upon the beholder is to suggest something of a cross between a penitentiary and a stockyard, but unsafe for criminals and too small for cattle."

30. "Regiment Returns," AGO.

31. *Wis. Hist. Colls.*, II, 149. Date given here (1821) must be wrong, for Findley signed official documents as late as May 12, 1823, as shown by records in the office of County Clerk, Prairie du Chien; *Minn. Hist. Colls.*, V, 390, 467; also, "Report of Major Cutler, 1825," Indian Files, Interior Department, refers to the death of these men at the hands of the Chippewa "last fall."

32. "Inspection Reports—1826," Inspector General's Office, AGO.

33. AGO. Letter to author.

34. See p. 160.

35. *Wis. Hist. Colls.*, V, 145-153.

36. St. Gabriel's Church Records, Prairie du Chien, Wisconsin. Photostat copies available at the Wisconsin Historical Library. Francois, born December 6, 1824; Marie Regis, born August 15, 1826.

37. Newspaper clipping from *The Statesman*, January 3, 1829, in James D. Doty's "Trials and Decisions in the Several Courts Held in the Counties of Michilimackinac, Brown and Crawford, 1823-1830," Manuscript volume in the Wisconsin Historical Library. John Scott, employed by the United States to prosecute eight Winnebago prisoners at Fort Crawford, charged the government $1000 for his services as prosecuting attorney. Charles Hempstead of Galena was paid $1050 for defending these Indians and Judge Doty also presented a bill in the case. He was a presiding judge at the trial held at Prairie du Chien in September, 1828. "Indian Files," Interior Department.

38. "Report of John Marsh—June 30, 1827"; *Ibid.*, July 4, 1827; *Ibid.*, July 10, 1827." Note discrepancy in dates. June 28 is correct. George D. Lyman, *John Marsh*, pp. 118-138; Burial Records, St. Gabriel's Church.

39. *Wis. Hist. Colls.*, II, 166-167.

40. Bruce Mahan, *Fort Crawford and the Frontier*, pp. 101-119; *Wis. Hist. Colls.*, V, 178-204; XI, 362, footnote; VIII, 264; *Annals of the Society for the Propagation of the Faith*, IV, 536-537.

41. "General Order Book—1825-1827," AGO.

42. "Post Returns—April 30, 1828," AGO; *Wis. Hist. Colls.*, VII, 265.

43. "Muster Roll," AGO; "Letters—Kearny," Letter File, AGO; *Wis. Hist. Colls.*, V, 238-239.

44. *Senate Document*, No. 191, 2nd Session 20th Congress.

45. *Wis. Hist. Colls.*, V, 238, footnote; "Letter Files—1832," AGO; "Surgeon General's Report, August 1, 1832," AGO.

46. Samuel Mazzuchelli, *Memoirs*, Chapter XXXVII, "The Temperance Society . . ."; Mahan, *Fort Crawford and the Frontier*, p. 262.

NOTES ON CHAPTER NINE

1. Mahan, *Fort Crawford and the Frontier*, p. 100.

2. See map, p. 187; "Deeds, Vol. D, Register of Deeds Office, Prairie du Chien; "Letters—1829," AGO; RDS 78 Flat, Engineers' Department, AGO. Photostat copy of map in possession of the author; *Wis Hist. Colls.*, V, 258.

3. "Letters," Letter of Garland, Quartermaster Department, Ft. Myers, Virginia. Photostat in possession of the author.

4. "Major Sherman's Report to Quartermaster General at St. Louis, July 13, 1856," AGO.

5. For sketch see *Appleton's Cyclopedia of American Biography.*

6. "Letters—1829," QM Department.

7. "Letters—1831," Letter of Garland March 20, 1831, QM Department.

8. *Wis. Hist. Colls.,* V, 243.

9. "Letters—1829," Letter of Garland to Jessup, August 30, 1829, and Letter of Garland to Jessup, October 9, 1829, QM Department.

10. *Ibid.,* Letter of Garland, August 31, 1829.

11. "Special Orders II, 1828-32," p. 188 and Letter of Taylor to Atkinson, May 26, 1832, AGO.

12. "Inspection Reports," Vol. III, p. 73, July 20, 1831, Inspector General's Office.

13. "Letters—1831," QM Department.

14. *Ibid.*

15. "Letters—1835," Letter of Stockton to Jessup, May 22, 1835, QM Department.

16. "Reports," Vol. III, p. 73, Inspector General's Office, AGO.

17. "Reports," Inspector General's Office, AGO.

18. "Orders, Western Department," June 26, 1830, AGO.

19. "Orders, War Department," August 4, 1830, AGO.

20. "Report of Street to Gen. Clark, May 7, 1830," Indian Files, Interior Department.

21. "Letter of Gen. Clark" dated St. Louis, May 28, 1830, Indian Files, Interior Department; *Wis. Hist. Colls.,* II, 170.

22. "Report of Street," August 1, 1831, Indian Files, Int. Dept.

23. "Letters," AGO, Letter of Taylor, October 30, 1833; Letter of Morgan, October 12, 1817; Letter of Street, October 24, 1831; Letter of Chambers, September 19, 1823.

24. See note 11 of this chapter.

25. "Old Records," AGO. Photostat copy in possession of the author. Likely half a mile north of Mt. Zion of today, at Mook's cemetery, next to highest point in Crawford County, about four miles from Soldiers' Grove.

26. *Niles' Weekly Register,* September 29, 1832; contains "Letter of Street dated at Prairie du Chien, August 27, 1832"; same letter in "Letters—1832," AGO.

27. *Wis. Hist. Colls.,* XII, 261; "Letters," Letter of Scott, August 10, 1832, AGO.

28. *Niles' Register,* September 1, 1832; *Mich. Pion.* XXXI, 345 ff.

29. "Post Returns, 1832," AGO: *Wis. Hist. Colls.,* II, 414, footnote; "Letters—1832," Letter of Street, July 24, 1832, AGO.

30. "Letters," Letter of Stambaugh dated at Cassville, August 11, 1832, AGO.

31. "Letters," Letter of Price dated at Cassville, August 14, 1832.

32. *Niles' Register,* October 20, 1832, "Letter of Colonel Loomis dated at Prairie du Chien, August 2, 1832; Indian Files, Int. Department, Letter of Street, August 2, 1832, Indian Files, Interior Department.

33. "Letters," Letter of Taylor, August 22, 1832, AGO.

34. *Wis. Hist. Colls.,* II, 259-262.

35. "Letters," AGO, Letter of Taylor, September 6, 1832; letter of Street to Scott dated at Rock Island, September 5, 1832.

36. "Orders and Special Orders, Eastern and Western Department," Vol. II, 1828-1832, Special Order No. I, p. 373, January 15, 1832; Special Order, p. 337. Photostats in possession of the author. "Muster Roll," April 30, 1832, shows E. A. Ogden Bvt. 2nd Lt. Co. B. This was Davis's position in the company and the "Brevet" shows Ogden as a substitute. "Muster Roll," June 30, 1832, shows Davis on leave of absence; left his post March 26, 1832; Ogden still Bvt. 2nd Lt. Co. B. "Muster Roll" shows that Davis returned to his company August 18, 1832. "Special Order" by which Col. Taylor put him in command of a detachment to accompany Black Hawk to Jefferson Barracks. Letter from *Annals of Iowa,* IV, p. 231.

37. "Muster Roll" of Fort Crawford for 1832 shows no one ill with cholera. It shows Dr. Beaumont present at the fort during May, June, July, and August up to August 23. "General Orders," 1828-1835, AGO. Dr. Beaumont went on leave of absence August 23, 1832. "Surgeon General's Report," 1832, AGO. Cholera first broke out among volunteer troops August 26 at Rock Island.

38. *Wis. Hist. Colls.,* V, 255-256.

39. "Muster Roll," Semi-annual report, June 30, 1832; "Regiment Returns," AGO.

40. *Army and Navy Chronicle,* I, 115, "Report of Quartermaster dated Washington City February 4, 1835," including undated report of commissioners Center and Doty; *American State Papers: Vol. V, Military Affairs,* p. 41. (This reference is to the Duff Green edition.)

41. "Order Book No. 2," 1830-1835, p. 308, Order No. 20, April 1, 1835, AGO; "Letters—1834-35," Book 15, Letter of Taylor, June 5, 1835.

42. *Wis. Hist. Colls.,* V, 258.

43. "Map" and "Field Notes" of J. A. Center on military road survey, Engineers' Department, AGO. Photostat copy of map showing original survey of military road in possession of the author.

44. "Envelope No. 203," Manuscript Department, Library of Congress.

45. "Regiment Returns," July, 1837, AGO.

46. *Wis. Hist. Colls.,* II, 157; Eng. Dept. B. 177, AGO, Letter of October 24, 1839; "Old Records," AGO, June 15 to July 3 [1840] "rest of the garrison engaged building road."

47. "Muster Roll," August 13, 1847, Remarks: Reference in AGO, July 11, 1846.

48. "Court Proceedings, Circuit Court, Prairie du Chien," 1853-54; also letter, December 9, 1858, Judge Advocate General's Office, AGO.

49. "Letters," QM Department, Letter—December 29, 1862; Letter—October 13, 1864; Letter—December 13, 1865.

50. "Deeds," Register of Deeds Office, Prairie du Chien.

51. For list of Commanding Officers, See Appendix B.

NOTES ON CHAPTER TEN

1. Charles J. Kappler, *Indian Treaties*, pp. 74-77.

2. *Ibid.*, Appendix, p. 1031; Coues, *Zebulon M. Pike, Expeditions*, I, 231, 269.

3. See Chapter XII, p. 184.

4. *Indian Treaties*, pp. 250-255; *Wis. Hist. Colls.*, II, 153.

Witnesses: Thomas Biddle, Secretary; R. A. McCabe, Captain, Fifth Infantry; R. A. Forsyth; N. Boilvin, United States Indian agent; C. C. Trowbridge, sub-Indian agent; Henry R. Schoolcraft, United States Indian agent; Thomas Forsyth, agent Indian affairs; Marvien Blondau; David Bailey; James M'Ilvaine, lieutenant United States Army; Law. Taliaferro, Indian agent for Upper Mississippi; John Holiday; William Dickson; S. Campbell, United States interpreter; J. A. Lewis; Wm. Holiday; Dunable Denejlevy; Bela Chapman.

5. Indian Files, Interior Department, Washington, D.C., "Report of Col. Morgan July 9, 1826." Photostat copies of testimony in possession of the author.

6. Caleb Atwater, *Remarks on a Tour to Prairie du Chien in 1829*, pp. 68-70.

7. *Indian Treaties*, pp. 297-300.

8. *Ibid.*, pp. 300-303.

9. Description of land as given in the Winnebago treaty: ". . . beginning on Rock River, at the mouth of the Pee-kee-tan-no or Pee-kee-tol-a-ka, a branch thereof; thence, up the Pee-kee-tol-a-ka, to the mouth of Sugar Creek; thence, by a line running due North, to the road leading from the Eastern blue mound, by the most Northern of the four lakes, to the portage of the Wisconsin and Fox rivers; thence, along the said road, to the crossing of Duck Creek; thence, by a line running in a direct course to the most Southeasterly bend of Lake Puck-a-way, on Fox River; thence, up said Lake and Fox River, to the Portage of the Wisconsin; thence, across said portage, to the Wisconsin river; thence, down said river, to the Eastern line of the United States' reservation at the mouth of said river, on the south side thereof, as described in the second article of the treaty made at St. Louis, on the twenty-

fourth day of August, in the year eighteen hundred and sixteen, with the Chippewas, Ottawas, and Potawatamies; thence, with the lines of a tract of country on the Mississippi river, (secured to the Chippewas, Ottawas, and Potawatamies, of the Illinois, by the ninth article of the treaty made at Prairie du Chien, on the nineteenth day of August, in the year eighteen hundred and twenty-five) running Southwardly, passing the heads of the small streams emptying into the Mississippi to the Rock river, at the Winnebaygo village, forty miles above its mouth; thence, up Rock river, to the mouth of the Pee-kee-tol-a-ka river, the place of beginning.

10. Atwater, *Tour to Prairie du Chien*, pp. 68-70.

11. Indian chief's welcome to Marquette and Jolliet. See Schlarman, *From Quebec to New Orleans*, pp. 62-63.

12. Half-breeds named in the Winnebago treaty: Catherine Myott; Mary, daughter of Catherine Myott; Michael St. Cyr, son of Hee-no-kau (a Winnebaygo woman); Mary, Ellen, and Brigitte, daughters of said Hee-no-kau; Catherine and Olivier, children of Olivier Amelle; Francois, Therese, and Joseph, children of Joseph Thibault; Sophia, daughter of Joshua Palen; Pierre Pacquette; his two children, Therese and Moses; Pierre Grignon L'Avoine, Amable, Margaret, Genevieve, and Mariette, children of said Pierre; Mauh-nah-tee-see (a Winnebaygo woman); her eight children, viz.: Therese, Benjamin, James, Simeon, and Phelise Leciiyer, Julian and Antoine Grignon, and Alexis Peyet; John Baptiste Pascal, Margaret, Angelique, Domitille, Therese, and Lisette, children of the late John Baptiste Pacquette; Madeline Brisbois, daughter of the late Michel Brisbois, Jr.; Therese Gagnier and her two children, Francois and Louise; Mary, daughter of Luther Gleason; Theodore Lupien.

13. Witnesses to the Winnebago treaty: Charles S. Hempstead, secretary to the commission; Joseph M. Street, Indian agent; John H. Kenzie, sub-agent Indian affairs; Z. Taylor, lieutenant-colonel, U. S. Army; H. Dodge; A. Hill; Henry Gratiot; Wm. Beaumont, surgeon, U. S. Army; G. W. Garey; Richard Gentry; James Turner; Richard H. Bell; John W. Johnson; Wm. M. Read; G. H. Kennerly; R. Holmes, U. S. Army; John Dallam; J. R. B. Gardenier, lieutenant, U. S. Infantry; Charles Chouteau; John Messersmith; John L. Chastain; Wm. D. Smith; Charles K. Henshaw; James B. Estis; Jesse Benton, Jr.; Jacob Hambleton; John Quaill; John Garland; Henry Crossle; J. L. Bogardus; B. B. Kercheval; Luther Gleason; Pierre Paquet, his (X) mark, Winnebago interpreter; J. Palen; Jacques Mette; Antoine Le Claire; Joge; M. Brisbois.

14. *Indian Treaties*, pp. 305-310.

15. Indian Files, Interior Department, 1835.

Signers: Gen. Taylor; Joseph M. Street; E. H. Hitchcock, Capt.

U. S. Army; T. M. Hill, Lt. U. S. Army; D. Lowry and Antoine Le Claire, Interpreters. Indian chiefs included Keokuk, Waukon, Wapello.

Claims allowed: 9 horses killed, Francois Duchoquette; one black mare killed, Louis Menard; hogs and canoe stolen, Charles Menard, Sr.

Claims disallowed: wood burned on Indian lands 12 miles above Prairie du Chien, Pierre La Chapelle; 2 stacks of hay burned, Jedediah P. Hall.

16. *Indian Treaties,* pp. 466-467.

17. *Ibid.,* pp. 498-500.

Claims presented: Nicolas Boilvin, $6,000; the other four children of Nicolas Boilvin, formerly agent $4,000 each; Catherine Myott, $1,000; Hyacinthe St. Cyr, $1,000; the widow of Henry Gratiot, late sub-agent, in trust for her eight children, $10,000; H. L. Dousman, in trust for the children of Pierre Paquette, late interpreter, $3,000; Joseph Brisbois, $2,000; John Roy, $2,000; Satterlee Clark, junior, $2,000; Antoine Grignon, $2,000; Jane F. Rolette, $2,000; George Fisher, $1,000; Therese Roy, $1,000; Domitille Brisbois, $1,000.

18. Manuscript Department, Congressional Library, "Envelope 207." List included recipients of $95,500: Theresa Paquette ($\frac{1}{4}$) daughter of Pierre; Moses, son of Pierre; Alexis Payer ($\frac{1}{2}$); Mary B. Gleason ($\frac{1}{2}$); Eliza Gleason ($\frac{1}{2}$); Wm. Gleason ($\frac{1}{2}$); Caroline Gleason ($\frac{1}{2}$); Sophia Campbell ($\frac{1}{2}$—late Sophia Palen); Mary Laurant ($\frac{1}{2}$); Antoine Grignon ($\frac{1}{4}$); Hypolite Grignon, brother—valuable service rendered by father; Archange Grignon ($\frac{1}{4}$); Mary Dougherty ($\frac{1}{2}$); Sarah B. Daugherty ($\frac{1}{4}$); James P. Dougherty ($\frac{1}{4}$); Mary Ann Dougherty ($\frac{1}{4}$); Leon Dougherty ($\frac{1}{4}$); Christine Laronda ($\frac{1}{2}$)—valuable services rendered by father and mother and other ancestors of claimant; Con Rasdell ($\frac{1}{2}$); Sarah Rasdell ($\frac{1}{2}$) William Chalifous ($\frac{1}{2}$); Louise Chalifous ($\frac{1}{2}$); Hannah Wood ($\frac{1}{2}$); Margaret Wood ($\frac{1}{2}$); Ho-no-nee-gah, wife of Stephen Mack ($\frac{3}{4}$); Rosa Mack ($\frac{3}{8}$); Mary Mack; Louise Mack; Thos. Mack; Antoine Grignon ($\frac{1}{2}$); Julia Grignon ($\frac{1}{2}$); Simon L'Ecuyer ($\frac{1}{2}$); Margaret L'Ecuyer ($\frac{1}{4}$); Mary L'Ecuyer ($\frac{1}{4}$); Julia L'Ecuyer ($\frac{1}{2}$); Lizette Thibault ($\frac{1}{2}$); Mary Myotte ($\frac{1}{4}$); Catherine Myotte age 49 ($\frac{1}{2}$)—important services to Indians; Margaret Deschamps ($\frac{1}{2}$); Michael St. Cyr, Sr. ($\frac{1}{2}$); Madeline Bauette ($\frac{1}{4}$); Baptiste Lasillier ($\frac{1}{2}$); Mary Bellair ($\frac{1}{2}$); Mary Bellair ($\frac{1}{4}$); Amable Grignon ($\frac{3}{4}$); Michael Brisbois age 22 ($\frac{1}{4}$); Peter Monague ($\frac{1}{4}$); Chas. Monague ($\frac{1}{4}$); Josette Benway ($\frac{1}{4}$); Benjamin L'Ecuyer, Jr. ($\frac{1}{4}$); Mary L'Ecuyer ($\frac{1}{4}$); Mary Ann L'Ecuyer ($\frac{1}{4}$); Benj. L'Ecuyer ($\frac{1}{4}$); James L'Ecuyer, Jr. ($\frac{1}{4}$); James L'Ecuyer, Sr. ($\frac{1}{2}$); David Twiggs ($\frac{1}{4}$); Therese Grignon (late Theresa Roy) ($\frac{1}{4}$); Sophia Paquette ($\frac{1}{4}$); Esther Paquette ($\frac{1}{4}$); Mary Ann Mitchell ($\frac{1}{4}$); Lewis Wood ($\frac{1}{2}$); Domitilee Legris ($\frac{1}{2}$); Joseph Legris ($\frac{1}{4}$);

M. A. Harrison (or Hanison) (¼); Wm. H. Harrison (¼); Jos. Harrison (¼); Lewis Pelkie (½); Peter Harrison (¼); John Funk, Jr. (½); Catherine Amelle (½); Louis Amelle (½); Joseph Amelle (½); Oliver Amelle, Jr. (½); Nancy Amelle (½); Francis Thibault (¼); Baptis. Thibault (¼); John Roy (¼); Catherine Roy (¼); Joseph Roy (¼); Simon Roy (¼); Jerome Roy (¼); Theresa Roy family; Theresa L'Ecuyer (½); Celeste Paquette (¼); Charlotte Carbona, Jr. (¼); Caroline Harney (¼); John B. Perault (¼); George Deseriviere (¼); (or Duevin); Christine Pallido (¼); Ah-hoo-pee-nee-kah (½); Joseph Thibault, Jr. (¼); Joseph Lasellier (½); John Bapt. Pion, Jr. (¼); Angelica Pion (¼)—services to Indians by mother and her own services as Indian interpreter at Indian school; Peter Roy (¼); Margarite LaChapelle (½); Baptiste Perault, Sr. (½); Baptiste Perault (¼); Florentine Perault (¼); Eliz. Perault (¼); Margarite Gruvelle (¼); Amelia Grunelle (¼); Francis Gruvelle, Jr. (¼); Bapt. Grunelle (¼); Mary Gunn (½); Louis Rob. Grignon (½); Charlotte Carbona, Sr. (½); Hu-tho-ke; Martha Boyd (¼); Angel Corbeille (¼). Added items: 5 children of F. Navalle; Frederick Oliva to make total of $100,000.

NOTES ON CHAPTER ELEVEN

1. *Indiana Historical Society Publications,* III, 110-112. Harrison was referred to at this time as "Governor of Indiana and Superintendent of Indian Affairs and Commissaire Plenopotentiary of United States."

2. *Wis. Hist. Colls.,* IX, 147.

3. Coues, *Pike: Expeditions,* I, 46, appendix.

4. *Wis. Hist. Colls.,* XIX, 314-316.

5. *Ibid.,* XIX, 323, footnote. See this on claim that Campbell was appointed Indian agent as early as 1802.

6. *Ibid.,* XIX, 324; *Mich. Pion.,* XL, 261.

7. *Mich. Pion.,* XL, 284.

8. *Wis. Hist. Colls.,* XI, 249-251.

9. See note 5 on Chapter VII.

10. *Wis. Hist. Colls.,* XIX, 342.

11. *Ibid.,* XII, 139-142.

12. "Old Records," AGO. Photostat copy in possession of the author.

13. "Dousman-Bailly Papers," Manuscript Department, Minnesota Historical Library.

14. *Minn. Hist. Colls.,* III, 168. Sketch of Faribault by Col. H. H. Sibley.

15. *Mich. Pion.,* XV, 246.

16. *Wis. Hist. Colls.,* XII, 125.

17. *Ibid.,* XIII, 46.

18. *Ibid.,* IX, 202.

19. *Ibid.,* XIX, 424.

20. *Ibid.,* II, 119.

21. "Records," St. Gabriel's Church.

22. *Minn. Hist. Colls.,* II, 56-64.

23. *Wis. Hist. Colls.,* VI, 263-264; *Wisconsin Magazine of History,* March, 1920.

24. Probate Court Records show this as one of the bills allowed against Aird's estate in 1819. "Record of Crawford County Commissioners," Office of County Clerk, Prairie du Chien.

25. *Wisconsin Magazine of History,* March, 1920.

26. *Wis. Hist. Colls.,* VI, 257; "Marriages," Register of Deeds Office, Prairie du Chien.

27. "Deeds," Book A, pp. 415-421, Office of Register of Deeds, Prairie du Chien; *Wis. Hist. Colls.,* VI, 244 ff. In 1822 the Land Office refused to acknowledge the claim, but certain interests persisted and in 1832 a New York group known as the Mississippi Land Company tried to revive it. They retained Doty as their agent but were no more successful then than earlier.

NOTES ON CHAPTER TWELVE

1. *Wis. Hist. Colls.,* II, 115-116.

2. Brisbois' commission does not seem to be preserved, but it is mentioned in a letter from the Hudson's Bay Company to the author dated London, February 10, 1931. This information and all other information from the Records of the Hudson's Bay Company are here reproduced by permission of the Governor and Committee of the Hudson's Bay Company.

3. For Lockwood's claim that it was Brisbois, see *Wis. Hist. Colls.,* II, 115-116; for Martin's claim that it was Boilvin, see *Ibid.,* II, 115, footnote.

4. *Mich. Pion.,* XXXVII, 210.

5. *Ibid.,* XXXVII, 548.

6. See Lee's map, p. 186.

7. His wife was one of the three heirs to the Basil Giard tract of land in Iowa one and a half by six miles in extent. See P. L. and Marian Scanlan, "Basil Giard and His Land Claim in Iowa," *Iowa Journal of Politics and History,* XXX, 219-247.

8. *Wis. Hist. Colls.,* XIII, 163 ff.

9. Deeds and transfers for Farm Lots 33 and 34, Office of Register of Deeds, Prairie du Chien.

10. See map of Borough of Prairie du Chien, p. 192.

11. *Minn. Hist. Colls.,* II, 107. The *Virginia,* a steamer 118 feet

long and 22 feet wide, Capt. Crawford in command, arrived at Fort Snelling May 10, 1823.

12. "Inspection Reports," 1826, Inspector General's Office.

13. *Wis. Hist. Colls.*, II, 156-157.

14. Atwater, *Tour to Prairie du Chien*, p. 178.

15. *Niles' Register*, 1826.

16. *Wis. Hist. Colls.*, II, 254.

17. *Ibid.*, XV, 232-233. This was in the summer of 1830.

18. *Ibid.*, IX, 241.

19. For complete census of 1836 see *Wis. Hist. Colls.*, XIII, 254-257.

20. "Deeds," Register of Deeds Office, Prairie du Chien.

21. "Sibley Papers," Manuscript Department, Minnesota Historical Library.

22. "Marriages," Register of Deeds Office, Prairie du Chien. A marriage performed by Fr. Lutz August 14, 1831, shows his presence at Prairie du Chien two weeks after the Menominee massacre.

23. Indian Files, 1833, 1834, 1835, Interior Department.

24. "Letter file—1858," Land Office, Washington, D.C. A reply from the Quartermaster said that he had no authority to sell.

25. *Wis. Hist. Colls.*, II, 147.

26. *Ibid.*

27. *Wis. Hist. Colls.*, V, 332-333.

28. "Record Book," High School, Prairie du Chien. District 1 was to include the town of Prairie du Chien and Farm Lots 35-40, lying south of the rock hospital of Fort Crawford and all of the fractional sections of 7, 8, 17, and 18 Township 6 North, Range 6 West.

29. *Prairie du Chien Patriot*, May 23, 1849.

30. *Ibid.*, December, 1846.

31. *Crawford County Courier*, Sept. 22, 1852.

32. Keating, *Narrative*, I, 235.

33. Atwater, *Tour to Prairie du Chien*, pp. 184-185.

Appendix A

The following names are of particular interest to this region. The French licenses from Montreal (1670-1778) are published serially in the annual *Rapport de l'archiviste de la province de Quebec,* 1929-1933. (The Quebec licenses were published in the same form in 1921-1922.) Some British licenses from Montreal (1769-1790) are available in manuscript at the Wisconsin Historical Library, Madison, Wisconsin. The British licenses are harder to follow than the French because they were issued not only at Montreal but also at other points when a commanding officer had licensing authority.

In 1716 Francois Baribeau, Charles Rainville, and Philippe Leduc came to Mackinac. Descendants of all these left their impress on the locality of the upper Mississippi and Prairie du Chien.

1717

A license to Jacques Arrivé (Lariviere) introduces the first of a long line of traders of that name who were antecedents of the Prairie du Chien family.

From 1718 on, many French licenses were given for the "Upper Country" but not many locate the exact place to which the trader was going.

1718

Louis Ducharme, perhaps an ancestor of Francois-Xavier, whose large family of sons and daughters were raised at Prairie du Chien, had a license. The Charrons, one of whom married Francois-Xavier Ducharme, also visited the Upper Country.

J. Bte. Rhéaume (Reaume) to La Baye (Green Bay) with a canoe belonging to Pierre de Lestage. No doubt he is the same man who was Indian interpreter at Green Bay for many years, who settled there as early as 1746, antedating the Langlades by several years.

1719

Augustin Langlois and a son of Claude Carron at La Baye.

1721

Charles Gautier (father of Charles Gautier) *voyageur* for Francois Montfort, Montreal merchant, to Mackinac.

1722

Employers: Joseph Brunet; Pierre Sarrazin.
Boatmen: Nicolas Roze, for Mackinac; Jacques Bourg *dit* LaChapelle.

Credit transaction: July 29, 1722 Augustin Langlois (Langlade, father of Charles Langlade of Green Bay fame) received credits for goods to the amount of 105 livres 4 sols and 6 deniers from Jacques Langlois, which he was to take to the Mississippi River.

1724

Employers: Amariton (commanding officer at Green Bay); Nicolas Sarrazin (one Sarrazin married a Cherrier at Prairie du Chien in later years); Constant Le Marchant de Lignery; Charles Deneau; Jean Baptiste Neveu; Joseph Denys; Joseph Tessier *dit* Lavigne; and Louis Hervé were all in one company but licenses were issued variously to one or more of the combination. Jean Lemire Marsolet (for Lignery, who engaged more than 15 men to go to Mackinac in 1724 and 1725).

Boatmen: Jacques, son of Jacques Tessier; Jean Mesny; Jean-Francois Sans-Soucy; Jean Baptiste Gadois; Francois Sincerny (Saint-Serny). All were listed for Mackinac, but doubtless they were going to La Baye and its dependencies. Jacques Beauchamp; Jean Baptiste Tessier; Francois Prejean (Prézeau); Louis Roulaud; Jean-Baptiste Augers, who may have been the father of Augustin Angé (a settler at Prairie du Chien as early as 1779); Charles and Etienne Le Maître *dit* Auger.

1725

Boatmen: Antoine Deschamps, Francois Lescuyer (L'Ecuyer); Jacques Pany, Pierre Sincerny, Francois Laviolette, Antoine Benoit *dit* Luvernois; Louis Brunet.

Credit transactions: May 25 Robert Reaume, representing Jean Baptiste Reaume, interpreter, got credits of Charles Nolan lamarque for merchandise valued at 4821 livres 14 sols and 6 deniers to be paid for by his son and brother at La Baye.

From Ignace Gamelin, over 5580 livres' worth for Green Bay trade, in care of Claude Caron and Philippe Leduc.

June 1 Dame Millon, wife of Amariton, sent 6270 livres' worth of goods to La Baye to her husband and his associates Nicolas Sarrazin and Francois Augé by Pierre de Lestage, their *bourgeois.*

1726

Employers: Lignery and Jean Lemire Marsolet, with Francois Augé's name included late in the year, although he appears as an independent trader before this, having apparently left the Amariton company. Duplessis (commanding officer at Green Bay) apparently was associated with Sarrazin and Rene Bourassa.

Boatmen: Louis Ménard (ancestor of the Ménard family of Prairie du Chien), Jacques Coiteux, Jacques Laprise, Jean-Baptiste Tessier, Jean Baptiste Trottier *dit* Lariviere, Jean Baptiste Charon *dit* Ducharme,

Joseph Desorsy, Francois La marque, Michel Germano, Pierre Fortin *dit* Paris, Francois Deneau, Nicolas David, Joseph Beignet, Guillaume Deguire *dit* Larose, Joseph Desrosiers Dutremble, Noel Baugy, Louis and Pierre Angers.

Credit transactions: May 25 Louis Ducharme, associated with Jean Baptiste Reaume got equipment from Charles Nolan to the amount of 4833 livres to go to La Baye. Jean Baptiste Ailleboust (Dailleboust) de Musseaux got credits from Alexis Lemoine for La Baye. He took 886 livres' worth of goods.

1727

Employers: Sieur Ignace Gamelin; Pierre Dumets (Dumay, Dailly), a member of the First Sioux Company; Francois Youville, a member of the First Sioux Company; Jean Garreau *dit* St. Onge; Jean Chevalier; Francois Campot; Etienne Petit; Alexis Lemoine de Moniere, one canoe for himself; Clignancourt, partner of Sarrazin, had 2 canoes for himself; and Maugras; Claude Marin (from which it may be concluded that it was he and not his brother Pierre Paul who went up with the Sioux Company. It is a noticeable fact that Paul and Claude Marin never appear as partners); Francois Lefebre; Pierre Boucher, son; Dame Charlotte Petit, wife of Joseph Desnoyelles; Nicolas Sarrazin & Co. (2 licenses).

Boatmen: Michel Pot de Vin (Portwine, perhaps the ancestor of the Prairie du Chien family) going to La Baye; Pierre Trutteau, first man listed as going to the Sioux; Jacques Bourg *dit* La Chapelle (a name prominent in Prairie du Chien early) going to the Upper Country; Jacques Gervais; Jean Leblanc; Paul Deneau; Pierre Garrau, Etienne Blot, Etiene Petit, and Jean Henry Duplanty, to the Sioux; Michel Jubinville, going to La Baye; Louis Lapron, going to the Sioux; Charles Boissel.

Credit transactions: Pierre Boucher, commanding officer, got credits for 1771 livres.

Francois Lefebre got credits of Julien Lariviere for 1970 livres for the post of the Sioux.

1728

No licenses for Green Bay.

1729

Credit transactions: July—Paul Marin and wife of Louis Hamelin got credits from Lemoine for 7725 livres for a voyage to the Poste of the Folle Avoines.

1730

Paul Marin's license was for the Upper Country. Marie Cardinal, widow of Pierre Hubert Lacroix, to the Upper Country. Dame Marie

Catherine Trottier Desruisseaux, widow of Belestre, commanding officer of Detroit. Credits from Julien Lariviere, probably her brother, a merchant outfitter of Detroit.

1731

Employers: Pierre Garrau, Francis Campeau; Pierre Robineau, sieur Portneuf; Nicolas Antoine Coulon de Villiers, commanding officer at La Baye.

Boatmen: J. B. Robilliard, Louis Langlois, Alexis Morant, Louis Chapus, J. B. Normandin, Alexis Arseneau for La Baye; Jean Landreville for Mackinac; for Sioux post, Pierre Leblanc; J. Fr. Mauricet, Charles Maurice, La Fantasie.

Credit transactions: Fran. Montfort & Co. gave credits: to Fr. Guion Desprey more than 3256 livres; to Pierre and Jean Chevalier (brothers) 2786 livres; to Pierre Richard 3056 livres; to Rene Godefroy, sieur de Linctot and his wife Marie Catherine D'Ailleboust 1201 livres; to Rene Godefroy sieur de Linctot and Sieur Exupère Linctot Picotté, his son, for Joseph D'Ailleboust, sieur de Coulonge, 3256 livres. Francois Poulin ·de Francheville gave credits to Augustin Mouet d'Englade (Langlade) 1823 livres.

1732

Employer: Paul Marin.

Boatmen: Pierre Majeau to Mackinac; Pierre Perrot, Rene Cadot, and Claude Biguot, going to Mackinac; Francois Perrot, and Etienne Belemare, going to the north; Louis St. Louis *dit* St. Louis, going to Nipigon.

Other employers: Antoine Rivard Lanouette, Pierre Chevalier, Augustin Mouet Langlade, Fr. Campot, Pierre Robineau, Toussaint Pothier, J. B. Giguere, Louis Ducharme.

Other boatmen: Fr. Beauchamp, Prisque Maisonneuve, J. B. Maisonneuve, J. B. Gendron, J. B. Denot, Pierre Leblanc, Jacques Leblanc, J. B. Blondeau, Louis Dumouchel, Jean Vanier, Paul Poupart Lafleur, Seraphim Lariviere. *Note:* For Rev. Fr. Guignace a canoe under Charles La Croix.

Credit transactions: June 4 Paul Marin received credits from Sieurs Moniere and Ignace Gamelin 5288 livres and 15 sols. August 20 J. B. Hervieux gave credits to Rene Messier *dit* Duchesne to go to the post of the Sioux.

1733

Employers: Ignace Gamelin, Mr. Foucher, Fr. Lefebre (Duplessis) and Company (Simon Guillory, Jacques Rouillard *dit* St. Cir), Fran. Campot and Pierre Chevalier, Toussaint Pothier, Mr. Mouet Danglade, Chas. Leduc, Portneuf and Garrau (St. Onge), Pierre Garrau.

Boatmen: Michel Ouisconsin, *Panis de Nation,* to go to the post of the North. Joseph Duclos and Rene Maurice La Fantasie (no doubt ancestor of Prairie du Chien family of that name who were early settlers) to go to la Baye des Sacquis (Green Bay). J. B. Cardinal to Green Bay. Pierre Le Sueur to the Sioux; Laurent Dagenais, son, Louis and Augustin Le Cuyer, Jacques Chevalier, Philippe Gervaise, Pierre Menard, Robert Bruillet.

Credit transactions: Charles Nolan gave credits to Fr. Lefebre sieur Duplessis for the post at La Baye 9068 livres.

Mr. Foucher gave credits to Alex Dagneau for voyage to Green Bay 9510 livres.

Fr. Guion Terbanna Deprez for Sioux 2136 livres.

J. B. Hervieux gave credits to Jean Giasson, a *voyageur* associated with Rene Messier (Duchesne) for the Sioux 2533 livres. J. B. Hervieux gave credits to Pierre Richard for 400 livres. Hervieux paid this to Joseph Vaudry for expenses and wages for the voyage. (Richard to the post of the Sioux.)

Maurice Blondeau gave credits August 24 to Joseph Duclos 127 livres and 10 sols as his equipment to go to the Mississippi River.

1734

Employers: Paul Marin, Pierre Richard, Caron, Lefebre, J. B. Hertel de Moncour, commanding officer of Green Bay, Jacques Legardeur sieur St. Pierre.

Boatmen: Pierre Carignan to Nipigon for Marin; Antoine Houle to Sioux fort, Joseph Rivard *dit* Laranger to Green Bay; Fr. Lefebre to Green Bay; Jean Cincirre (St. Cyr) and Louis Basil Lefeuillade; Pierre Barrette and Francois La Tulippe *dit* Juneau.

1735

Employers: Mr. Marin (Paul?) ; Hertel, sieur 'e Moncour; Caron, and Lefebre, Louis Nolan.

Boatmen: Joseph Tessier, Lavigne, Charles Ange, Joseph Migneron to Mackinac; Andre Janot Lachapel to Green Bay; Joseph Couillard, Pierre Sanspitié, Charle Dube to Green Bay, Charle Latreille to Green Bay, Charle and Alexandre Larchevesque, Pierre Matte, Fr. and Joseph Lefebre, Pierre Joseph Renville (no doubt the father by a Sioux wife of Joseph Renville, once a citizen of Prairie du Chien), Rene Dupuy, Francis Jandron, Jacque of Huron nation, Michel Grignon.

Credit transaction: "engagement de Marin Masta a Claude de la Margue pour faire de voyage a Michipicaton." (June 5)

1736

Employers: Srs. de Moncour and others; Jacques Gaudry Bourbonniere; Sieur Giguiere; Srs. Alexis Trottier Desaunier; Pierre Giguiere; J. Bte. Giguiere Co.

Boatmen: Pierre Cloche *dit* St. Pierre to Green Bay; Baptiste Lebeau, Antoine Giguaire, Louis Marcheteau to Sioux.

Credit transaction: Alexandre Lemoine Moniere and Fr. Malhiot gave credits to Jean Giasson 6221 livres for equipment for Sioux voyage.

1737

Employers: Pierre Lestage; La Martiniere, commanding officer at Green Bay (1737-39); Jean Garreau *dit* St. Onge, LeDuc; Jean Noel Desriviers, license to Green Bay.

Boatmen: Louis Coton *dit* Fleurdepee; Joseph Le Roux (probably grandfather of Augustin La Rocque); (Fleurdepee for La Baye); Jacques L'Arrivee.

Credit transaction: Jean Baptiste Blondeau gave credits to his brother Thomas Blondeau for 4355 livres for trade at La Baye.

1738

August, Paul Martin had several licenses to the village "des Sakis et Renards."

1739

Employer: Lestage. *Boatman:* Andre Prezeau for La Baye.

1740

Employer: Charles Texier and Company of La Baye.

Boatmen: Paul Desrochers, Louis Joseph Houde, Antoine Rivard *dit* Feuilleverte of Loranger.

1742

Employers: Nicolas Lefebre *dit* St. Ustache, Alexis Lemoine Moniere.
Boatman: Stanislaus Circe for La Baye.

1743

Employers: Charle Texier & Co.; Alexis Texier & Co.; Charle & Alexis Texier & Co.; Louis D'Ailleboust, sieur de Coulogne; Jean Bte. Lefebre; Fr. Ange; Fr. Ange & Co.; Jean Garau *dit* St. Onge; Garau & Co.; Rigault (Rigaud) Vaudreuil; Louis Ducharme (apparently an independent trader at La Baye).

Boatmen: Boucher, Alexis Dany, Ambrose Trouillet *dit* Lajeunesse, Ignace Tibaut, Simon Favreau, Louis Chrestien, Nicolas Domay, Louis Rockbert, Jacques Chevalier, Ant. Hue Paul *dit* La Traverse, Jean Baptiste Jourdain, Joseph Papineau *dit* Montigny; Francois Mousseaux, Bernard Dumouchel, Jean Baptiste Daunier, Pierre Joly, Claude Lamirande.

Credit transactions: Company of the Indies gave credits to Messrs. Ange, Texier, and Co. 1800 livres powder and 27 "pieces de drap."

1744

Same as 1743. Jean Lefebre, Sieur Thos. Le Cavelier. Paul Leduc became a Green Bay trader this year, having 4 *engagées*.

1745

Employers: Lefebre, D'Ailleboust, licensed for La Baye.

1746

Employers: Leduc, Garreau, D'Ailleboust. (Ange & Texiers had dropped out during this time.)

1747

Employers: Lemoine, Lechelle.
Boatmen: Louis Damour, Sieur Clignancourt, Jean Garreau St. Onge, Etienne Ange, Paul Leduc.

1762

Moran & Co., Goddard & Co., Abeal & Co., Messrs. Lery & Ezekiel Solomon, and Henry Bostwick all have bills for goods sold at Green Bay to be used as presents for the Indians.

July 15, French license for La Baye issued to Samuel Holmes. His men included Henry La Fantaisie who spent the winter of 1762-3 trading on the Wisconsin and who was later a resident of Prairie du Chien. Other boatmen were Amable Lariviere, Alexis Campion, J. B. Dagenest, Augustin Dubreuil, Laurent Dagenest.

1763

February, engagement of Joseph Charbonneau to Jean Orillat & Co. to take a canoe of goods to the post which is indicated ("au poste qu'il luy sera indique").

Orillat also had a license for La Baye. His men included Louis La Croix *dit* Seraphin, Jacques St. Yves, Jean Baptiste Seraphin, Joseph St. Michel, Jean Louis Menard, Nicolas Amiot.

French license for La Baye granted Nicolas Marchesseau. He was a prominent independent trader who operated from 1763 to about 1790. He was at Prairie du Chien much of this time but also traded up and down the Mississippi as far south as Cahokia (see *Mich. Pion.*, X, 508) where he spent the winter of 1783-84 and as far north as St. Peter's River, a tributary of which was named after him. The Rush River of Wisconsin also bore his name on the early maps. He seems to have had an agent with the Sauk at Turkey River in 1783-84 and appears in the records as certainly having a trading-place at Prairie du Chien in 1786-87. (See *Wis. Hist. Colls.*, XII, 94.) In 1783 he built a house at Mackinac and seems to have lived there part of the time until he sold the house in 1806. After that there is no record. He was an uncle of Joseph Laroque and perhaps of a Lamarche who traded along the Mississippi. Marchesseau's men in 1763 included Charles Albanel, Pierre Entaya, Julien Thiery, Andre LaVigne, Rene Aubain, Nicolas Perrilard, Michel Robert (an Acadian), Joseph Lorion, Louis Loiseau *dit* Cardin, Antoine Lariviere, Jean LaMarche.

English permit to La Baye granted Laurent Ducharme "esteemed above all the other French." One of his men was Knash Bray.

1774

Etienne Campion had a license to La Baye but whether he reached Prairie du Chien or not does not appear.

Laurent Ducharme, Recollect Lariviere, J. Bte. Teboux, Jean Calvet, Charles Latour, Gabriel Cota were all trading in Wisconsin.

1775

Jacques Venier claimed to have come to Prairie du Chien in 1775.

Paul Tessier (descendant of a long line of Wisconsin traders) visited Green Bay. (Tessier Islands—fourth ward of Prairie du Chien and Horseshoe Island—were so named as early as Le Sueur's 1700 map. From them a trail led westward as far as the Missouri River.)

Joseph Biron and Laurence Durocher; Wm. La Motte; Jo Carignan; Michel Labatte; Hypolite Janis; Ignace Petit; Barthelmy Janis; Gabriel Cotte; J. M. Ducharme; Pierre Dumas: all were trading in Wisconsin this year.

1776

Jean St. Friole was a boatman in the employ of Letang *dit* Brunet this year only. (Frequently when a man lost his life at a particular place the place was given his name. May this be the origin of the name given to the slough at Prairie du Chien, the Marais St. Friole? Another reference shows this name for a parish in Canada.)

1778

John and William Hay of Detroit, license.

Robert Aird had a license to Prairie du Chien.

Several licenses to the Mississippi River and Illinois, among them John and William Kay and McCrae, who, in 1777, had sent out Gratiot who did not return for many years.

Etienne Campion, native of Montreal, was a Prairie du Chien trader in 1778. Later he had trade connections at Detroit and Mackinac. He was one of three men sent out by the Society of Merchants at Mackinac in 1784 to superintend western trade. The other two men were Michel Labath at St. Peter's and Sayers on Lake Superior. Campion was on the lower Mississippi. He died in 1790 (?). He had at least one brother,

Alexis, in the western country and one sister; the latter married Pierre Ignace Dubois of Mackinac.

1779 licenses

Finley & Gregory, 2 canoes to the Mississippi; Wm. & John Hay, 2 canoes to Prairie du Chien; Et. Campion, 4 canoes to La Baye and Mississippi; Marchesseau, 5 canoes to La Baye and Mississippi; Hypolite Lariviere, 3 canoes to La Baye and Mississippi; Ben Lyon, 1 canoe to Prairie du Chien; Joseph Sangennet, 3 canoes to La Baye; Jean Callot, 2 canoes to Mississippi; Jean Marie Ducharme, 2 canoes to Prairie du Chien; J. P. Lavigne 2 canoes to Green Bay; Joseph Biron 1 canoe do; C. Lamarche, 1 canoe do; Alexis Campion, 1 canoe to La Baye; Robert Aird, 1 to Prairie du Chien; Pascal Pillet, 1 to La Baye; Pierre LaCroix, 2 to La Baye.

Appendix B

IN COMMAND:

Brevt. Brig. Gen. Thomas A. Smith—June 20, 1816 to July, 1816

Lt. Col. Wm. Sutherland Hamilton—July, 1816 to August, 1816

Capt. Willoughby Morgan—August, 1816 to October, 1816

Capt. W. L. Dufphrey, serving in the absence of Capt. Morgan— October, 1816 to April 22, 1817

Col. Talbot Chambers appointed August, 1816, but reporting— April 22, 1817 to June, 1818

Capt. Llewellyn Hickman—June, 1818 to June 30, 1819

Col. Henry Leavenworth—June 30, 1819 to August 8, 1819

Maj. Peter Muhlenberg, Jr.—August 8, 1819 to June 21, 1821

Maj. John Fowle, Jr.—June 21, 1821 to April 26, 1822

Maj. Willoughby Morgan—April 26, 1822 to June, 1825

Capt. Robert McCabe—June, 1825 to January, 1826

Maj. Willoughby Morgan—January, 1826 to August, 1826

Capt. Wilcox—August, 1826 to September 30, 1826

Post abandoned September 30, 1826 under orders issued by the War Department August 14, 1826.

Post occupied by the Prairie du Chien militia under Capt. Thomas McNair under orders of Gov. Cass who called out the militia— July 4, 1827 to July, 1827

Capt. Abner Field's arrival with the Galena militia July, 1827 to July, 1827

Col. Josiah Snelling's arrival with four companies of the Fifth Infantry, U. S. A. July, 1827 to July 29, 1827, arrival of

Gen. Atkinson—July 29, 1827 to August 29, 1827

Maj. John Fowle—August 29, 1827 to April 30, 1828

Maj. Fowle arrived August 21, 1827 but was not in command until Gen. Atkinson left. Fort Crawford was ordered garrisoned by United States troops September 6, 1827 and Maj. Fowle and his command remained at the fort. (About a week in September 1827 Atkinson was again in command by reason of being superior officer.)

Col. John McNeil of the First Infantry—April 30, 1828 to September 10, 1828

Maj. Stephen W. Kearny—September 10, 1828 to July 16, 1829

Col. Zachary Taylor—July 18, 1829 to July 4, 1830

Col. Willoughby Morgan—July 4, 1830 to June 27, 1831 when he left with soldiers for Rock Island. Troops returned July 5, 1831 but Morgan went from Rock Island to Virginia on leave of absence.

Capt. Barker (in the absence of Col. Morgan)—June 27, 1831 to July 5, 1831

Capt. Gustavus Loomis—July 5, 1831 to October 10, 1831

Colonel Willoughby Morgan—October 10, 1831 to April 4, 1832 when he died.

Capt. Gustavus Loomis—April 5, 1832 to August 5, 1832

Col. Zachary Taylor—August 5, 1832 to July 18, 1837

Brev. Brig. Gen. Geo. M. Brooke, Fifth Infantry—July 18, 1837 to July, 1837

Capt. Wm. Alexander—July, 1837 to July 1, 1838

Gen. Brooke—July 1, 1838 to September 1, 1841

Capt. A. S. Miller, First Infantry—September 19, 1841 to November 19, 1841

Brevt. Col. Wm. Davenport—November 19, 1841 to October 22, 1842

Lt. Col. Henry Wilson—October 22, 1842 to September 17, 1845

Post abandoned September 17, 1845.

Lt. Philip R. Thompson, First Dragoons—December 6, 1845 to May 11, 1846

Capt. P. St. George Cook, First Dragoons—May 11, 1846 to June 6, 1846

Post abandoned June 6, 1846.

Capt. Wiram Knowlton, Dodge Guards, (Volunteers)—July 11, 1846 to December 21, 1846

Brevt. Maj. A. S. Hooe, Fifth Infantry—December 21, 1846 to September 15, 1847

Capt. W. Knowlton—September 15, 1847 to August, 1848

Post abandoned August, 1848.

Lt. Col. Gustavus Loomis, Sixth Infantry—September 6, 1848 to April 25, 1849

Capt. C. S. Lovell (substituting)—October, 1848 to April 24, 1849

Post abandoned April 25, 1849.

Maj. Ed R. S. Canby, Tenth Infantry—October 19, 1855 to December 3, 1855

Lt. Col. C. F. Smith, First Infantry—December 3, 1855 to June 9, 1856

Post abandoned June 9, 1856.

Note: In the absence of the commanding officer at any post, the ranking officer assumes command.

Index